IT'S
RISING
TIME!

A CALL FOR WOMEN

WHAT IT *REALLY* TAKES
FOR THE REWARD OF
FINANCIAL FREEDOM

IT'S
RISING
TIME!

A CALL FOR WOMEN

WHAT IT *REALLY* TAKES
FOR THE REWARD OF
FINANCIAL FREEDOM

PLATA
PUBLISHING

Published by Plata Publishing, LLC

Rich Woman, CASHFLOW, Rich Dad, Rich Dad Advisors, ESBI, Triple-A Triangle, and B-I Triangle are registered trademarks of CASHFLOW Technologies, Inc.

are registered trademarks of CASHFLOW Technologies, Inc.

Plata Publishing, LLC
4330 N. Civic Center Plaza
Suite 100
Scottsdale, AZ 85251
(480) 998-6971

Visit our Web sites: PlataPublishing.com, RichWoman.com, RichDad.com

Printed in the United States of America

First Edition: November 2011
ISBN: 978-1-61268-085-9

Cover photo credit: Seymour & Brody Studio

Do

Act... Apply.

Without action—the *do*—the best education, coaches, mentors, support team, and all the commitment in the world will not move the needle on your Dream Meter.

Do... Aspire to your dreams.

Do... Acquire the knowledge and skills to build your confidence and become better equipped to make sound, informed decisions.

Do... Apply all that you learn and rise up to meet your challenges, your intelligences—and your dreams.

You can do it.
I know you can.

It's Rising Time!

PREFACE

It's Rising Time!

A call for women...
To rise up to what it really *takes for the reward of financial freedom.*

To rise up... means "to become powerful, to grow larger, to stand up, to move upward, and to soar." *It's Rising Time!* declares your commitment to not quit, to move beyond the obstacles, and to keep moving upward, even in times of doubt. This is an agreement with yourself to do whatever it takes to reach your financial dreams. *It's Rising Time!* is about you being true to who you are and going for what you want.

... to what it really *takes...* What does it *really* take? It takes all of you—your body, your mind, your thoughts, your emotions, and your spirit. Going for your financial dreams, your financial freedom, is a fantastic journey! I have tremendous respect for the women who take it on. It is no small feat, yet one of the most rewarding. You cannot help but grow mentally, emotionally, and spiritually from your experiences on this quest. It *really* takes more than the data of how to find, buy, hold, and sell investments. It will take more than study and research. Data and information alone will not get you there. It takes gathering the facts and figures, and then stepping out and putting it into practice—actually doing it. It is in the doing that true learning occurs. You will hear from many women throughout this book who did just that and succeeded. You'll also hear about the challenges they faced, and yet they kept going. That is the key. It is because of what it *really* takes—dealing with the obstacles, the fears, the unknowns—that some women never start, or else they stop at some point before achieving their dreams.

The purpose of *It's Rising Time!* is to give you tools, real-life stories, inspiration, and encouragement to rise beyond whatever stands in your way and to keep going, no matter what.

... for the reward of financial freedom. The reward is the achievement of your dream. But you get even more than that. Financial freedom is really well beyond financial. It is a woman free to be who she really is. Sometimes we are so busy putting everyone else first—husbands, partners, children, parents, bosses—and playing so many different roles in life—mother, wife, businesswoman, employee, daughter, sister—that we lose sight of who we really are and what we want. *It's Rising Time!* will clarify that. You see, by achieving your financial dream, who you have to become in the process is not the same woman you are today. You will have to grow, get better, and get spiritually and emotionally stronger in this process. In other words, whatever has held you back in the past or kept you less than who you really are will have to vanish. The powerful, happy, playful, brilliant *you* will emerge. That truly is the reward.

How will you do it? By taking one step, doing one thing every day that will get you closer to your own financial dream. The key lies in taking action. You simply cannot *have* something without *doing* something to get it.

It's Rising Time! truly is a call for women—for women who want more in their lives, for women who are not afraid of a challenge, for women who are willing to stand up and be role models, for women who are willing to do what it takes today for their freedom and happiness tomorrow, for women who want it all!

If this is you, then welcome to an incredible adventure. *It's Rising Time!*

Dedication

To women throughout the world
who want a shot at their dreams!

Be the kind of woman that,
when your feet hit the floor each morning,
the devil says, "Oh, crap, she's up!"

CONTENTS

Epigraph v

Preface vii

Dedication ix

Introduction 1

PART ONE   *Aspire: Choosing Your Dream*

    Chapter 1   Money Does Not Make You Rich 11

    Chapter 2   Seeing the Invisible 19

    Chapter 3   Courage and Consequences 27

    Chapter 4   It All Starts Here 35

    Chapter 5   The Money Question No One Asks 45

    Chapter 6   Two Life-Changing Words 53

    Chapter 7   Shift Your Focus 63

    Chapter 8   It's All About... You 71

PART TWO   *Acquire: Gaining the Knowledge to Make It Happen*

    Chapter 9   Question the "Expert" Advice 83

    Chapter 10   Finding <u>Real</u> Advisers 95

    Chapter 11   Sending Out an SOS 107

    Chapter 12   Expect Unexpected Turbulence 117

    Chapter 13   Figure-atively Speaking 125

    Chapter 14   Take the "Numb" Out of the Numbers 133

    Chapter 15   Debt Is Not a Four-Letter Word 145

    Chapter 16   The Investor's Prize 151

    Chapter 17   A Different State of Mind 161

    Chapter 18   A Recipe for Raising Capital 171

    Chapter 19   Good Partners = Good Deal 179

PART THREE   *Apply: Bringing It All Together*

    Chapter 20   Four Assets Are Better Than One 191

    Chapter 21   Good Deal to Great Deal 201

CONTENTS

Business

Chapter 22   Getting Started… in Business............ 213

Chapter 23   Ruffles to Riches............ 217

Chapter 24   Choices and Journeys............ 221

Chapter 25   A Self-Fulfilling Prophecy............ 227

Chapter 26   Sweet Inspiration............ 231

Real Estate

Chapter 27   Getting Started… in Real Estate............ 241

Chapter 28   Turning Problems Into Profits............ 247

Chapter 29   Taking Calculated Risks............ 253

Chapter 30   Partners in Life, Partners in Business............ 257

Chapter 31   Practice Makes Perfect............ 265

Paper Assets

Chapter 32   Getting Started… in Paper Assets............ 271

Chapter 33   Focus on the Fundamentals............ 275

Chapter 34   Bouncing Back from Broke............ 279

Chapter 35   Taking Stock of Your Life............ 285

Commodities

Chapter 36   Getting Started… in Commodities............ 293

Chapter 37   The Silver Lining............ 301

Chapter 38   Assets Are a Girl's Best Friend............ 307

PART FOUR   *Achieve: Realizing Your Financial Dreams*

Chapter 39   Aligning All the Pieces............ 311

Afterword............ 319

Final Thought............ 321

Acknowledgments............ 323

About the Author............ 325

References and Resources............ 327

INTRODUCTION

It's Rising Time! is a call to action for women who are ready to take that next meaningful leap in life. *It's Rising Time!* is for women who want to grow and expand beyond where they are today. *It's Rising Time!* is for women who have a vision of what they truly want in life and are willing to go after it.

The Economist magazine recently stated: "… the next giant economic growth wave won't come from the Internet or China or India, but from empowering women."

The CEO of Coca-Cola, Muhtar Kent, said in a speech not long ago: "The truth is that women already are the most dynamic and fastest-growing economic force in the world today. The 21st century is going to be the 'Women's Century.'"

It's Rising Time!

It's Rising Time! focuses on that world that you and every woman throughout the planet live on today—our financial world. It's about money, yet, as you will find throughout this book and as you apply this information, I think you'll find that it's about so much more than that. *It's Rising Time!* is the affirmation with yourself that this is your time, no matter what, to reach *your* dreams.

Why "no matter what"? Because reaching a big dream takes daring, resolve, and old-fashioned guts. This game is not for little girls. As my friend Dionne says, "It's time to put on your big-girl panties."

Why "no matter what"? Because too many women quit. They quit on their dreams and, more importantly, they quit on themselves. Many women love the idea of being financially secure and independent. They get excited. They get started. They may read a book or attend a seminar. They begin their process, and then they hit a bump in the road. They make a mistake or life just interferes, so they decide, "This is too hard." And they quit.

This book is not *It's Lazing Time*. This book is *It's Rising Time!* To become powerful, grow larger and soar requires rising above what is comfortable and known and stepping into what may seem at times foreign and clumsy.

It's Rising Time! is about what it *really* takes to go from where you are today financially to where you want to be. And what it takes may surprise you. Whether you are a novice to the world of money or are actively pursuing your financial dreams, *It's Rising Time!* will challenge you to continue to rise up and move beyond where you are now— beyond what you think you can achieve—so you can have what you want.

I will share real-life stories, stories from businesswomen and investors who are open and candid and tell it like it is. This is not theory or academia. Understanding what it really takes in the world of money can only come from people who practice what they preach, who are out there every day doing what they talk about in this book.

I will include the facts, the figures, the data—the left-brain information that you will need to achieve financial independence. But I will go well beyond that. *It's Rising Time!* will involve all the senses—the thoughts, the mind, the emotions, the heart, the body, and the spirit. Accomplishing any valuable and meaningful goal takes all of you.

Achieving requires action, and action will open doors you never anticipated. This is the exciting part because this is where true growth and learning occur. It's in the real-life *doing*.

You Must Do *in Order to* Have: *The Triple-A Triangle*™

You cannot *have* what you want unless you *do* something. It's impossible. Think of some "wants" in your life. Maybe it's success, wealth, health, joyous relationships, and fun. In order to accomplish any one of those goals requires that you *do* something. Success requires accomplishments. Wealth requires delivering a product or service that someone is willing to buy. Health requires eating well and exercising. Whatever you *have* is a result of what you *do*.

The definition of *do* is "to perform, to execute, to accomplish, to exert, to be the cause of." There are three types of *doing* necessary to reach a goal. Some women start, but do not reach, their financial goals because they are only focused on two of the three *dos*.

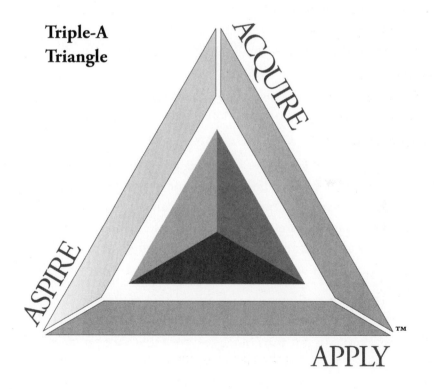

Triple-A Triangle

ACQUIRE

ASPIRE

APPLY™

There are three parts to the Triple-A Triangle:

1. **ASPIRE**

   This is the dream, the vision, the want. It is more than "I want a million dollars." It is what you will ultimately have when you reach your financial goal. The dream may be, "I will have the freedom to sail around the world." "I will take up photography." "I will have the time to spend with my granddaughter." "I will open my gourmet food shop." "I will contribute my time to Habitat for Humanity." Although the goal is financial, the dream is much more than money.

   The *do* of ASPIRE is that you must:

   • Choose your dream or your want.

   • Have a clear vision of what the dream looks like in your mind. You can create this visual in your mind or create a physical drawing or collage of pictures and words that represents your dream.

   • Refer to this visual regularly, ideally every day. This is the vision of why you are doing what you are doing.

2. **ACQUIRE**

   This is the education part of *do*. Acquiring knowledge includes reading books, attending seminars and classes, online research and study, talking with experts, working with coaches and mentors, and on and on. You are gathering the information you need in order to take action. Which leads us to step number 3…

3. **APPLY**

   This is the put-what-you've-learned-into-action stage. Applying the knowledge is where you do such things as make the offer to purchase, put your money on the table, take on your first client, buy the stock shares or gold, make the sales call, or ask for investment dollars. The technical phrase for applying knowledge is "putting your butt on the line." Without the APPLY step, nothing happens.

True knowledge comes from putting what you've learned into real-world practice.

It takes all three parts of the Triple-A Triangle to achieve your goals and dreams. Many women accomplish the ASPIRE step and move into the ACQUIRE step and get stuck there. They attend all the seminars, read all the books and are online constantly researching. The problem is they never move into the APPLY stage. Why? My guess is fear—fear of making a mistake, fear of losing money, fear of looking stupid, fear of people saying, "I told you so!"

Confucius said it best:

"To know and not do, is to not yet know."

It is only by *applying* the knowledge after you *acquire* it that those fears will dissipate. All three steps are necessary to achieve your financial dreams. It is primarily the *apply* stage that stops so many women.

The purpose of *It's Rising Time!* is to offer clarity to define what you ASPIRE to, to offer information for you to ACQUIRE and then, and most importantly, to use real-life stories and encouragement as the catalyst for you to APPLY the knowledge in your life to have what you want.

These three stages are constantly in motion. You don't move from one to the second and then to the third and then you're done. You aspire, you acquire, and you apply. Then you acquire more and apply more, and acquire more and apply more, all the while holding onto your vision of what you aspire to. It's an ongoing dynamic cycle. And while you have your big dream and aspiration, you also have many smaller goals leading up to your main dream. Each one of these goals has its own Triple-A Triangle.

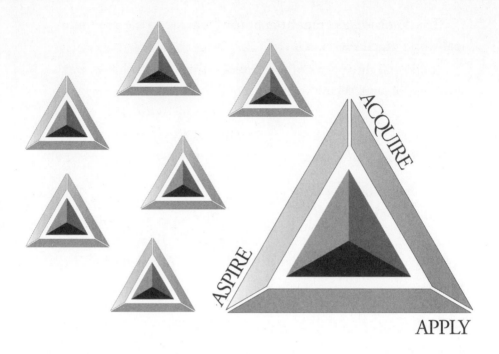

As you move towards achieving your financial dreams, pay attention every now and then to how much of your *doing* is spent in *acquiring* knowledge and how much is spent in *applying* knowledge. If you notice one is becoming much more weighted than the other, you may want to make a slight adjustment. You should notice a constant flow between all three stages of aspire, acquire, and apply.

What It Means to You Today

As I write, it is September 2011 and the United States and the world economy are… (How can I put this politely?)… one huge mess. My prediction is that the global situation will get quite a bit worse, long before it gets better.

What does that mean to you and me? Given where we are today, it means three things:

1. I am not waiting for, or depending upon, the government or government legislation to solve any of my financial concerns. I do not believe they have the answers that will help you or me.

2. Now is the best time to take your financial life into your own hands, to not depend upon the government, your spouse, your parents, or some financial "expert." Your financial future is up to you.

3. Your financial life, your wealth, does not have to be at the mercy of the economy. Yes, it's important we pay attention to what is going on, but the economy does not have to have any significant impact on you, your money, or your financial well-being. You can prosper, no matter what the economy is doing. You will see evidence of that throughout this book.

To the Adventure!

As you embark on this financial journey, you will find that your financial life is an essential part of, and not separate from, your day-to-day life. Face it, your financial life will always be with you. It is not a hobby or something you work on once or twice a year. It is ongoing and alive. If you give it daily attention and do one thing every day that brings you closer to your financial goal, then you will see other areas of your life rise up as well.

I promise you this: Whether you are brand new to the world of finances and investing or you have been successfully investing for years, *It's Rising Time!* will speak to and support any woman striving to elevate her financial life. The women who share their stories do so with a passion to light a spark in other women to take control of their financial lives, as they themselves are doing.

I also promise you this, that in pursuing your financial dreams, you will experience countless rising-time moments, those personal breakthroughs where you will grow mentally, emotionally, physically, and spiritually. That is the beauty of true knowledge. That is the hidden magic of this journey.

So women, I applaud you. *IT'S RISING TIME!*

PART ONE
ASPIRE

Choosing Your Dream

CHAPTER 1

MONEY DOES NOT MAKE YOU RICH

To rise to your money smarts and more takes...

The headline read: "Eddie Murphy's ex-wife is broke!"

A 2010 news story reported that Nicole Murphy received a $15-million divorce settlement from Eddie Murphy in 2006. She opted for that one-time payment instead of monthly installments. In less than four years, she spent the entire $15 million and still has a few outstanding bills to pay. She now owes $846,000 to the IRS (Internal Revenue Service), $600,000 to a law firm, and $60,000 to a landscaping company. She was forced to put her home (on which she owes $5 million) up for sale. She not only spent the $15 million, but accumulated at least another $6.5 million in bad debt.

So what's her financial plan now? The story stated: "Nicole Murphy is engaged to former NFL football great, TV commentator, and celebrity Michael Strahan."

It seems Nicole clearly does have a plan, but her plan has nothing to do with taking financial matters into her own hands. Rather, she will depend upon her next Prince Charming.

Nicole is young, gorgeous, and well connected in celebrity-ville. I'm sure she will be just fine. The toll it may take on her personal self-esteem and the example she is setting for young women throughout the world is another issue. I'll leave it at that.

Granted, I am an outsider looking in. Yet, as an outsider, this story illustrates to me some common choices many women make, such as:

- A man is my financial plan.

- I choose to be financially ignorant. Maybe if I ignore it, the problem will go away.

- I'll take what appears to be the easy road today, although it can very likely become the hard road in the future.

Nicole's story also reveals another truth: If you don't know where to put your money, it will be gone. Nicole had a lot of money but, because she did not know where to put it to create a secure financial life for herself, she lost it. She not only lost it, but she ended up in even more bad debt.

Money Does Not Equal Money Smarts

Whether you have a lot of money or a little money, one fact remains: If you don't know what to do with the money you have, it will be gone.

Ed McMahon, Johnny Carson's famous sidekick on *The Tonight Show* for many years, was a perfect example. Mr. McMahon made millions of dollars throughout his lifetime. He was an icon of American television—a bright, charismatic, respected, and well-liked gentleman.

> *If you don't know where to put your money, it will be gone.*

But just because a person has a lot of money doesn't mean they know much about money.

Towards the end of his life, Mr. McMahon faced foreclosure of his multimillion-dollar Beverly Hills home and owed American Express $747,000. Those were only two of his many financial troubles.

How could that happen? Mr. McMahon put it quite succinctly when he said, "I made a lot of money, but you can also spend a lot of money." His was a simple case of overspending. Well, maybe not so simple… when you're talking about millions!

The stories of Nicole Murphy and Ed McMahon illustrate that having a lot of money does not ensure that you are financially independent—or even financially secure, for that matter.

Women and Money Today

Today women rank "financial issues" as the number-one most pressing concern in their lives—more pressing than family, health, or time.

We women know we need to do something, so why don't we?

What holds women back from getting actively involved in building their financially secure future? A 2010 study found these top three reasons:

1. Women have little knowledge about money and investing.
2. Women find the subject of finances too complicated, confusing, and overwhelming.
3. Women say they have no time to devote to their financial life because of children, job or career, and daily obligations. (Yes, we women are pros at putting everyone else first and ourselves last.)

It's not difficult to see why women place money at the top of their worry list. The facts regarding women and money, especially as we get older, are downright scary.

1. **Women are poorer in retirement than men.**
   - Women are twice as likely to live their retirement years in poverty.

   - In the United States, an alarming 87% of the elderly living in poverty are women.

   - Even more surprising is that the majority of these women now in poverty were not poor when their husbands were alive.

   - Here's an interesting twist: A woman might go through the couple's nest egg paying for the healthcare costs of her ailing partner and deplete the financial resources she needs for the rest of *her* life.

- Not only do women live longer than men today, but women often marry older men. That means many women will be widows who will have to support themselves for 15-20 years.

2. **Women are poorer in divorce than men.**
   - Divorced women with children are four times more likely than married women to have an income that is under the poverty line.

   - In the United States, in 2000, the average income for a middle-aged, divorced woman is only $11,000 per year.

Here is a shocking study that made my jaw drop. This article is from the *Saturday Star* newspaper in Johannesburg, South Africa, dated January 19, 2008.

> *They may promise to have and to hold for richer and for poorer; but wives seem most interested in the richer part. In a study of married men and women in Britain, 59% of wives said they would divorce immediately if their future economic security was assured.*

Almost 60% of the women surveyed said they would leave their marriage if they could afford it!

A similar study was done in Sweden where 37% of women stated they would divorce if they had the money to take care of themselves. Not as high as in Britain, but still a big number. It's pretty clear that women, money, and marriage are closely related.

3. **Women, on average, are financially unprepared.**
   - 58% of female baby boomers have less than $10,000 in retirement plans.
   - 33% of women investors admitted they avoid making financial decisions out of fear of making a mistake.
   - Women tend to own investments and securities with a very low rate of return.
   - Women are three times more likely than men to NOT know what types of investments offer the best returns.

According to the research of authors Christopher Hayes and Kate Kelly, "Women's decision-making tends to be based on security and concern for others. Their decision-making tends to be directed toward gaining enough money to get by rather than to get rich. This desire for security also means that most of their decisions favor 'safe' investments rather than those that might return more."

What It Really Takes

I won't go on and on about the horrific state of affairs so many women fall into when it comes to their financial lives, especially as they get older. I'm assuming that you have already made your decision to move forward in improving your financial life and achieving your financial dreams. You should not need to be convinced on why this is important. You know it's important to you. (Do, however, please share these statistics with women who might be unaware.)

So what does it *really* take to have your financial dreams come true? Do you remember from the study what things hold women back?

- Lack of knowledge
- Too much overwhelming information
- No time

The reality is that any woman can acquire the knowledge. Any woman can sift through the information to find what she needs. It starts with learning the vocabulary of money and investing. Just learning the definitions of financial words will greatly increase your knowledge on the subject.

And the issue of no time? What if your house were on fire? Would you say, "Sorry. I don't have time to put out the flames."? No, you would immediately stop whatever you were doing and take action. Your burning house becomes your number-one priority. Unfortunately, too many women do not make their financial lives a priority until their financial house is on fire, which, in most cases, is too late.

I have no doubt that these women gave truthful answers in this survey, yet, are these the things that are *really* holding women back? Are these *really* the causes?

I believe there are two major missing pieces in the puzzle that explain what's really holding women back from *aspiring, acquiring* the knowledge, and then *applying* that knowledge.

The first missing piece of the puzzle is *financial education*. The reason there is so much confusion around the term "financial education" is because most people do not have a clear definition of what it is.

The word "education" comes from the word "educe" which means "to draw out, to develop." Education is a process of discovery. It is not a process of sitting silently in your chair, memorizing, and then regurgitating what you've read and heard from the teacher. That falls under the definition of "brainwash: to impose beliefs on somebody or to condition somebody to behave differently."

True education is meant to draw out the information so that students learn through their own discovery process. The traditional education system will often tell you the answer such as: "The burner on the stove is hot. Don't touch it." True education is when you see the burner for the first time, and you're curious. You walk to it and touch it. You get burned. Where is the greater learning? True education is discovering things for yourself. And sometimes the process is painful.

What about financial education? The school system will bring a banker into a classroom of 10-year-olds to explain how they can open a bank account. Or they bring a stockbroker into a high school to explain stocks and mutual funds while handing out their business cards and encouraging the teens to open a trading account. This is not education. This is a sales pitch.

Financial education is discovering where you are and what you have financially and then determining where you want to go. The key word is *you*. Everyone's financial situation is different. I hear financial "experts" declare to everyone, "You should not have more that 15 percent of your portfolio in gold." How in the world do they know what's best for every individual? Or "Pay off the mortgage on your primary residence." That may be good advice for one person, but bad advice for someone else. You have to find out what you need and want when it comes to your money and your financial future. Then seek out the knowledge that will get you there.

But what kind of knowledge should you look for, and where do you find it? In school, we usually don't have much of a choice about whom we will listen to. The information comes from classroom teachers, already pre-selected. But outside of school, we do have a choice of what teachers we want to listen to. We can choose our mentors, our advisers, our coaches, our "teachers." Most of my teachers don't even realize they are teachers. They are simply passing on their experience and real-world knowledge to me.

This freedom to choose also brings with it a certain level of confusion, at least in the beginning. That's because there is no one place, such as a physical school building, that has all the information and knowledge you need to become financially independent. You will have to search for it.

And where should you search? In books, seminars, meetings, and investment clubs. In online research, videos, and chats. In discussions with experts in their fields—people who are doing what you want to do. In finding mentors and coaches who can guide you through your process and in networking with other investors. These are just a few places to look. Nothing can replace this kind of financial education. It is a step that cannot be bypassed or delegated to someone else. This is a must-do, because the rewards are so worth it.

Lorraine Stylianou of London, England, shares her story of the value she got from her own financial education.

I am the breadwinner for my family with two small children under five years old. I had just started working a second job to pay for my newly acquired mortgage on a family home in North London, a very modest three-bedroom terraced family house. However, I had little time to spend with my children since I worked over 40 hours a week in a full-time job and then worked every weekend in a self-employed administrative role.

I was on a huge hamster wheel and had to watch every penny.

One Saturday I took my children shopping and found I had only one £2 coin left in my purse. We were hungry and decided to share one kid's meal in that famous burger chain. We each had one chicken nugget and about four fries each!

From that moment, I realized something had to change. I decided I would go to the business section of the local library and read every finance and business book I could get my hands on. I enrolled in a women's money-and-investing weekend that year and later signed up for four property courses. I purchased my first tiny one-bed rental flat in Scotland four months later as a no-money-down deal.

Only 18 months after my first property purchase, I now have eight investment properties and have resigned from my full-time job. We live temporarily in one of our investment properties while I'm renting out my family home. I have experienced a huge improvement in my quality of life by doing so. My painting hobby is now turning into a lucrative business, and I've ditched the hamster wheel of daily commutes into Central London. I no longer feel miserable in a job that made life unbearable.

Today I am my own boss. I accomplished all this primarily with the financial education I acquired through books, seminars, and just getting out there and doing it.

That is the value of seeking out the financial education that works for you.

The second missing piece of the puzzle that holds women back is *the invisible.*

Beyond the knowledge that comes from financial education lies the invisible, where the "secret formula" is found. This secret formula has very little to do with facts and figures. It's invisible because it cannot be seen, and it's secret because it's hidden from most of us.

A woman's true strength, purpose, and genius reside in the invisible. The secret is to make the invisible visible. And that is what we will do.

To realize your financial dreams, you must blend the information of what to do and how to do it with the thoughts, emotions, and spirit of the invisible. We'll explore the details of this invisible secret next.

CHAPTER 2

SEEING THE INVISIBLE

To rise beyond what's visible to you takes...

Y ou have your left brain—the logical, analytical, practical side of your world. And you have your right brain—the creative, innovative, intuitive part of your world. And then you have the physical, the spiritual, and everything in between. Rising to meet your financial dreams takes all of it. It takes all of you.

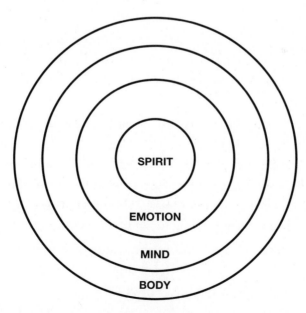

Body

We obviously need our body to get anything done in this physical world we live in. It doesn't have to operate perfectly, but it's an important tool for our financial journey.

Your body will give you signals. Have you ever had a moment when you had a physical sensation in your heart that something was wrong? Or you suddenly felt queasy in your stomach when you were around someone you didn't trust? This is your body giving you clues. Trust those signals. Your body is the physical conduit of your thoughts, emotions, and spirit.

Mind

The brain, a critical part of the body, collects, stores, organizes, and recalls the facts, figures, stories, and information that we need to make sound decisions. Your physical brain is a mass encased in your skull, but have you ever seen a mind or a thought? Your thoughts are part of your invisible world, but they are ever so powerful. They are a driving force in determining the results you have in your life. The tricky part is that some of our thoughts are conscious thoughts, while other thoughts are subconscious and lie hidden under the surface. These hidden thoughts have as much, if not more, power than the thoughts we are aware of.

For example, when you hear the word "investing," what immediate thoughts come to mind? Are they positive thoughts? Negative thoughts? Does the idea of investing excite you, or put you to sleep?

When you hear the words "financially independent," what thoughts do you have? Do you say to yourself, "Yes! I can do this! This journey will be fun!"? Or are you saying, "I'd rather be happy than rich. This sounds too hard. I don't want to lose money."? It's the "I-can't-do-it" or "I-don't-know-how" thoughts in your mind that will prevent you from having the financial success you want.

Janet, a friend of mine, and I were talking about what kind of car she should buy. She is young, bright, single, and attractive. I asked her, "Have you ever test-driven a Porsche?"

She immediately got flustered and irritated. She snapped at me, "I don't want a Porsche!" I was taken back by her instant emotion around this.

"Why?" I asked.

"Because I'm not that kind of woman!" she said quickly.

I had to do my best to keep my cool because—I had a Porsche! I kept calm and curiously asked, "What kind of woman?"

She looked at me like I should know the answer, "The kind that is flashy, loose, flaunts her sex, has no brains, and wants to be seen."

"Wow!" I thought to myself. "How in the world does she associate Porsche with all that?" That thought made no logical sense at all to me, but somewhere in Janet's subconscious, the idea that a female Porsche driver equaled a stupid sex bimbo made perfect sense to her. I decided to skip the psychoanalysis and stop talking cars with her altogether.

The Power of Your Thoughts

One of my favorite books of all time is *As a Man Thinketh* by James Allen, written in 1902. He explains that the purpose of the book is "to stimulate men and women to the discovery and perception of the truth that—*They themselves are makers of themselves.*" He goes on to say, "A man is literally *what he thinks*, his character being the complete sum of all his thoughts." He puts this concept into a poem:

> *Mind is the Master-power that moulds and makes.*
> *And Man is Mind, and evermore he takes*
> *The Tool of Thought, and, shaping what he wills,*
> *Brings forth a thousand joys, a thousand ills;—*
> *He thinks in secret, and it comes to pass:*
> *Environment is but his looking-glass.*

We Hear What We Want to Hear

According to Allen, your thoughts create your world. Your thoughts also determine how you process the information you take in.

Let's talk about this in relation to money. Imagine that the glass in the diagram represents your thoughts, beliefs, opinions, and judgments—in other words, the foundation or context of your viewpoint on money.

The water being poured into the glass represents information and data you are learning on the subject of money. Let's say we are talking about "financial independence." If your secretly embedded thought is that "I will never become financially independent," then it's quite simple. You will not. If your thought is, "I don't have the time," then you will not have the time.

No matter what information is poured into your glass, it has to pass through your context, or your filter, around money and financial independence. Like brewing coffee, the flow of information is filtered first through your thoughts, opinions, and beliefs before it lands in your glass. The information that does not match up with your core thoughts and beliefs around money will either be rejected or filtered out so that the information can be made to fit your context.

Your context, how you think about money and investing, is often more important than the actual content of investing information. All the data in the world will be of little value to you if your filters, your invisible thoughts, are at odds with your stated goals. When you change your context or thoughts to be supportive and aligned with your goals, then the invisible becomes visible.

How Do You Make the Invisible Visible?

It's not difficult. The first thing is to begin to watch your thoughts. Listen to that little voice in your head. In 1985, a friend challenged me to "spend the next hour catching glimpses of your thoughts." I did, and it changed my life. I had no idea how many self-defeating thoughts were floating around in that head of mine. I challenge you to do the same.

You may also want to write down your thoughts in a journal. When fear sets in, ask yourself, "What am I afraid of?" and just start writing. Don't think about what you're writing. Don't edit it. Don't judge it. Just write. Write until you come to an aha, or realization. You'll be amazed at how much clarity will come through.

Emotion

Your emotions are typically driven by your thoughts. For example, if someone says something very mean and hurtful to you, you will probably get upset because your thought may be that you would never speak so rudely to anyone. What if, on the other hand, you grew up in a society (or family) where really rude remarks were a sign of affection? If that were the case, instead of getting upset, you might actually feel loved. It all depends on your context, which is created by your thoughts.

The primary emotion that comes up for women around money is fear—fear of making a mistake, fear of losing money, fear of what other people might think. One of women's greatest fears today is running out of money during retirement. It's a bit of a Catch-22: One fear is the fear of not having the money to support us as we get older. The other fear is the fear of actually doing what we need to do so that we have that money as we get older. The thing we need to learn is that fear, and then breaking through that fear, is a tremendous catalyst for our own personal development.

I do not know of one woman investor who did not have some, or a lot of, fear in the early stages of her investing life. Even today, given how volatile and uncertain the economy is, I get nervous venturing into new areas of business and investing. It's natural. The problem arises when the fear paralyzes you to the point that you do nothing because you are frozen in your tracks. Or you turn your financial responsibilities over to someone else because you fear making a mistake or losing money. Shelby Kearney of New York City learned that lesson the hard way.

I read Rich Dad Poor Dad *and believed every word, but fear had me paralyzed from taking any action. However, a couple of years later, my boyfriend, who was a realtor, encouraged me to buy a duplex and a triplex. I felt he knew a lot about rental properties, and I was less fearful investing with someone I knew. He also offered to manage the properties for me so I turned over all management responsibilities to him and paid no attention to it.*

Needless to say, both properties went into foreclosure because of mismanagement. I was able to sell one property, but lost the other. After that devastation, I knew I had to educate myself and not rely on anyone else's judgment of a good deal or good management.

In the last few years, I have attended several seminars and read many books on real estate. I tried purchasing several four-plex properties in the Atlanta area, but either got out-bid by other buyers or discovered something unappealing during my due diligence. I figured it was a sign from God and turned my focus to Pennsylvania, which is much closer to where I live in New York City.

Earlier this year, I closed on a single-family property and a duplex in Harrisburg, Pennsylvania. It's been a long time coming, but I'm on my way and it feels soooo good!

Shelby got her lesson. Her solution to reducing her fear came from getting financially educated, trial and error, and then securing her two current properties. There will be no stopping her now.

Spirit

In times of pressure and emergency, you often see a woman's spirit rise to the occasion. When there is a crisis in the family, such as a job loss or a home foreclosure, it is frequently the woman who will step up and do what needs to be done. Her natural instinct is to protect herself and her children. It is her spirit, not her mind, that takes over.

Our spirit also shows us that we are capable of achieving more than we would ever believe. It gives us strength, energy, and focus. There will be times throughout your financial journey when you will call upon your spirit to provide the courage and willpower to take that next step.

Here is a compelling poem about the power of spirit.

Will

You will be what you will to be;
Let failure find its false content
In that poor word, "environment,"
But spirit scorns it, and is free.

It masters time, it conquers space;
It cows that boastful trickster, Chance,
And bids the tyrant Circumstance,
Uncrown, and fill a servant's place.

The human Will, that force unseen,
The offspring of a deathless Soul,
Can hew a way to any goal,
Though walls of granite intervene.

Be not impatient in delay,
But wait as one who understands;
When spirit rises and commands,
The gods are ready to obey.

The river seeking for the sea
Confronts the dam and precipice,
Yet knows it cannot fail or miss;
You will be what you will to be!

— *Ella Wheeler Wilcox*

"The human Will, that force unseen" is the invisible power within you that emerges when you are tested at critical times.

"Can hew a way to any goal, though walls of granite intervene." Your spirit can do whatever it takes, even though it may seem impossible. This is the magic that emerges for something of great importance and meaning to you.

It is when your "spirit rises and commands" that the invisible becomes visible. And it is brilliant.

It Takes All of You

Pursuing and attaining your financial vision will take all of you: body, mind, emotions, and spirit. Achieving your financial dreams is a process. It is an incredibly enlightening, frustrating, eye-opening, and honest process of self-discovery and personal development. There is so much to learn. But in the learning come the growth, the confidence, the fun, and that special freedom.

CHAPTER 3

COURAGE AND CONSEQUENCES

To rise up to your inner strength takes...

C ourage is a broad term. Courage may be reflected in acts of heroism, overcoming tremendous odds, physical bravery, or going against the status quo. No matter how courage reveals itself, there is always one thing that every act of courage has in common—fear. It wouldn't be courage unless you were scared.

When it comes to money and investing, fear is the emotion that tops the list. That means courage will play a big role in achieving your financial dreams.

What kind of courage will be required of us? Most of us know what we need to do. The question is: Do we have the courage to accept the consequences?

There must be an unknown for there to be fear. And the unknown is the possible outcome or consequences we might face. Fear exists because we don't know what the outcome will be.

The Consequences

For acts of physical courage—diving off a 75-foot cliff, jumping into a raging river to save a child, or thwarting a store robbery—there are three possible consequences:

1. Survive unharmed
2. Get hurt, injured
3. Die

Feats of mental and emotional courage actually have similar consequences. The fear of public speaking is one of the greatest fears for many people. You walk up on stage for the first time, notes in hand, face a group of strangers, and begin talking. For many people, this would be a very scary undertaking—scary because you don't know how it will turn out.

What are the possible consequences?

1. The audience likes your presentation. (You survive unharmed.)

2. The audience isn't wowed. Some fall asleep. (You're hurt, injured.)

3. The audience boos you off the stage. (You're completely humiliated. You die.)

Common Fears for Women Today

A study was conducted recently among 4,000 women in the United States asking them what they feared most. Surprisingly, 50% of the women surveyed (almost 2,000 women) fear becoming a bag lady. The "bag-lady syndrome" is the fear that they will end up alone, destitute, and homeless. What's even more surprising is that this fear is prevalent among women with high incomes and net worth. (And I'm certain this fear is worldwide.) Becoming a bag lady would, for many women, be the ultimate death. This fear alone may be why so many women are hesitant to venture too far into the investing world. Instead, they play it safe which, in the long run, could be the riskiest thing they could do.

Facing Our Fears

Even though we may not have the courage to face the consequences, most of us know the things we need to do. What might some of those things be?

- Speak the truth or stand up for what you believe in, even if you fear people may not like you or agree with you.

- Pursue your dream, even if you fear the resistance and rejection you may encounter, especially from those closest to you.

- Get out of a toxic relationship, even if you fear you're unable to survive financially or you fear being alone.

- Leave a job where you are unfulfilled and feel unappreciated, even if you fear the loss of a steady paycheck.

- Make a financial decision, even if you fear you might make a mistake.

What about confrontation? For many women, it is the fear of confrontation they're not willing to face. I do not like conflict. I'm the kind of person who works to find the common ground when ideas or people are at odds. I do like to keep the peace whenever possible. I will not avoid a confrontation if the situation calls for it. God knows I've had my share. Yet, I can name many women who will avoid a confrontation, especially with their spouse or partner, at all costs, including the cost of themselves.

There's Going to Be a Fight

Cathi is a bright, successful entrepreneur. She's owned her own PR (public relations) company for 17 years. We were talking about investments one day, and she told me, "My husband and I are pretty conservative when it comes to our investments. We have mutual funds, some stock shares, and we each have our own managed retirement plan."

She went on, "I like to do my homework so I began learning about investments that seem to deliver a better return than we are currently getting. After looking at several options, I've decided I want to invest in a specific real estate project that was presented to me. I know the people who are putting the project together, and their investors are extremely happy with them. I weighed all the pros and cons of the project, and I've made up my mind that this is the investment for me."

Cathi's plan was to pull her money out of her retirement plan, which had gone down about 30 percent in value the previous year, and put the money into this project which was on track to deliver a 10- to 12-percent return. Cathi confessed, "There's just one problem."

"What's that?" I asked.

She sighed, "My husband. Jack's going to look at this investment and immediately sum it up as 'too risky.' There's going to be a fight. It's not something I look forward to. This is what has stopped me from doing this sooner. I hate the idea of a fight. But I also want to be sure he doesn't talk me out of it. I know this is what I need to do. It's my first real investment. It's my start."

I asked her, "Are you willing to have this investment cause an upset in your marriage?"

She hesitated. "I am," she replied. "I don't like it, but I'm willing."

Then Cathi came up with an idea, "I'm going to do this one way or another so I've decided that I'm going to invest my money first and then tell my husband." And that's exactly what she did.

Later, she told me how her discussion with Jack went. She said, "I rehearsed all day about what I would say and carefully chose my words to lessen the blow and hopefully lessen the upset. When I walked in the room to talk to Jack, I took a deep breath and then just blurted out as fast as I could possibly talk: 'I-pulled-all-my-money-out-of-my-retirement-plan-and-put it-all-into-a-real- estate-investment. I'm sure I'll get a better return on my money. I don't think it's a risky investment at all. The people managing the project have been doing this successfully for years and they told me all the negatives and the positives on the property. And besides, it's my money, and I should be able to do what I want with it!'

"I finally exhaled and then I just stood there," she said, "waiting for Jack to erupt. He looked up at me from his desk and said, 'Okay, if that's what you want to do.' Even though there was skepticism in his voice, I just about fell over."

She laughed. "All that fear and worry, preparing for a big fight… and none of it happened. I actually almost didn't go through with it because I hated the thought of a fight. But what made all the difference for me was that I was willing to have the fight if I had to."

Truth or Consequences

Oftentimes we get so wrapped up in imagining the worst possible consequence and convincing ourselves that the worst will happen, so we do nothing. The reality is that the worst-case scenario very rarely plays out.

For you to be willing to accept the consequences of whatever stand you take, there must be something more important to you than the potentially dire consequences. There must be something more important to you than what you fear. For many women, what's more important is our self-esteem, standing up for what we believe in, and being true to ourselves.

Here is a story of a famous woman who knew what she needed to do for herself and who was willing to accept the consequences.

Tired of Giving In

Her name is Rosa Parks. On December 1, 1955, Rosa Parks, a black woman, boarded a bus in Montgomery, Alabama, just as she did most days. But this day was different. The civil rights movement, led by black citizens to obtain equal rights in the United States, was just heating up. At that time in Montgomery, buses were segregated into "whites" and "colored" sections. If the bus got crowded, the African-American passenger was asked to give up his or her seat to a white passenger. Rosa Parks took her seat that day after a long day of work as a seamstress at the Montgomery Fair department store. As the bus took on more passengers, the bus driver approached Rosa and asked her to give up her seat to a white passenger who was standing. Rosa refused. The driver demanded, "Why don't you stand up?" to which Rosa replied, "I don't think I should have to stand up." The driver called the police and had her arrested. Later, she explained that her refusal wasn't because she was physically tired, but because she was "tired of giving in."

It certainly would have been easier for Rosa Parks to simply stand up and move to the back of the bus. Instead, she was willing to accept the consequences of standing up for her rights as a human being. Her immediate consequences were her arrest and fines. She was also fired immediately from her job. But what was more important to Rosa Parks was that she stood up for what she believed in. She stood up for herself and her dignity. She was true to herself. Today Rosa Parks is remembered as "the mother of the civil rights movement."

When life is going well and we're comfortable and happy, it's easy to overlook what we know deep inside that we should do for ourselves. For Rosa Parks, she kept giving in until she got to the point where she was just too tired to give in one more time. Some women know exactly what they need to do as soon as the thought appears, while others have to get to the point where they are just too tired to give in any more.

Do we have the courage to accept the consequences?

Rising Moments of Courage

You wouldn't need courage if you weren't scared. To be courageous is to triumph over fear. Every time you face a fear, consider that a "Rising Moment." With every rising moment, you become more of who you are—more confident, more creative, more "out there," more complete.

It is those courageous rising moments that show you who you really are.

An Exercise in Courage

We know what we need to do. The question is: Do we have the courage to accept the consequences?

Maybe you're saying to yourself, "What if I don't know what I need to do? How do I figure out what I should do?"

First off, when you have a quiet moment to yourself, which may be a feat in itself, ask yourself, your intuitive self, your heart-based self, "What is the one thing I need to do to improve my life?" The first answer that pops into your mind is probably the thing you need to do. Trust your inner voice.

Here is another way to uncover your must-do. Grab a pen and paper and write without thinking. Just let your thoughts and pen flow with the answers to these questions. (Take it one question at a time.)

If money were no issue and you had all the money you needed (and assuming you have already taken your much-deserved extended vacation), what would you be doing differently regarding...

- *Your profession or career?*
- *Your health and fitness?*
- *Your financial life?*
- *Your personal and spiritual well-being?*
- *Your marriage/primary relationship?*
- *Your children?*
- *Your other family members?*
- *Whatever else is important to you?*

The most important element of this exercise is that you tell yourself the truth. Do not filter your answers to be politically correct. Do not write what you think others want you to think. *Whatever* comes up for you, write it down. Do not analyze it. This is for your eyes only.

Out of this process, you are sure to reveal to yourself one or two things that, if acted upon, would greatly improve your life forever.

CHAPTER 4

It All Starts Here

To rise to where you **really** *are takes…*

I t is in the courageous rising-time moments that you see who you really are. But, you must also see *where* you really are.

It doesn't matter if you are a seasoned financial expert or you just opened your first checking account, you always, always, always need to know where you really are financially.

Sounds simple enough. What's so difficult about determining *where* you are financially?

The (Brutal, Honest) Truth Shall Set You Free!

Imagine this (which for most of us women is probably not much of a stretch). You want a new dress for a special charity gala you are attending. You try on several dresses in your size. Most of them are a little snug. "They must be sizing them smaller nowadays," you say to yourself. Then you slip on a dress that you don't really love but, lo and behold, it fits perfectly. Do you really like the dress? Not so much. But you buy it anyway. Why? Because it tricks you into believing that maybe, just maybe, you really haven't gained any weight and you really are still the same size. You can proudly state that yes, indeed, you still are "a size X." Has your weight increased? Not according to that dress size. Has your body shape changed? Apparently not. You are still a size X.

What has this scenario got to do with your financial situation? People do the same thing when it comes to facing up to how much money comes in and goes out every month. People pretend they just woke up one morning and, clear out of the blue, half of their annual salary is racked up in credit-card debt for clothes, vacations, and household items. "How did that happen?" we innocently ask. It happened because you did it. I have no problem with credit cards. I love my American Express, Visa, and MasterCard. The problem is spending a lot of money on things that do nothing to improve your financial situation.

The first key to financial success is taking a good hard, truthful look at where you are now. Once you know your starting point ("You Are Here"), you can plan a strategy on how to move forward.

Lie to Me, Please

The subprime disaster that began in 2007 is a good example of people lying to themselves about their finances. This happened in many countries, but it was rampant in the United States. *Subprime* means "less than great." Lenders want "prime" borrowers, people with track records of paying their loans back. Borrowers are labeled "subprime" when they have a poor history of repayments. What happened in the financial world was that government policies made it easier for lenders to lower their standards and allow people with poor credit to borrow money to buy a home. This created a real estate bubble which benefited lenders in the short term. What kind of benefit? They could collect more in fees and commissions. They offered mortgage loans which required little-to-no money as a down payment and very low interest rates… initially. The financial institutions made a lot of money for themselves.

And what did our subprime borrowers exclaim? "Yippee! I can finally afford to buy a house!" Although it sounded too good to be true, thousands of people climbed on board. They didn't seem to question the fact that, even though their financial situation remained the same and they had been unable to qualify for a home loan before, now they were miraculously qualified. They didn't question it because they were happier with the lie than the truth. They simply closed their eyes to the fact that somewhere down the road, they would eventually have to pay. And pay they did. Had they asked the questions, they would have discovered that, in the fine print of their loan documents, it said that, at some point down the road, the low interest rate would disappear and be replaced by a much higher interest rate. Because so many of these borrowers did nothing to improve their financial situation, they were later faced with higher mortgage payments they could not afford. Many paid the piper and lost their homes to foreclosure, bankruptcy, and financial ruin. As my stockbroker friend tells his clients and me, "If it's too good to be true, then it is. Walk away."

Even today, in the midst of this global financial fiasco, people simply want to believe that everything will be all right. The government will fix it. Somebody will come to their rescue. They live in hope and do nothing differently related to their own financial situation.

When it comes to money, many people are lazy. It's not that they are not working hard. Many people today are working two or three jobs. It's that they are too lazy to learn something new. (Obviously you are not one of them because you are taking action and learning what you need to do for you.)

To Stay Balanced, Keep Moving

In October 2010, Robert and I and four friends sailed a new 58-foot Beneteau sailboat from Los Angeles, California, to Honolulu, Hawaii. The opportunity appeared and, even though I had almost zero sailing experience, I figured this was a once-in-a-lifetime opportunity. Count me in.

The boat was delivered to Los Angeles from France and all the necessary work to get the boat voyage-ready was done in Marina del Rey, California. Robert and I arrived in Los Angeles five days before we set sail, buying provisions, working with the team, and supporting the final preparations. I was anxious to set sail for Honolulu.

You have to understand, I have never been so far out on a boat that I could not see land. I wasn't sure how I would respond or what to expect. One thing was glaringly apparent once we were out of port and under full sail—you were not, even for one second, standing still... ever! Depending on the winds and the waves, the boat was either on a slant to the left (port) or a slant to the right (starboard), and sometimes it was a back-and-forth motion. I was always grabbing onto something to keep my balance. Making coffee in the morning was a monumental feat. We lost the French press to a swell the first day. Thank God I brought my stainless steel coffee pot and filters along. No one would want to be with me for 14 days in confined quarters without coffee.

Everything I take for granted on land was now a task to be mastered at sea—washing my face, clearing dishes off the table, carrying a glass of wine up five steps—all took extreme concentration and balance. There was one night where the weather had turned, and the rain was coming down pretty hard, so we were all eating dinner below in the main cabin. Four of us were seated around the table. JM was sitting on the steps with his plate in his lap, and Chad was carrying his dinner to the table. Just then a large swell hit the boat and Chad, looking as if the scene were choreographed, lightly stepped, stepped, stepped carefully not to lose his balance and fell into the couch on the opposite side of the cabin, holding his plate full of food balanced over his head. He didn't spill a drop. We all applauded his dexterity. In the middle of the applause as I was standing up, a much larger swell hit the boat, sending me and JM flying across the cabin. No applause here. Only spilled food and several bruises.

I was always on guard because the boat, the foundation I was standing on and my only physical safety, could shift at any time. I could never be complacent or assume that things would remain calm. I was never standing still, always moving to keep my balance.

Nothing Happens Until Something Moves

Women seem to be constantly looking for balance in their lives. While many think balance is a stillness, a calmness, I think balance takes constant movement. If you're standing still, then there is no movement. When an unexpected event occurs, you're thrown off your feet. You're thrown off balance. So one of the keys to dealing with whatever comes at you is to always keep moving. As Albert Einstein said, "Nothing happens until something moves."

Your financial statements are never standing still. They are constantly changing.

To know where you are today is a snapshot in time. But you have to take that initial picture. It is the foundation for your voyage, for where you want to go. To have a strong foundation requires:

- Knowing what makes up the foundation you have
- Getting rid of whatever makes the foundation weaker
- Building and adding what will make your foundation stronger

If you build your house out of sticks and straw, like in the fairy tale, your foundation will be weak and the house will eventually collapse.

That is why, no matter where you are on your own journey, you need to do a complete financial assessment of where you are today. I review my income, expenses, and cash flow twice a month. Yet I easily can, and sometimes do, lose track of where I am today when it comes to my investments, assets, and accessible sources of money. If I'm not prepared for a great opportunity when it appears, I will miss it.

What Do You Need to Know?

The question to ask yourself is this:

*If an investment opportunity that I want appears today,
do I know what I have and don't have available financially,
and do I know what funds I need in order to own this investment?*

There are two parts to this question:

1. **Know what you have**

    What funds do you have available to put towards this investment?

2. **Know what you don't have and still need**

    Just because you may not have the money doesn't mean you can't still do the deal. It may be a matter of knowing how much money you need to raise in order to make the deal happen.

What Is Your Financial Truth?

It's so easy to lie to ourselves about what we really spend on eating out, on clothes, or vacations. And it's easy to pretend our investments are making money, or at least breaking even. It can be uncomfortable to face the facts and learn that you're actually spending more every month than you're making, or that the money you placed in that mutual fund, which the "experts" told you would *make* 10 percent, actually *lost* 20 percent last year.

Jamie got a surprise when she took a closer look at her finances.

One day my husband and I were having a conversation about our future and planning for retirement. We have no savings, no investments, we don't own any properties, and we live paycheck to paycheck. We are both very naive when it comes to finances and have absolutely no knowledge about investing or creating financial security.

We were expecting to receive our tax return soon so we talked about opening an individual retirement account (IRA). We knew absolutely nothing about this except that people opened these to save money for retirement. We went to our bank to open an IRA. They were more than happy to assist us. We sat down with the regular bank teller and went through the steps with little to no explanation of what this process means and what really happens with our money. I was a little concerned that someone in the financial advising area did not come out and speak with us to make sure we fully understood what we were doing. They were quick to take our $500 and have us sign papers. Even so, after the process, we walked out of the bank thinking we had made the right decision and that our financial future was going to be great.

*A year later, I was working on my financial statement with a mentor
and we discussed the IRA. I pulled out our statement and showed her
that we had made 41 cents last year. She responded, "You know that is a
return on your money of about zero. Silver went up 31 cents in the past
24 hours, and 75% in the last year."*

*What an eye opener! I thought the 41 cents was what it was supposed
to be. I thought I was doing well! My husband and I are now getting
ourselves educated through, books, seminars, and mentors. We play
the* CASHFLOW 101 *game often with our entire family. We are
determined to be financially free together.*

Not only do you have to know where you are financially, but
you also need to understand what "where you are" means in this
financial world. Jamie thought that where she was, earning a 41-
cent annual return on $500, was a good investment. As you will
learn in this book, there are investments that any woman can
participate in that will earn much greater returns… as long as
you know what you're doing.

Some Steps to Take

- Tell yourself the truth about any and all income that comes
  into your household.

- Be brutally honest about your expenses. What exactly do you
  spend every month? This is not a matter of your numbers
  looking good (although we women *do* like looking good). It's a
  matter of knowing where you are—period.

  Important: If you enjoy eating out every night, then financial
  freedom for you had better include eating out every night.
  Financial independence means having the money to live the
  life you want, not just having enough to survive. Financial
  independence is not living below your means. I would rather
  expand my means and have my money work hard for me so
  that I can create the financial life I want for myself and my

family. Being honest about your expenses now is important, because this sets you up to have the financial future you desire.

- What investments do you own? Do you have stocks, bonds, mutual funds, retirement plans, real estate (other than your home), business investments, gold, or silver? What do you have that is making you money without you working for it? What price did you pay for the investments? What is happening with that investment today? It's not uncommon to not want to open that investment-fund statement when you're guessing it may be worth a lot less than you put into it. Look at every statement. That one action alone can be a valuable eye-opener.

If, for whatever reason, you don't know what you have or what it's doing, FIND OUT.

Warning: If you have not been handling your finances and have put them in the hands of your husband, a family member, or a financial manager, this could cause some tension, especially if this is the first time you are asking about them.

Why? Two reasons:

1. The person handling your money may not want you know what your financial situation is.

2. The person handling your money may feel threatened that you are questioning his or her ability to manage your money.

My suggestion: Simply be up-front, and tell the truth. It's your financial life, and you have a right to it. If the resistance is strong and continues, then chances are someone is hiding something from you. All the more reason to find out the facts.

What outstanding debt do you have? What do you owe money on today, such as your house, car, credit cards, student loans, and loans to individuals (no matter how far back they go)? Any money you borrowed and need to repay should be included here.

If you have never done this before, stick with it until it's complete. If you've compiled your financial snapshot before, then please update it. If you are fully up to date, congratulations. Please teach and support a woman who needs your guidance.

Note: In the References and Resources section in the back of this book, there is a sample financial statement. You may use that as a template for your finances.

Keep Your Numbers on a Tight Leash

Finding out exactly where you are today financially is like a breath of fresh air. It's a relief. Don't invalidate yourself or beat yourself up if your finances are not where you want them to be. So what? It's where you are. It is what it is. Now that you know what it is, you can deal with it. Until that time, you were only wishing and praying. Every time I review my numbers, I learn something new, and I've been doing this for just about 25 years.

Remember that your numbers are dynamic. They are always changing. They are never static. As long as your numbers keep moving, you need to keep moving to direct them where you want them to go. If you let a puppy run free, he runs in all directions and you don't know where he'll end up. But if you're guiding him on a leash, then you both end up where you want to be.

CHAPTER 5

THE MONEY QUESTION NO ONE ASKS

To rise to your financial "wants" takes…

Warren Buffett, thought of as one of the top investors of all time, said it best, "There are many ways to get to financial heaven."

The first question to ask yourself is, "What is my financial heaven? What does financial heaven look like to me?" Financial heaven will be different for each woman, depending upon where she is today and what she wants in her life. Your financial heaven may be to never have to worry about money again. Financial heaven may be to wake up every morning without having an alarm clock telling you it's time to go to work. Financial heaven may be first-class travel, first-class hotels, and first-class restaurants whenever you want. It's your financial heaven. Make it what you want.

Years ago in the late 1980s when Robert and I were broke, it was hard to imagine such a thing as financial heaven. We were living a financial hell. We were in the early stages of building our new business. We were hundreds of thousands of dollars in debt from Robert's previous business which had gone bad, and we were committed to paying that back. We had very little income trickling in and no white knight riding towards us on the horizon. We knew we had our work cut out for us. We just took it one step at a time, and I kept taking deep breaths.

What did I consider my financial heaven at that time?

Zero.

My financial heaven would be the moment we climbed out from that massive financial hole and paid off that last debt so we could move forward.

I still remember the day I sat down with our bookkeeper, and we wrote that last check. It was to an old friend of Robert's who had loaned him money for his now-failed business. That evening I pulled a bottle of champagne out of the refrigerator, poured two glasses, and Robert and I toasted to zero. Today I'm happy to say that my financial heaven is much more abundant and bright.

So, what would you say is your financial heaven?

The All-Important Question

To reach your financial heaven, you have to start from wherever you are today. So where are you today? We have already talked about the importance of knowing what you have in terms of income, expenses, assets (i.e., investments), and liabilities. I strongly recommend you gather that information as soon as possible if you have not done so already. This will put you one step closer to arriving at your financial heaven.

Now let's take it a step further to give you a vivid, and very revealing, picture of your current standing. In other words, let's make it real for you. The question is this:

If you (or you and your partner/spouse) stopped working today, how long could you survive financially?

This is a crucial question and one that most people will never calculate. This is why, when the unexpected happens—like a job layoff, an illness, or a divorce—so many people are not prepared. This is one reason why so many people are struggling in this economy. It's at the time of the unexpected event that most people, for the first time, are forced to face the truth of where they are and how long they can survive.

This calculation is important because most people calculate what they want and need in terms of money. "I need $1 million to live on for the rest of my life." When you talk with financial planners, they talk to you about your nest egg, how much money you will have to set aside to retire.

However, instead of measuring your wealth in terms of *money*, we're going to measure your wealth in terms of *time*.

There are two parts to this question:

1. **If you stopped working today…**

   That means there is no more salary, no more paycheck. For whatever reason, you can no longer work for a business or job so no income is coming in from those sources.

2. **How long could you survive financially?**

   We're talking about survival at your current standard of living, not if you downsized your house, sold your car and rode the bus, stopped eating out, and so forth. Given your *current* level of expenses, how long would your money last? Remember, this is about reaching your financial heaven, not living in financial shackles.

For our purposes here, your money consists of your savings, CDs, retirement accounts, liquid stocks (stocks you could sell today), physical gold and silver you have in your possession—anything that can be converted into cash today. It does not include selling your jewelry, your furniture, or your second car, for example, because that would lower your current standard of living. It does include cash flow from dividends, rental real estate, and other investments that produce income without your effort.

If you have done this calculation for yourself before, then I encourage you to do it again now. Why? Because your finances are dynamic. They are continually changing. You may come up with a similar answer, or you may be surprised by your new outcome.

Do the Math

The equation goes like this:

$$\text{Your Wealth Number} = \frac{\textbf{Your Available Money}}{\textbf{Your Monthly Expenses}}$$

Note: Remember, it's easy to lie to yourself about how much you actually spend on monthly expenses. Include all your expenses because you want to expand your financial means to meet the lifestyle you desire, not live below that lifestyle.

Once you do the math and divide how much money you have available by your monthly expenses, you end up with your wealth number. What does that mean?

Your wealth number is measured in time—in this case, in months. So if your wealth number is 24, that means 24 months. If your number is 6, that equates to 6 months. And what does that mean?

Your wealth number is the number of months you could survive if you (or both you and your partner) stopped working today. What's your number?

For most, this calculation is sobering. It brings you and your money face to face. It is the most realistic and telling demonstration of exactly where you stand today financially.

For a lot of people, their number is 3 or less. That means they could only survive without paychecks for three months or less. They are pretty much living paycheck to paycheck. Some actually have a negative number, which means they are spending more every month than they are bringing in.

If you are unhappy, or even upset and disturbed, about that number in front of you—good. This exercise is meant to shake you up if that's what you need. You see, it's not until a person is uncomfortable that they begin to take action. Think about it. You're sitting in a chair for 20 minutes. You suddenly realize you're uncomfortable because you've been in the same position for so long, so you move.

You do something different. That is the purpose of determining your wealth number. To realize the position you've been sitting in for so long may, all of a sudden, be uncomfortable. And it should be uncomfortable enough for you to do something about it.

It really doesn't matter what your number is. Your number is simply your number. You don't need to make it right or wrong or continually stress over it. It is what it is. Period. Now you know. Now you know something that most people will never take the time to figure out. And most importantly, now that you know, you can take action and change it if you choose.

What Is the Ideal Wealth Number?

What do you think the ideal wealth number is? Remember, we're talking in terms of *time*, not money. If you're 30 years old and you stopped working today, do you want to survive financially for 10 years? Twenty years? Thirty years? I don't think so. If you're 60 and want to retire and you stopped working, how long do you want your money to last? Whether you're 20 years old or 70 years old, the answer should be the same. You want to survive forever. You want your money to live as long, or longer, than you do. The optimal wealth number is *infinite*. The word *infinite* means "boundless or endless." Infinite wealth means, if you stopped working today, you could survive at your current standard of living for as long as you live, *whether you work or not*.

> *The number-one fear in America is the fear of running out of money during retirement.*

Setting Your Infinite Wealth Goal

The difference between the Rich Woman philosophy and other financial philosophies and strategies is that most financial planners, experts, spokespeople, and journalists plan on two things happening upon your retirement:

1. You will have a fixed amount of money to live off of that earns you a small amount of interest, and

2. You will have a lower standard of living during retirement than when you were working, due to the loss of a salary or paycheck and rising medical expenses as you age.

The Rich Woman philosophy does not make those assumptions. Instead we assume:

1. You have income coming in every month that equals or exceeds your living expenses… forever, In other words, you never have to worry about running out of money once you retire or stop working, and

2. Your standard of living remains the same or, in many cases, increases.

That is why we measure wealth in terms of *time*—specifically, *infinite* time. I can't imagine a more horrible money problem than being 70, 80, 90 or 100 years old and knowing you are just about out of money.

I was in Honolulu meeting some friends at a beachside restaurant. I took a seat at the bar to wait for them and began talking with the gentleman sitting next to me. He and his wife had both recently retired and they were living their dream of retiring in the islands. They bought a house on the island of Kauai and were on their way to their new life in a few days.

We had not discussed money, retirement, or the economy, yet out of the blue, this man said to me, "I am just a bit concerned."

I asked him what he was concerned about, and he told me, "My wife and I have looked forward to our dream retirement for many years, and now here we are. My worry is that we may not have put aside enough money to last through our retirement. I guess time will tell." There was a sadness in his voice.

Here he was, after a lifetime of working hard towards his goal so he and his wife could live their retirement dream in Hawaii, and he was already worried before they had even begun. He was in his first week of retirement and already he was fearful of running out of money. That is not a way to live out the years that are supposed to be your reward for a lifetime of hard work.

Reaching your financial heaven requires determining your infinite wealth goal and *aspiring* towards your dream, and then *acquiring* and *applying* the knowledge to achieve it. Simple? Yes. Easy? Not necessarily. Worth it? More than you can imagine.

Now let's figure out how you can do that.

CHAPTER 6

TWO
LIFE-CHANGING
WORDS

To rise to the investor within takes...

Y ou will not get to financial heaven by saving money and investing in 401(k)s and mutual funds. It is virtually impossible. Yet, that is what most financial experts and planners tell you to do. That advice will not get you there.

Investment plans such as 401(k)s in the United States, Japan, and England; superannuations in Australia and New Zealand; or RSSs in Canada were never designed to be vehicles for retirement. They are basically savings plans, and not very good ones at that.

Today, it is nearly impossible to save your way to retirement. Can it be done? For some, yes. For most, no. It's unachievable for the majority of us because of:

- Rising taxes
  (Did you know that the average person in the United States works four months, from January to April, just to pay taxes? This varies from country to country. Check out the statistics in your country.)

- Inflation,
- Lack of pensions,
- Future rising interest rates,
- Devaluation of the dollar and other currencies,
- Insolvency of Social Security, Medicare, Medicaid, and other entitlement programs,
- Insufficient personal retirement accounts.

There was a time when our great-grandparents, our grandparents, and, in many cases, our parents could save their way to a very comfortable retirement. But what worked then does not work now. That is why we have to look at our financial lives differently from the old, outdated, and no-longer-relevant conventional advice.

Where Does the Income Come From?

If the monthly income of your infinite wealth plan does not come from a job, a salary, or you working for it, then where does it come from? It comes from you putting your money to work, instead of putting you to work. It comes from investing your money where it will deliver a consistent return of money back to you. Different investments produce different results. The question is, what results do you want?

There are two primary outcomes an investor invests for:

1. **Capital Gains**

   Capital gains is the game of buying and selling for a profit. You have to keep buying and selling, buying and selling, buying and selling, or the game and the income stop.

   Capital gains occurs, for example, when you buy a share of stock for $20. The stock price goes to $30, and you sell it. Your profit is called capital gains.

   The same is true with real estate. You buy a single-family house for $100,000. You make some repairs and improvements to the property, and you sell it for $140,000. Your profit is termed capital gains.

Let's say you bought 10 one-ounce silver coins for $15 each. You sell the coins for $40 each. Your profit is called capital gains.

Any time you sell an asset or investment and make money, your profit is capital gains. Of course, there are also capital losses. This occurs when you lose money on the sale.

Unfortunately, many "flippers"—people who buy a real estate property and quickly turn around and sell it for a profit, or capital gains—got caught when the real estate market turned. The mindset for many was that the market would continue to go up. When the market reversed and crashed, the properties were no longer worth what the flippers bought them for, and there were no buyers to flip the properties to. This is one reason why we are seeing so many foreclosures and people just walking away from homes.

Most investors today are chasing capital gains in the stock market through stock purchases, mutual funds, and 401(k)s. These investors are hoping and praying the money will be there when they get out. To me, that's risky.

As long as market prices go up, capital-gains investors win. But when the markets turn down and prices fall, capital-gains investors lose.

2. **Cash Flow**

   Cash flow is realized when you purchase an investment and hold on to it, and every month, quarter, or year that investment returns money to you. Cash-flow investors typically do not want to sell their investments because they want to keep collecting the regular income of cash flow.

   If you purchase a stock that pays a dividend, then, as long as you own that stock, it will generate money to you in the form of a dividend. That is called cash flow.

To cash flow in real estate, you could purchase a single-family house and, instead of fixing it up and selling it, you rent it out. Every month you collect the rent and pay the expenses, including the mortgage. If you bought it at a good price and manage the property well, you will receive a profit or positive cash flow.

The cash-flow investor is not as concerned as the capital-gains investor whether the markets are up one day or down the next. The cash-flow investor is looking at long-term trends and is not affected by short-term market ups and downs.

A Third Way Investors Invest

There is a third way investors invest, and that is called a *hedge*. A hedge is like insurance. It is used to offset possible losses.

For example, with every rental property I own, I create a reserve account. The reserve account ensures against unforeseen repairs and drops in income. The money is set aside to cover emergency expenses or a loss of rental income in case the tenants move out. It is a hedge against those losses.

We have a large commercial property with one tenant. If this tenant moves out before their lease expires, we are left with a gaping hole in our income which we use to pay our mortgage. We would then be at risk of losing the property. The reserve account we have on this property is a hedge, or insurance, that if that happened, we could still pay the mortgage.

Silver and gold are two other examples of a hedge. Robert and I buy gold and silver not because we think the price will continue to rise, even though we do think that will be the case. We buy it mainly as a hedge against the dollar losing its value. Historically, when the dollar declines in value, people look to real money, such as gold and silver. Generally, when the dollar goes down in value, the price of gold and silver goes up. To us, gold and silver are a hedge against the devaluing dollar. We buy gold and silver to offset possible losses of the dollar.

Stock options are another hedge that investors use. A stock option is the right, but not the obligation, to *buy* a stock (a *call*) or to *sell* a stock (a *put*) at an agreed-upon price within a certain time period or on a specific day.

A stock option is a hedge because, if you buy a call option, you are betting that the price of that stock is going up. The price of the option is a small fraction of what the actual stock would cost you to buy. For instance, the stock may be selling at $30 per share, but the option might cost only $1. If the price of the stock goes down $10, then you forfeit the cost of the option at $1 per share instead of losing $10 per share. The option is a hedge against possible losses. Of course, if the stock does go up, then you can use, or exercise, your option and buy the stock at the lower agreed-upon price. Stock options are a science all to themselves.

Two Words You Should Grow to Love

Capital gains, cash flow, and hedges all have a place in the world of investing. I use all three. However, to accomplish my goal of financial independence and infinite wealth, my two favorite words when it comes to money are:

CASH FLOW

Cash that flows in every month without you working for it is produced by investments, or assets, generating cash flow. That cash flow is called passive income. That's not to say you won't also use investments to produce capital gains or as a hedge. They are all important. The primary focus in building infinite wealth, however, is on cash flow. Why? Three reasons:

1. *Most people cannot save their way to retirement today.* It's not easy—in fact, I would say it's almost impossible—to save the amount of money you will need to retire. Unfortunately, way too many hardworking people who were planning on retiring in the next few years are finding out that they cannot afford to do so. Too many people will be forced to work, literally, until the day they die.

A better focus would be to acquire the amount of cash flow, or passive income, you want per month that will last as long as you own the investment.

For example, when Robert and I retired back in 1994, we did not have a huge amount of money in savings. As a matter of fact, we had very little in savings. Our stock portfolio was almost nonexistent, and we did not have mutual funds or a 401(k). What we did have was $10,000 per month in cash flow coming in every month from our investments, primarily real estate at the time. Our living expenses, on the other hand, were only $3,000 per month. At that point, we were financially free. Our passive income was greater than our living expenses. My point is, it wasn't millions. It was $10,000 per month. That, and more, is very doable today.

2. *I like control.* I do not like to invest in things where I have no control, especially when it comes to my money. I am not a stock trader or a flipper (one who constantly buys and sells property). I am not good at timing the highs and lows of the stock market or the real estate market. I'm just not that smart. My cash flow from my investments is not dictated by the daily fluctuations of the market. I cannot control the markets. I can control my rental properties. I can control my businesses. The majority of stock shares that Robert and I own are shares of companies we own. And although I may not be able to control the oil production of our cash-flowing oil wells, I can pick up the phone and talk with the owners of the company at any time.

3. *I want to determine when I retire or, better yet, have the choice to stop working or not.* I can achieve my goal of building up my cash flow to equal or exceed my living expenses much quicker than I can amass a set amount of money to live on for the rest of my life. Cash flow also frees me up to get on with my life and do what I really want to do, not dictated by the constraints of money.

Cash Flow Breeds Cash Flow

Cash flow breeds more cash flow. My first cash-flow investment was a small two-bedroom, one-bath house in Portland, Oregon, in 1989. My monthly cash flow averaged a massive $50 per month. Not a lot, but it gave me my start. And that first step was, by far, the toughest. I wasn't sure if I could actually go through with it. I had enormous amounts of fear.

So that $50 was much more than a few dollars in my pocket. It was the first building block towards the cash flow I enjoy today. There comes a point in your investing life where the cash flow from your investments supports, not only your living expenses, but also your next investments. Your cash flow breeds new assets which, in turn, breed more cash flow.

Here's the key. To pave the way to your financial heaven, you've got to understand these two things:

1. **You must know if an investment will give you cash flow, capital gains, a hedge, or any combination of the three.**

    A stock can give you cash flow in the form of a dividend. If the stock price goes up and you sell it for a profit, then you will have capital gains.

    You may hold 100 ounces of silver as a hedge against the falling dollar. If at some point you sell the silver, then any profit will be capital gains.

    Robert and I bought 10 apartments in a 300-unit apartment building that was being converted into condominiums. Those 10 units gave us cash flow because the developer rented them from us to use as models for prospective buyers to walk through. Once the project was completed, we sold the 10 units which produced capital gains. We immediately reinvested the capital-gains profit into a cash-flowing apartment building that we still own today. In this one deal, we went from cash flow to capital gains to cash flow. The key was that, even before we sold the 10 model units, we already knew where that money would be invested next.

Remember, if you don't know where to put your money before you get it, your money will be gone.

2. **You must decide which result you want from your investments—cash flow, capital gains, or a hedge.**

What's your plan? What's your goal? What do you want?

When I began having my money work for me, my goal was this: To acquire two rental units per year for 10 years. At the end of 10 years, I would have 20 units, all cash-flowing. The beauty of a goal is, once you are crystal clear on what you want and you work towards it, magic often happens. Or as my friend Paula White, a well-known minister, says, "When you are clear on what you want, God will send you opportunities." In my case, I did see opportunities, and it didn't take me 10 years to reach my goal. It took me 18 months. It came much faster because, when I set the goal, I wasn't sure how I would achieve it. But, as I kept working towards my goal, I learned new strategies that sped up the process tremendously.

Then I immediately set the next goal—to acquire more investments to increase my cash flow so that the cash flow was greater than our living expenses. I gave myself five years to accomplish this. We actually reached our infinite wealth goal in only three years, and we were free.

A Distinction About Goals

My fitness trainer taught me something valuable about setting goals. JR works with a lot of tri-athletes and marathoners. He noticed a pattern in the athletes after they completed a major goal, such as running a marathon or competing in a triathlon. He often saw the athletes lose their drive and interest in training after their event. In fact, the motivation of some athletes decreased within days of finishing the event. Sometimes the athletes experienced deteriorating moods and even depression.

In talking with the men and women he trained, he discovered that these athletes trained at a very high level for months towards their goal of winning the event, beating a certain time, or simply completing the event. The training was demanding.

He began to realize that these athletes, who were driving towards their goals for months, now had no goal. They were drained from the event and needed time to recuperate, so it was tough for them to get excited about the next event. Yet the more time that passed, the more their interest waned, as did their fitness. He said it would shock him to see a person who was at the peak of fitness right *before* his or her event put on 30 pounds and decline in health in just a matter of months.

His solution? About one or two weeks before the athlete's event, while the athlete is still excited about his or her upcoming event, JR sits them down and makes sure they set their next goal. They set their next goal *before* accomplishing the goal at hand. Do you think this strategy could work with anything in life? It does for me.

Your New BFF

I assume you want your freedom as soon as possible and that you want to live at your current standard of living or higher. And I assume you want to be the one in control of your financial destiny, not someone else. If those assumptions are correct, then the rest of this book is dedicated to you and your infinite-wealth goal.

I know it's been said that diamonds are a girl's best friend, but I would argue that your real BFF (Best Friend Forever) is CASH FLOW because cash flow will get you to your financial dreams. And then you can treat yourself to all the diamonds you want.

CHAPTER 7
SHIFT YOUR FOCUS

To rise above the need for a paycheck takes...

I f you are familiar with the Rich Woman and Rich Dad philosophy, then some of the concepts in this chapter will be a review—with a twist. When it comes to your education, repetition is one effective way to learn.

Information about money that does not match up with your core thoughts and beliefs will be filtered out. But as your mind is opened, you may see familiar concepts in a new light.

Financial Statements Made Simple

In the Rich Woman world, there are fundamental principles that are impossible to omit when we're talking about women, money, and investing. It begins with the financial statement: the income statement, the balance sheet, and the statement of cash flow.

You'll notice that the financial statement shown here is not your traditional accounting financial statement. That is because we like to keep things simple.

The Income Statement

The Income Statement is made up of:

- Income (money flowing in), and
- Expenses (money flowing out).

Income

All income that flows into your household flows through the income column of your income statement. This includes all three types of income:

1. Ordinary earned

This is income that you work for and includes your wages, tips, salaries, and commission from your job or business.

2. **Portfolio**

   Portfolio income includes profits from any investment sales. These capital gains can come from the sale of stocks, businesses, and real estate.

3. **Passive**

   This is income from rental properties, limited partnerships in which you invest money but are not actively involved, and other similar enterprises. Passive income can also come from interest on savings accounts, bonds, certificates of deposit (CDs), stock dividends, patent royalties from inventions, and royalties from books, songs, and other original works.

Your job as an investor is to convert your ordinary earned income into portfolio and passive income.

It's important to note that each of these types of income is taxed at a different rate. Ordinary income is taxed at the highest level. The government takes the biggest chunk from the money you work so hard for in your job or business. Portfolio income is taxed at a lesser rate. Passive income is taxed at the lowest rate. When you invest for passive income, your money is working for you, plus you get to keep more of that money since it will be taxed at a lower rate.

Expenses

These are the monthly expenses you pay out each month, including such things as your mortgage payment (or rent payment), car payment, student loans, food, car and gas, utilities, insurance, clothes, eating out, medical bills, and so forth.

The Balance Sheet

The Balance Sheet is made up of:
- Assets (things that put money in your pocket), and
- Liabilities (things that take money out of your pocket).

Assets

The Rich Woman definition of an asset is not the definition you'll hear from your traditional accountant. The conventional accountant will tell you that an asset is "something of monetary value that is owned by an individual or company." By that definition, your alarm clock and your everyday dishes could be considered assets!

Most accountants go crazy with this definition because they want to classify your shares of stock, your jewelry, your personal residence, your cars, and your mutual funds as assets. To us, none of these things has any value until the day you sell them. If you sell something and make money, it's an asset. But if you sell something for a loss, then it most definitely is not an asset.

Using the Rich Woman definition:

An asset is
something that puts money in your pocket,
whether you work or not.

Why use such a definition? Because a clock and some plates and bowls will not get you closer to your financial dream, but *something that is putting money in your pocket whether you work or not* will.

Liabilities

Again, we go to battle with the traditional definition of a liability. Most accounting professionals will tell you that a liability is "an obligation to pay an amount you owe to creditors, be it an individual or an organization." The Rich Woman definition begs to differ.

A liability is
something that takes money out of your pocket.

You can see the dilemma. Most would list their Mercedes as an asset or something of value. We, however, would list the Mercedes as a liability because every month it takes money out of your pocket. "But it's paid for!" you argue. The car loan may be paid for, but what about gasoline, tune-ups and repairs, and insurance?

The biggest fight we get is when we tell people your home, your personal residence, is not an asset. We received a lot of flack for that, especially when times were booming and people were taking out loans against their home, sometimes two or three times. It wasn't until the real estate market crashed and people found out that they owed more on their house than it was worth before they started to understand this principle.

The problem with people calling their liabilities assets is that they believe they are financially better off than they really are. When the economy turned, many people were forced to face reality. They are now realizing what they have and how long they actually can survive financially.

This is why the concept of "net worth" means very little in the real world. When accountants calculate your net worth, they list everything but the kitchen sink. In most cases, to have the dollar amount your accountant attaches to your net worth, you would have to sell just about *everything* you own—at whatever the market will bear at the time.

This does not mean you shouldn't buy a house or a BMW or a new Cartier watch. It just means you shouldn't fool yourself into thinking that your liabilities, items that take money out of your pocket, are assets.

Pocket Science

Assets and liabilities are not difficult to understand. Many people have commented that "it's not rocket science." And it's not. I think of it as *pocket science*—specifically "put-it-in-my-pocket" science. So as you pursue your financial goals, see, feel, and hear that money flowing into your pocket.

A Different Focus

Here is the revelation I had when looking at the income statement and balance sheet.

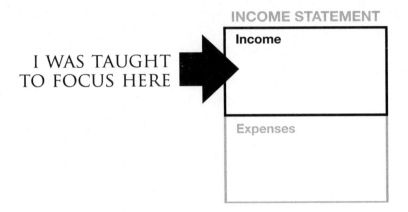

The key to financial well-being is to focus on acquiring assets.

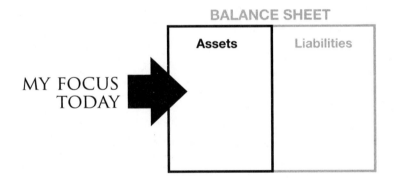

I was always told to focus on the income column. I was taught to get a job and work hard and keep getting pay raises. Or if I worked on an hourly basis, I should put in more hours or increase my hourly rate. The focus was always on income, specifically ordinary earned income—increasing my salary, wages, or commission. As long as I put my focus and attention there, then I would be working hard for that income all my life.

The lights came on when I realized that the key to financial well-being is not to focus on acquiring income, but to *focus on acquiring assets.*

When I made that connection, life became easier, both in my personal financial life and in our Rich Dad Company business. I focused on acquiring assets personally and also focused on the assets we were building within our company. Yes, our books and board games are assets because every month those products generate cash flow in sales to the company and royalties to me and Robert. But the question we began asking throughout the company was: What new assets are we building today? It is simply a different way at looking at the world.

Let me tell you about our new venture, an asset-in-the-making, into digital games... and introduce Nicole Lazzaro.

> *Nicole is extremely smart and talented and is recognized as one of the top women in the world of digital games. She owns a consulting company and her expertise is in demand by well-known, influential companies all around the world.*
>
> *She and I were having breakfast one morning, and she pulled out her iPhone to show me a new game she was developing. She was really proud of this game. She said, "In my consulting business XEODesign, my clients hire me. I love what I do, and I love my clients. They want my knowledge and experience to help them make their games more fun. However, I only earn money when I work for them. So I saved up for several years to self-finance an iPhone game called Tilt World. This is my first asset that puts money in my pocket!" she declared triumphantly. "For me, having my own assets gives me the financial freedom to pursue my own creative designs and dreams."*

You see, a job, even if you are the owner of the company, is not an asset. You're the one doing all the work. A savings account may not be an asset if you're paying more in bank charges than you are collecting in interest. If that's the case, then it's a liability.

Carrie, a woman I've met a few times, overheard me talking with my friend about assets. She jumped into our conversation and said, "I'm so fortunate. I just received a big asset, a large inheritance from my uncle."

My friend asked her, "What are you going to do with it?"

She said, "Well, the first thing I'm going to do is take 20 family members and friends to Hawaii for two weeks. First-class hotels, yachts, whatever they want. I've budgeted about $300,000." Our jaws dropped open.

"And then what?" my friend just had to ask.

"After Hawaii," she said, "I'm going to start looking for a new home with a big swimming pool."

We smiled, wished her well, and moved on. Even an inheritance may not be an asset.

The strategy to achieve infinite wealth, where the cash flow coming in is equal to or greater than your monthly expenses, is very simple:

Acquire assets that give you cash flow.

It's no secret that wherever you put your time, energy, and focus will grow in your life. So if you want to achieve your financial dreams, you may want to put your time, energy, and focus on acquiring assets.

Asset-Column Tip

Here is one rule you may want to adopt that Robert and I have held to since that first two-bedroom, one-bath house. Once a dollar (or a peso, euro, yen,…) goes into the asset column, it *never* leaves the asset column. You may sell an asset, but that money then buys another asset. Too often I hear a woman say, "I bought my first asset!" only to learn that, one year later, she sold it to buy a new house or car for herself. So I'll say it again:

Once a dollar goes into the asset column, it stays in the asset column.

CHAPTER 8

It's All About...
YOU

To rise to your #1 asset—you—takes...

S tepping out there and going after your financial dreams take
GUTS. It takes daring, chutzpah, strength of character and,
above all, the ability to laugh. Call it what you will, but this game is not
for whiners, sissies, or teachers' pets.

We've seen the TV ads and infomercials promising you "financial
freedom" for five easy payments of $29.99. Really? They kind of remind
me of this cartoon: Yes, there seems to be something missing.

"I THINK YOU SHOULD BE MORE
EXPLICIT HERE IN STEP TWO."

I'm Afraid You *Are the Miracle*

If you're looking for that financial savior to come to your rescue, guess what? Tag, you're it. Not that you'll be figuring out this miraculous equation all by yourself. Just the opposite. You will definitely want a support structure of friends, experts, brokers, mentors, and teachers with you on this journey. When I say, "You're it," that means this is your journey, and you are the architect.

However you choose to embark on this journey, your success depends on one very important factor. It depends upon you creating what you want and figuring out how you will get there in a way that fits your values, your spirit, your interests, and your passion. In other words, it comes down to you.

Being True to You

It's rising time for you. It's not rising time for who people want you to be. It's not rising time for you the mother, or you the wife, or you the businesswoman, or you the daughter, or you the artist, or you the homemaker, or you the best friend, or… It's rising time for you! No label attached.

We women get so caught up in playing so many roles for so many people in our lives that we often lose track of who we really are and what we want. My girlfriend told me that days after her divorce was final, she was shopping at her local grocery store and her eyes started welling up with tears. At first, she didn't know why she was crying. Then as she was pushing her shopping cart down the aisle, she realized that she was so used to shopping for what her kids (now grown) and her husband wanted that, for the first time in a very long while, she was actually shopping for herself. She was crying as she looked at all the food on the shelves because it dawned on her that she didn't know what food she wanted. She was so conditioned to put everyone else's needs and wants before her own that she had completely lost track of who she was. That was the start of her rediscovering herself.

Who are you? When I say you, I am speaking of your innermost person, your spiritual being.

How do you know when you are being true to you? You can tell because magic happens. Things just seem to go right. You think a thought, and it manifests instantly. You are "in the right place at the right time." Things occur effortlessly. You are happy and enjoying life. That is the true you.

Be True to Your Financial Life

How in the world does "being true to you" fit into money, finance, and investing? Simple. Your plan has to fit you. The subtitle of *It's Rising Time!* is "A Call for Women—What It Really Takes for the Reward of Financial Freedom." Not the dreams of your parents, your siblings, your spouse, or your friends. To realize your reward of financial freedom really demands that you stay true to your values, your loves, your dreams, your talents, your wit, your silliness, and everything that makes you, *you.*

This is a big dream. And it will take all of you. It will test you at times. If you're doing this for anyone other than you, then you won't make it. You will quit. *This is why your reason for pursuing your dream, your purpose for your financial journey, has to be what you really want deep down in your heart and soul.* It's your drive and passion that will get you through the rough patches, the doubts, and the setbacks. But every success you experience will propel you forward.

No One Is More Important Than You

No one and no thing is more important than you. Not your children, your spouse or partner, your religion, or your mission in life.

"Heresy!" some of you might say. "How selfish is that? How arrogant!"

Not really. When you make some one or some thing more important than you, then you give that person or thing power over you and allow them to have control over you. You lose a piece of yourself to whatever you grant the power to. Your children, your spouse or partner, even your purpose in life may all be very important to you, but they are not more important than you, the being.

Think of a time when you were really happy. What were you doing? How were you feeling? Were you more productive? More fun to be around? Willing to help others? Did things seem to happen effortlessly? This is you being all of you and making you most important.

Another kiss of death to being true to who you are is when you take on someone else's dream. You either adopt it or pretend that it's your dream. A good example is from a movie about a famous golfer entitled *Bobby Jones: Stroke of Genius*. Bobby Jones, as a very young boy, is enamored with the game of golf. He sneaks around the golf course, peering out from behind trees to watch the great golfers play. Someone gives him a few handmade clubs to play with. He loves the game of golf… but he also wants to please his family. He becomes a lawyer because that makes his mother happy. His father is a lawyer. His grandfather thinks golf is a waste of time, and he should have a "respectable profession." Even after winning tournament after tournament, he quits the game to make his wife happy because she doesn't like him on the road all the time. He loves the game of golf yet, throughout the movie, you see him struggle with his internal conflict because he is taking on the dreams and desires of those around him instead of doing what he loves and being who he is.

The classic scene is when he is in the lead of a major golf tournament. Up to this point, he has yet to win a major event. On the final day of the tournament, he receives a telegram from his grandfather, who had never supported Bobby's love of the game. In fact, he actually belittled it. The telegram read: "Win this one, Bobby!" He finally had the approval he had been seeking from his grandfather. Because of that, he won his first major tournament that day.

Be True to You… or It Can Kill You!

My dear friend, Dr. Radha Gopalan, is a heart transplant specialist at Mayo Clinic in Scottsdale, Arizona. After completing graduate school and his residency in the United States, he returned to Sri Lanka, where he was born, to learn acupuncture and Eastern medical practices. Dr. Radha's passion is blending Eastern and Western medical theories and philosophies. He says, "When a person comes to me with serious heart problems, oftentimes the only solution is surgery. The surgery fixes the immediate problem but does not address the cause, which may be found in the ethereal, the energy, the thoughts, the emotions, the invisible."

This is one of the most profound statements I heard from Dr. Radha. He said that *if you're doing something that you don't want to do, that goes against who you are at the core, then that causes conflict within the body and the spirit, which leads to disease.*

"It takes courage to grow up and become who you really are."
— *e.e. cummings*

A devoted vegetarian serving up burgers every day at McDonald's would most likely experience conflict. A woman who constantly puts up with demeaning comments from her husband has conflict. When we experience something, anything, that is out of sync with our personal values and ethics, it creates a battle within us.

Thank you, Dr. Radha, for giving us the best argument for staying true to who we are. If we don't, we will die! And sometimes it's not a physical death, but an emotional or spiritual death within.

One Smart Young Woman

You will enjoy Alecia St. Germain's story.

When I was in college, I thought I had it all figured out. I was going to graduate from college, get a job, get married, have children, and have a wonderful life. I was right on track when I met my fiancé my senior year. He was in the same program as I was, and we quickly found we had so much in common. After college graduation, we sought out employment that allowed us to travel the country together. We had a great time seeing new places and going on vacation. I also racked up a whole lot of debt trying to keep up with his lifestyle. I was never bad with money until I met him. One thing is for certain—my heart is a terrible money manager! It didn't seem like a big deal at the time because I would just *put it on credit cards and then make payments. I had a great-paying job and more money than I was ever used to having. It was no big deal— that is, until I realized I had accumulated over $45,000 debt in less than three years and had nothing really important to show for it.*

I am lucky to have a mom who taught me rules of financial freedom throughout my teenage years because it might have taken me a lot longer to come to this sobering reality. I sat over my finances and sulked about the mess I had gotten myself into. Sure, I could be mad at him, but I did it to myself. I remember I would say, "I can't afford to do that." And he would say, "That's okay, I'll pay for the flight and hotel. You just pay for the food and fun while we are there." Seemed fair enough, but it really added up.

The other problem for me was that I don't like handouts. So mentally, I was keeping track and then paying for other things in our daily life to try to make up for it. The realization was starting to creep into the pit of my stomach that we wanted two very different things in life. We always kept our finances separate so, to this day, I couldn't tell you how he afforded the things he did.

When you're in debt the way I was, it's easy to feel angry and trapped. You want to blame someone else for your misfortune. That's much easier than putting it on you and feeling like a failure. Driving home, I contemplated what my life had become. I realized if I stayed in this profession, living my life the way I was living it, that I had already arrived at my final destination.

I was raised that if you don't like something, then change it. Don't whine about it. I enrolled my fiancé and me in a weekend financial seminar. I decided that weekend that I wanted to live my life financially educated and working towards my freedom. I made a plan to pay off my debt that wasn't putting any money in my pocket.

Education is one thing, but emotional fears are the hardest to overcome. At the core of it, it's the confidence to stand up to others who are holding you back and not fulfilling you the way you need to be fulfilled.

Remember that my fiancé took the class with me. I told him, "No more trips, and no more spending money frivolously." He gave me so much support as I started the new venture into investing. By "support," I mean he was content to let me work for financial freedom for us. But he would still go ahead and do whatever recreational activity he wanted to do on his days off. It didn't take long to figure out that he wasn't raised with the same values I had and that I wanted for my future children.

The final straw came as a birthday gift about one month after my change in focus. He surprised me with a trip to Hawaii. He said that all I had to pay for was the food and fun. Sounds familiar, doesn't it? Any other person looking in on this situation would think I was so ungrateful, but this time I was wiser. It became crystal clear that he did not support the vision I had. Just because someone says they are on board with you doesn't mean that they actually have the same commitment you do.

There are many ways that someone could have handled a situation like this, but for me, I broke it off. I remember trying to decide how to explain why it was over. How many times has a woman said to a man, "It's not you. It's me."? We say it because it's a nice way of letting someone down. Right or wrong, I said, "It's not me. It's you."

For me, financial literacy isn't just your education. It's a lifestyle that affects the way you live, love, and grow.

A Tool to Validate You

There is a lot of stress and effort that goes along with acting like somebody other than your true self. Let's face it. There is no such thing as a perfect daughter, perfect wife, or perfect employee. Being true to who you are is key because, in order to have financial freedom, you must also have the freedom to be yourself.

Kathy Kolbe is an expert on human instincts and has dedicated her life to helping people find the freedom to be themselves. Kathy created what she calls the Kolbe Index, which is a tool to identify a person's natural, innate, and unchanging talents. In essence, it validates you for being you.

Our entire company took the Kolbe Index because it is also an excellent business tool to ensure that you have the right people in the right jobs where they will excel. When Kathy saw my Kolbe assessment, she asked me, "Kim, have you attempted to be organized in your life?"

"I have," I replied.

"And how's it going?" she asked.

"Terrible!" I exclaimed. "I've taken seminars on how to be organized. I've read books. I bought so many planning manuals and gadgets that promised to make me organized. But my office still looks like a bomb exploded in it. Nothing has helped."

Kathy started laughing and then gave me a gift. She looked me in the eye and said, "Kim, you will never be organized. It's not who you are."

I was stunned. I felt like this tremendous weight had just been lifted from me. "It's not who I am?" I questioned.

"No. So stop wasting your time and effort on being something you're not." She then pointed out three people in our company who love to organize, and one of those three was assigned the task of keeping me organized. The real beauty was that I could now focus on what I do best.

The president of our company at the time always thought of himself as a nerd growing up. He was into books and studying while his friends were into sports. After he saw his Kolbe results, he realized that he wasn't a nerd. What he loved and excelled in was research and collecting data.

Learn more about the Kolbe Index at kolbe.com/itsrisingtime

It was also clear to him and to us that the role of president, which he had been struggling in, was not where he would excel. He went on to work with a development company researching new markets for the company's expansion. He did very well there because he could be himself and put his true talents to work.

A Rising-Time Tool

Have you ever journaled? It is a simple and extremely effective tool for discovering the truth about yourself and the environment you're in.

All it takes is:

- Something to write in, (It could be a spiral-bound notebook, a legal pad, or a hardcover book with blank pages. You can go to an office-supply store and buy a journal book specifically for this purpose.)

- A pen,

- You and your thoughts.

I journal when I'm looking for an answer. It's a type of meditation for me. I may have a question I'm struggling with, an upset I'm not over, or a habit or behavior I've noticed that's not serving me. I break open my journal, state the issue in writing, and then just write.

My rules are:

- I don't analyze, question, or filter what I write. I write down any and all thoughts that come out. There is nothing politically correct here. This is for my eyes only. It's about getting out whatever is in my head so that the truth can come out.

- I write until I get an answer. There is no time limit. Write until the issue is complete. You'll know and feel when you have the answer. That will be a rising-time moment. There may be a sense of relief, excitement, calm, or even laughter, depending on the situation.

For example, the other day I came home from the office and noticed I felt "blah." My energy was low, my mood was off, and at 2:00 in the afternoon, I was done for the day—no motivation. I didn't know why. I walked into my home office and started journaling. Anger, blame, self-pity—it all came out in the writing. My rising-time moment was when I wrote: "I thrive in a creative environment—people brainstorming, free to share all ideas, all opinions valued, working together to come to the best solution. This is the environment I will, and choose to, play in. If that is not the environment, then I will change it."

The story is that the day before, we'd had a Rich Woman creative meeting with six of us working on a new project. This project had been in the works for eight months, and we were close to unveiling it. We decided to walk through the entire project to be sure it was delivering what we originally intended. The meeting was lively, loud, fun, insightful, and tense at moments. As a group, we came up with solution after solution that no one person could have imagined on their own. It was magical.

Later that same day, I was asked to join a meeting. There was a problem to be solved. I barely knew the people in the meeting. The atmosphere was very different. Instead of working through the problem to come to a solution, the meeting was filled with blame, invalidations, "my way or the highway"-type language, and no collaboration. The space was heavy. It felt miserable. I sat there quietly and let them fight it out. I said very little. In my journaling, I realized that it's up to me to choose the environment I want to play in AND that sitting quietly and doing nothing was the lazy way out. It turned out I was actually angry at myself for not speaking up. By saying nothing, I had actually condoned the behavior that played out. That goes against who I am, and that is where the upset was within me.

I knew I had my answer through my journaling because immediately I got brighter, happier, and empowered to get back into action.

It's Your Dream

Being true to yourself is a must in reaching your financial dreams. First, it has to be your dream, not someone else's good idea. Second, in this process you will be faced with choices to make, sometimes tough choices. Your best choices will be those that resonate with your values, talents, instincts, and passion.

What type of asset should you pursue? What kind of ongoing education plan should you follow? What tools do you have in place to keep you on track? How do you acknowledge and celebrate your wins along the way? These, and many more choices, will be answered according to who you are. Every one of us is a very unique and gifted woman. This is *your* journey, *your* dream, *your* process. Make it true to you. It's rising time!

PART TWO
ACQUIRE

GAINING THE KNOWLEDGE
TO MAKE IT HAPPEN

CHAPTER 9

QUESTION THE "EXPERT" ADVICE

To rise above all the financial noise takes...

The June 2010 cover of *Fortune* magazine read: "You can still... Retire Rich." Good, hope-minded title since the world was in the middle—or possibly the beginning—of a financial recession / depression / disaster / or whatever you want to call it. Many people didn't see "rich" as an option. They were battling not to lose everything. This was one year after the infamous Bernie Madoff was sentenced to 150 years in prison for cheating people out of billions of dollars in a pyramid investment scheme. It appears that *Fortune* magazine was doing its best to breathe life into a sick economy.

The story begins, "Admit it: You feel you've been lied to... you were told that stocks are your best investment for the long run. But the S&P (Standard & Poor) 500 has gone exactly nowhere in 12 years. You were told... pile into stocks when they bottomed on March 9, 2009... You were sold a bill of goods! And now... who can you trust?

"The answer is that, despite your feelings of betrayal, the classic advice is still valid."

Really? So what is this "classic advice" they are referring to? The journalist writing the story came up with three must-do's for a person to "still retire rich":

1. *Diversify*
2. *Save more ferociously*
3. *Live below your means*

"Diversify"

Yes, this is the same old, tired advice: Diversify (which means don't put all your eggs in one basket) and spread your money among various investments. However, usually when most financial "experts" talk of diversification, they are saying to vary your investments among different stocks. The author here takes a grand leap and instructs people to diversify among *global* stocks, not just *U.S.* stocks. (This is a very U.S.-based publication.) So basically, the classic advice still is: Invest in stocks. (Didn't their story begin by telling us that the S&P 500 has gone nowhere in 12 years???)

When the financial media (TV, print, radio) talk about investing, they are typically talking about paper assets—stocks, bonds, and mutual funds. About 95 percent of investors are in paper assets.

Now, investors are starting to pay more attention to commodities, such as gold and silver, than they have in the past. They cannot ignore the fact that the S&P 500 has gone nowhere in the past 12 years while, at the same time, the value of gold has increased over 700 percent and the price of silver has shot up over 800 percent. It seems like there just may be much better investment opportunities out there other than stocks, bonds, and mutual funds.

"Save More Ferociously"

Ever since I knew what a dollar was, I was taught to save money. I remember walking into our local bank with my mom to open up my first savings account. In those days, it was all manually done. I received my passbook with my initial deposit. I think it was $10.

It was official. I had now entered the world of money. I felt very grown up.

The old advice to save money has echoed from generation to generation throughout countries and throughout history. It is still being echoed today. But is this good advice today or simply a familiar refrain repeated by people too unconscious to question its validity?

The *Fortune* magazine writer says we're not saving enough. The assumption he and most financial "experts" make is that the only way a person can retire is to save their way to retirement. First of all, that would take an awful lot of savings.

Consider the statistics for women. In the United States, the average woman has a life expectancy of 80. This is the *average* age. Let's say you're a healthy old broad, and you live to 95. You retire at age 65. That is 30 years of retirement. Given the standard of living you desire, how much money would you need to save to live the life you want for 30 years? My guess is, it's a pretty large number.

Rich Woman makes a very different assumption. We assume that women, not the government, dictate when we want to retire—possibly before age 65—and that we'll retire via investments that are under our control, not via savings that are under Wall Street's control.

What's Wrong with Saving Money Today?

Many things are wrong with the traditional advice of saving money:

- **The interest you earn on savings**
  Interest rates on savings throughout much of the world are extremely low, almost nonexistent in some parts. Your savings account is actually a loan to your bank. The bank takes the money from your savings account and loans it out to its customers at a much higher interest rate than they are paying you. You are basically financing your bank's business for a ridiculously low rate of return on your money.

  If you were going to invest your money into a new electric-car start-up company, would you accept a return of 1 percent or less for your investment? Probably not. Yet that's what happens when you put your money into your bank's savings account.

> *Susan, a general surgeon, wanted to teach her two children about money. She took her son and daughter into her bank to open their first savings accounts. When the bank statements arrived, she and her kids reviewed them together. After three months, she noticed a disturbing trend. The fees the bank was charging to manage the accounts were greater than the interest her kids were earning. She shockingly realized that her two children were actually losing money every month! She quickly took her two kids back to the bank and closed both savings accounts.*
>
> *Where did she and her kids put their savings? Together they began to learn about gold and silver. Instead of going to a bank, she and her children went to a precious metals store and purchased one-ounce silver coins. This was back in 2005 when the price of silver was around $7 per ounce. Today as I write, the price is $41 per ounce. I'd say that's a much better return than 1 percent!*

- **Quantitative easing (aka, the government printing money)** Governments who fear that their countries will fall into a depression are printing money to artificially prop up the economy and give the illusion that the economy is stronger than it really is. What happens if a government decides to stop printing money? It is quite possible that the economy would fall into a depression, due to high unemployment and poor economic strategies. This is a scenario the government doesn't want to see happen since it would likely cause an economic collapse that could lead to national, and possibly worldwide, revolt and unrest.

So what's the likely scenario if the government keeps printing more and more money? (In the United States, it's the Federal Reserve that prints all the money.) It is speculated that the more money the Fed prints, the greater the odds that it will lead to…

- **Inflation**

  What does inflation mean? It means that your favorite brand of shoes or jeans will cost you many more dollars, euros, yen, or pesos in the future than they do today. Why would printing money lead to inflation? Here is a simplified explanation:

  Let's imagine that in all the world, there is $100. And in all the world, there are five products available. That would mean that, on average, each product would cost $20. The world government decides to print more money, thus putting more money into the world economy. It prints an additional $900. However, that money does not go to create more products or to grow the economy. It is used to pay off debt and prop up failing banks and businesses. So nothing new is created. Now, instead of $100 circulating in the economy, there is $1,000. Yet, there are still only five products available. Those five products are no longer valued at $20 each, but are now valued at $200 each. That is how inflation works, and that is the result of the government printing more and more money.

- **Worth-less money**

  If inflation, especially high inflation, does occur, then it will cost you much more to buy the same items you purchase today. Instead of $3 for a loaf of bread, you may be shelling out $12, for example. That dollar, euro, yen, or peso that you saved would then be worth only one-quarter of what it was previously worth.

Saving for retirement just got a whole lot harder. Not only is it difficult to save as much money as you will need, but the money you *do* save may be worth less and less as you get older and older. No wonder the greatest fear among Americans today is running out of money during retirement.

Should I Never Save Money?

Saving money, for me, is a short-term proposition. I save money while looking for my next investment. When the investment appears, I invest the money I've been saving. I invest it in something that will give me a solid return on my money. How difficult do you think it would be to find an investment that delivered a rate of return better than the 1 percent that your bank's savings account is earning you? It's not difficult. It can be as easy as buying a silver coin.

The third piece of classic advice the journalist offered was…

"Live Below Your Means"

Of course, you will have to live below your means if you follow this "expert's" advice because you'll soon discover that the money you saved and diversified to last you through retirement isn't enough. Time to downsize!

Living below your means is common everyday advice the financial "experts" serve up. Instead of just blindly accepting this advice, the question to ask is, "Why do they say that?" Jean Chatzky, well-known financial author and speaker, uses the words, "Live modestly." When asked why, she said, "Because 41 percent of people in the United States will run out of money during retirement." It goes back to assuming that people have to save their way to retirement.

Another assumption the "experts" make is that we don't know how to control our spending. We want instant gratification. In other words, we are spending more than we are bringing in.

"Live below your means" assumes the solution is to cut your expenses. I suggest the solution is to increase and expand your income.

Excuse me, but any mindless person can cut her expenses. It takes creativity, knowledge, and daring to grow your income. Instead of live below your means, why not *expand your means*?

Do I Live Above My Means?

A gentleman I know, Kevin, has lived above his means all his life. When he was younger, his income was high. He wined and dined beautiful women, drove the expensive sports cars, and lived near the ocean in Malibu. He lived a lavish lifestyle. As he got older, he had one problem: His lifestyle continued, but his income did not. Everything he owned was leveraged, or financed, to the hilt. His credit cards were always maxed out. He would ask to borrow money from his friends in order to support his extravagant lifestyle. "It's just a temporary setback," he'd tell them.

But it wasn't temporary. When it came to making money, he always went for the long shot, the big deal, the gamble. He lived well above his means. He just could not admit to himself that he was broke. He lived in an illusion for years. He refused to get a job. That was "beneath him," in his mind.

Today, his beautiful home has been foreclosed. He, his wife, and three children are basically homeless, living in inexpensive motels and staying with family members. He is 65. What surprises me, although I guess it really shouldn't, is that he still insists, "This is just temporary." Kevin definitely lived above his means.

Robert and I lived in a small house with a $400 mortgage for 10 years. Most of our friends during that time had high-paying jobs and were driving the newest Porsches, Mercedes, and BMWs. They were taking the expensive vacations to the trendy hotspots around the world. They lived in the McMansions.

Robert and I were not suffering by any means. Our house, small and inexpensive, was in a lovely resort with a water park, shops, and restaurants. The restaurant would deliver room service to our front door on a golf cart. We traveled the world. The difference between our travel and our friends' travel was that businesses paid us to travel to meet with them. Our friends paid their own way. We had a great lifestyle even though our expenses were low. We did all of this by design.

The money we could have spent on the big house and fancy cars went instead to buying our investments. At first, we invested primarily in rental real estate. Then we expanded our investments across all asset classes. It was definitely a case of delayed gratification. We continued buying investments and living where we were until the day came when the cash flow, or monthly income, from our investments could pay for the big house and fancy cars. Today, we still adhere to that strategy. We continue to increase our income and expand our means to create the lifestyle we want for ourselves. We did live below our means in the short term, as part of our long-term plan to expand our means. We have no intention of our income decreasing as we get older, as most financial planners and advisers assume. We intend that our income will continue to expand, thanks to the beauty of cash flow.

It is the live-below-your-means mindset that I oppose. For many people, including those offering the advice, this is a permanently poor mindset.

> *"Live below your means" assumes the solution is to cut your expenses. The solution is to increase and expand your income.*

But even more damaging than the poor mindset is that this advice kills the spirit. It contracts you. It makes a woman less of who she is, not more of who she is. It sentences a person to a life of mediocrity. And if you ever thought that you had to spend the rest of your life living below your means… then it's rising time! It's time to grow bigger, get smarter, and expand not only your means, but expand you as an individual as well.

More "Expert" Advice

Recently I was watching one of the national morning TV talk shows. The host said, "And stay tuned for our next segment on what you should do today to ensure your financial security!" So I tuned in, wanting to hear what new advice the expert had to offer. I had my pen and paper ready. Here was the fresh and innovative advice.

- *"Live humbly. Keep your life simple and mediocre."*
  I looked "humble" up in the dictionary. One definition is "to make somebody feel less important." I think that is the

perfect definition because, if you choose a mediocre life, then you will most likely feel less important.

- *"Have a budget."*
  This is *new*?

- *"Catch up. If you haven't been saving, then you'd better save, save, save! If you're in your 40s or older, then save even more."*
  Well, that's original!

- *"Work longer. The longer you can postpone taking your Social Security or government payout, the better."*
  You've gotta love that one. How inspiring!

This is the "newest" information being spouted on how to ensure financial security.

Is it new? No. Thought-provoking? No. Worthwhile? Not in my opinion. This advice may be good for people who want to "get by" or just survive financially. But this advice will not bring you financial independence.

I read it, I hear it, and I feel heavy, like there's a huge weight I have to take on for many years. It does nothing to excite me to take action. Where's the drive, the passion, the excitement for life? I feel like a school child being scolded by the teacher, "Sit down! Be quiet! Do as I say!" I want no part of it.

How to Tell Good Advice from Bad Advice

The first thing you have to know is what advice or information you're looking for. This depends on the dream and goal you *aspire* to. It also depends on your plan to get there.

Your plan is simply what you have to do to attain your dream. It primarily involves the *acquire* and *apply* elements of the Triple-A Triangle. Your plan does not need to be complicated. For instance, if you decide you want to be a tennis player, that's the dream. Your plan is to buy a tennis racquet, tennis balls, tennis shoes, and a tennis outfit and to take lessons three times a week. That's the plan.

There is one other piece to add to your plan—a way to keep score to tell you whether you are winning or losing. In tennis, the barometer could be the number of times you consistently hit the ball over the net. In your financial plan, the indicator may be the number of consecutive days you learn something new to bring you closer to your dream. Second, you have to know who you want to take advice from. You, and no one else, choose what information you want to put into your brain and which teachers you want to learn from.

Third, you have to know which advice and information are relevant and meaningful to you, and which are not. For example, the advice from the morning TV show is not relevant or meaningful to me because first, it puts me to sleep, and second, it is not aligned with my goals or my values. There is a ton of information coming at you at high speed these days about investing, the economy, and money. Your job is to decipher what's important, and what's not. One way to do that is to ask yourself…

What Does That Mean to Me?

Your financial life has to be part of your everyday life. It's not something you do on the weekends, because opportunity shows up on weekdays too. I do my best to learn something new about money and investing every day.

For example, today as I write, I learned about some of the horrors of school loans in the United States. Did you know that even if you declare bankruptcy, your school or college loan remains intact? It is the only thing that must be paid back. AND if you take out school loans to become a doctor, lawyer, or accountant, did you know that your professional certification could be pulled out from under you if you do not repay your student loans? If you have children who are in college or will be going to college, you may want to look into this further.

The world of money is fascinating. I think many of us probably lose interest or have that eyes-glazed-over syndrome if what we're reading or watching seems to have no relevance to us. If I'm listening to a radio show and the upcoming guest is going to talk about how to train a hamster, then I'll switch stations because I don't have a hamster. But we all have money, so when I'm watching a financial news show or reading a newspaper article about the economy, the question I ask is, "What does that mean to me?"

For example, there is a lot of talk about possible inflation. So what does that mean to me? It means that everything will cost more. It also means that the value of the dollar will continue to drop. And what does that mean to me? It means that interest rates will likely increase. And what does that mean to me? It means that I may want to fix the interest rate on my home mortgage soon so that I won't get caught in the future with a much higher mortgage rate that will cost me more money.

How you respond to the question, "What does that means to me?" also depends upon your mindset. Are you looking at this with the mindset of a poor person, a middle-class person, or a rich person? The news flash might read: "The price of oil skyrockets!" So what does that mean to me? A poor person might respond with, "That means I'll ride my bike or take the bus to work." A middle-class person may decide, "I'm trading in my BMW for a Prius hybrid car." And a rich person may decide, "I'm going to invest in oil." Which of those three answers most closely matches how you would respond?

When you ask, "What does that mean to me?" you may answer, "I don't know." That is often my answer. But that's when the learning begins.

Question Everything

Question, question, question… and challenge the same old repetitive advice that you hear every year. Question all advice that you hear and read. Question the "experts." Question me and my team. *Think for yourself.* Ask the questions:

- Does this make sense for me?
- What are the pros and cons?
- Will this get me to my financial goal?

Sometimes you may not know what questions to ask. Just keep asking because every question you ask is the right question if you're smarter as a result and if it leads you to make better, more informed decisions about you and your money.

It's rising time to think for yourself and question the routinely accepted traditional advice so many people blindly follow. It's rising time to discover which advice, information, and strategies work best for you.

CHAPTER 10

FINDING
<u>REAL</u> ADVISERS

To rise to an authentic advantage takes...

Fact versus Opinion

As you listen to all the financial advice online, on TV and radio, and in print, an important question to ask is, "Is this advice based on fact or on opinion?" Many people offer their opinions, disguised as facts, such as:

- "Men are better investors than women." Fact or opinion?

- "Women don't take risks when it comes to money." Fact or opinion?

- "Chocolate is good for you." "Chocolate is bad for you." Fact or opinion?

"Do you think it will rain today?" my neighbor, Ben, asked me as I pulled out of my driveway. Ben owns several car washes in town and, of course, he wanted me to reassure him as he looked at the rain clouds in the distance.

"No, Ben. I don't think it will rain." That was my opinion. If he wanted a factual answer to the statistical chance of rain that day, then he needed to consult a meteorologist. We often seek out opinions that match what we want to hear.

A personal finance "expert" was being interviewed on TV. She was asked about stock options as an investment vehicle. Her immediate comment was, "Options are very risky." Fact or opinion?

She revealed during the interview that she had never invested in stock options. She formed her opinion based on stories and news reports she had heard.

Someone who is very educated and experienced in trading stock options will say, "Stock options are not risky." Fact or opinion? This is where you have to draw your own conclusions. For me, if I were to trade stock options today on my own, it would be risky because I do not have the knowledge or experience to consistently make successful trades. If I choose to learn that, then I already know the course I would attend.

Have you watched any of the financial television shows? In almost every broadcast, there comes a point when the commentator will turn to his esteemed guest and ask a question like, "Do you think the stock market is at the bottom? Is the market finally rebounding?" And the guest confidently gives his reply—or rather, his opinion. It's an opinion because he or she doesn't know what the stock market will do. No one can state with 100-percent certainty that "the market will do this." It's all opinion based on a variety of factors and historical trends. That is why, whenever you hear someone touting a stock, or any investment for that matter, and she says, "This stock is going to the moon!" or "This investment is a sure thing!" you better do your homework, get the facts, and come to your own conclusion.

You'll hear this from many financial planners, "Mutual funds go up an average of 8 to 12 percent per year." Is that a fact or an opinion? Anyone can sway the facts to fit their argument. Why would a financial planner even say that? Because he sells mutual funds and makes a commission on every sale. To find out the facts, simply look up a specific mutual fund's performance for the last three years, and that will tell you the truth. You may also want to ask your financial planner how much money is taken out of your returns in fees and expenses. Those deductions are not included in the stated returns.

As you gather your own information, ask the necessary questions and think and decide for yourself. First consider: Is the statement I just heard a *fact*, or an *opinion*?

The Four Tests to Find Good Advice

1. Choose your advisers wisely.

Four girlfriends and I took a magnificent bike trip through the Loire Valley in France. The Loire Valley is known for its delicious wines and beautiful scenery.

The five of us are all entrepreneurial women. Kathy owns a branding and marketing company. Lisa owns several upscale drug and alcohol rehab facilities. Ronda owns a school dedicated to the troubled students that the public school system will not accept. Lee Ann is a business consultant to several major corporations. We all started our businesses from the ground up. We all made a ton of mistakes, but even the biggest fiascos didn't beat us, although there were times when every one of us wanted to quit. There was no safety net, nothing to fall back on, which was all good because it forced us to keep moving forward.

The bike tour was organized by a company that offers biking, hiking, and walking trips all over the world. Everything was first class. There were two women who were in charge of our Loire Valley group, 25 of us in all. These two women were responsible for our hotels, transportation, meals, biking itinerary, and most importantly, making sure we all made it to the next destination along our journey. The five of us were a bit of a challenge because, being independent and curious, we were always the last ones in at the end of day. We were, however, dubbed "The Fun Group" by the other bikers.

Over the course of six days, we got to know our two group leaders pretty well. The last evening of our trip, the entire group gathered for dinner in the dining room of a beautiful historic boutique hotel where we were staying. At the end of the meal, Emily, one of the group leaders, sat down next to me, and we talked. She said, "I love what I do, and I'm very good at it. Yet I'm ready for my next phase in life."

I asked her, "Do you have any idea what that next phase is?"

Emily nodded. "I want to start my own business. It's along the lines of what I do now, but a completely new and unique market. I've been researching it for about a year."

"What's your next step?" I asked.

"I think I'm going to go back to school," she replied, "and get my MBA (Masters of Business Administration)."

I was a little surprised and asked, "Why do you want an MBA?"

She replied, "I believe an MBA will give me the skills I need to be an entrepreneur." That was all I needed to hear.

The next morning was going to be the last ride of our trip. "Emily," I told her, "tomorrow you are biking with the girls!"

The next morning at 7:30, the six of us women got on our bikes and rode off. The discussion started. I asked Kathy, "Kathy, you have an MBA. Did it give you the skills to be an entrepreneur?"

She just laughed. "No! An MBA is designed for people who want to work in the corporate world. It trains you to be a corporate employee, which is where I started."

Lisa turned to Emily, "Do you want to be a corporate employee?"

Emily looked a bit stunned, "No. I want to start my own business."

Ronda asked Kathy, "Was the MBA education worth it?"

"Interesting question," Kathy replied. "The education is good. It will give you tools and strategies you can use in your business. But I don't know of an MBA program that will teach you how to start and run your own business—how to be an entrepreneur. You also need to look at the time and money you will spend on your MBA versus putting that time and money into your start-up business."

We biked for three hours. The conversation was non-stop, lively, and very candid. We laughed about the trials and tribulations of being an entrepreneur. Every new story seemed better than the last. The five of us were having such a good time reliving our past business adventures that we didn't notice until we stopped riding that Emily had become very quiet. Her eyes were as wide as they could be. "No one's ever told me this before!" she exclaimed. "And I've spoken to quite a few people about this."

"I'm curious, Emily," I asked. "Who suggested that you go back to school and get your MBA?"

"Several of my bike-tour clients, "she answered.

"What business were these clients in?" I prodded.

"They were retired," she said.

"Retired from what?" I kept pushing.

Emily started to laugh. "They all had successful executive corporate jobs!"

Lisa jumped in, "So they were giving you advice on how to do what they did—not knowing what it is you want to do."

"That's exactly right," Emily realized, "because what the five of you are saying makes sense to me. I was always a bit confused about the MBA path."

I added, "That's because we are all doing what it is you want to do. If I'm going to ask someone for advice, I seek out people who have actually done what I want to do. I want to learn from people who are out there doing it."

Emily was starting to realize that her current job of leading groups of adults, handling budgets, working with vendors, and dealing with emergencies on a daily basis was probably the best education she could get towards her dream of becoming an entrepreneur.

One Success ≠ Success in Everything

Emily told us she assumed that if a person was successful in their profession, they were smart in all areas. She had been taking advice from successful people who were employees of companies. They have a much different mindset than a person who owns the company.

This is also true for investors. Kyle was a very successful restaurateur. He and his wife, Diane, had three well-known restaurants in their city. They decided to sell the restaurants and enjoy what they had worked so hard for. When the sale was completed, Kyle and Diane had about $10 million. They figured they were set for life.

Kyle, being a successful businessman, decided he needed to invest a good portion of this windfall to sustain them through their retirement. Kyle is a very hands-on, do-it-yourself entrepreneur, and he approached his investments in the same way. He did it himself.

Unfortunately, what made Kyle a great entrepreneur did not necessarily make him a great investor. He had very little education in the investment world and almost no experience. He jumped in, assuming his business skills would carry him through. He lost half of their fortune. The other half? Assuming that the investments would pay off, Kyle and Diane spent the other half.

Just because a person is successful in one aspect of their life does not mean they know everything about everything.

2. **Practice what you preach.**
   Along this same theme, but with a twist, is seeking out advisers who may not be *preaching* what they *practice*. How is this different?

Often times those who are practicing what you want to do may not be preaching their advice. They may be quietly doing what it is they are so good at. You may need to do some searching to find these people, and then approach them and ask for their guidance. This is an excellent way to find mentors.

Practice what you preach is about distinguishing between those people who are openly giving their advice, such as a financial "expert," a speaker or instructor, or a media commentator. Many of these people make a living from sales made by offering their advice. The question I would ask before acting on their advice is:

Are they taking their own advice?

In other words, are *they* investing in what they recommend you invest in? Are they practicing the habits and strategies they are advocating? Are they living their message daily?

When it comes to brokers, does your real estate broker invest in real estate? Did your stockbroker purchase the same shares of stock she is recommending you to buy?

If a person does not follow his or her own advice, then something is amiss.

3. **Consider the source.**

   My friend Amy emailed me a survey about the current status of women and money. I read through it and found some interesting statistics and facts that they uncovered. As I read, it was clear that the survey questions were written in order to elicit a certain response so that the reader would draw the planned conclusion that… every woman needs a financial planner! Of course, in the fine print it stated that this survey was conducted by ABC Financial Planning Services.

   Have you ever watched the commercials on a financial television show? The ads typically feature mutual fund companies, stock brokerage firms, and investment banks. It's no wonder that most of the information from these shows favors mutual funds, stocks, bonds, and related financial instruments. If their number-one advertiser is a mutual fund company and their advertising dollars are keeping their television program (or magazine) afloat, are they going to speak out against mutual funds? Probably not. Instead, they'll promote why mutual funds are such a great investment and that you need to keep buying them.

Is your adviser free of any paid endorsements, advertisers, or associations with the investment world? Is the person on stage touting insurance products because she is their paid spokesperson, or because she actually believes they are the best investment vehicle for you? Is the financial TV anchor able to speak candidly about his recommendation, or are his hands tied by the network and their advertisers?

Sometimes it's just downright obvious. "Residential real estate is on the upswing!" stated a survey on the front page of a national newspaper at the end of 2010. The study said that the real estate market had reached its bottom and was now improving. In other words, now is the time to buy a house. The fine print wasn't even that fine. The study was done by the National Association of Realtors.

Consider the source of the information you gather.

4. **Adviser or salesperson?**
    Follow the money of the person selling you the investment. There is a big difference between a true financial adviser and a salesperson. Does the person advising you have no agenda (meaning they do not financially benefit, directly or indirectly)? Or do they have an agenda of their own (meaning they will make a commission or fee from what they are selling you)? Don't get me wrong. There are many excellent salespeople in the world. I work with them regularly. They make me money, and I make them money. The warning lights go off for me when the person comes across as a "financial adviser" but, in reality, they are only

recommending what they are paid a commission on. Just ask the question, "How do you get paid?"

For example, Jane has her first meeting with Sarah, a financial planner. After one hour of questions, Sarah recommends that Jane invest in an insurance annuity. Jane is to make ongoing payments to the insurance company. At retirement, she will receive monthly income checks. This advice sounds good to Jane so she signs up for it. Later, Jane discovers that Sarah's advice was not neutral. The insurance company pays Sarah a healthy commission for every person she signs up for this particular plan.

Was this a bad investment for Jane? Maybe, maybe not. Jane would need to compare it to other possible investments. The problem lies in the fact that Sarah wasn't giving Jane financial advice that was necessarily best for Jane. It was advice that was best for Sarah.

Some advisers are paid a flat fee for their advice and are not commission-driven. If that is the case, then I go back to the principle of "practice what you preach." Does the person advising you actually invest in what they are recommending that you invest in?

There is no good adviser or bad adviser here. The point is to separate the real advice from the sales pitch. Just be aware of what and whom you're dealing with.

Transaction versus Relationship

When it comes to brokers—stockbrokers, real estate brokers and business brokers, to name a few—you can generally separate the good from the not-so-good by how they approach your potential purchase. If you're talking with a broker or agent whom you've never met before and the conversations are only about this one deal, this one buy, then chances are she's only in it for the short-term commission from that one _transaction_. You may never hear from her again.

If, on the other hand, she's talking about other future potential purchases and asking you lots of questions (instead of doing all the talking), then she is probably more interested in developing a long-term business *relationship* with you.

Imagine you are driving to a vacation spot eight hours away from your home. You're going through a small town and you feel the car jerk, the steering becomes harder, and you know you have a flat tire. You pull off the road and, miraculously, there is a service station within sight a block away. You approach the man behind the counter. "I have a flat tire just down the road. Can you replace it?" you ask.

"Sure," the salesclerk says. "Where are you from?"

"About eight hours from here," you reply.

"Come through here often?" he asks.

"Never," you answer. The sales clerk just smiles.

What's about to happen? You're about to get ridiculously overcharged, and there's not a lot you can do about it. Many salespeople focus only on the short-term commission. "Let me make this one sale and collect my pay." That is a transaction sale.

The same is true of sex. Most women are looking for a long-term commitment, and most men just want a one-night stand. Fact or opinion? It all depends upon the woman and the man, right? As Chelsea Handler said, "Men don't realize that if we're sleeping with them on the first date, we're probably not interested in seeing them again either."

Great salespeople understand the power of building an ongoing relationship with their customers to serve them over many years. Relationship-based brokers will put much more attention on your wants and needs than on a short-term commission. The most talented brokers are not looking for a one-deal client either. They want the client who will buy from them again and again.

The point is not to walk away from a deal just because it's a one-time transaction. The point also is not to do a deal just because the salesperson wants to build a long-term broker-client relationship. The point is to know the difference between the two and seek out the best brokers and salespeople who will want to be part of your investment team over time.

Whom Do I Take Financial Advice From?

An adviser can be a person who personally counsels you on a regular basis, someone you listen to on TV, a stockbroker or real estate broker, an acquaintance, even an author. An adviser is anyone whose advice you use.

Here are five simple questions to help you evaluate the financial advice you receive:

1. Is the person offering the advice successfully doing what I want to do?

2. Does the adviser practice the advice they preach?

3. Is the advice clean of commercial ties, biases, and paid endorsements?

4. Is it really financial advice or a sales pitch?

5. Finally, do you trust this person? In your gut, do you feel they are ethical, moral, and forthright? Do you trust him or her to tell it like it is—the good, the bad, the pretty, and the ugly? Just as every coin has two sides, so does every investment.

You will kiss a lot of frogs to find your financial princes and princesses. Know that as your knowledge, experience, and cash flow grow, you will require smarter and more talented people on your team.

Team is the key word. Your team of advisers is in no way limited to only those giving you information and advice about specific investments. Your team will also include accountants, tax strategists, attorneys, and estate planners, to name a few. Robert and I have been through many advisers throughout the years, some good and some horrible. The best we've found are those who are smart and talented, but who are also generous—generous with their time, generous with their knowledge, and generous in knowing that if you win, then they win.

CHAPTER 11

SENDING OUT AN SOS

To rise up and keep going no matter what takes...

Yes, you are a Superwoman. And we Superwomen accomplish a helluva lot. There's no question about that. After all our crusading and taking on all that must be right in the world... let's face it, we're exhausted! The bottom line is this: For you to get from where you are financially right now to achieving your financial dream, you cannot do it all by yourself. It is impossible. And I'm usually pretty optimistic when it comes to doing the impossible. You must, must, must (I know, I sound very preachy right now) have some sort of support structure that you can rely on for moral, mental, and emotional backing and encouragement.

A support structure is different from a team of advisers. Your support structure is your go-to people whom you trust and respect and who will be a combination of confidante, sounding board, and feedback provider. They are there to support you in times of distress or "turbulence." They are aligned with you to accomplish your goals, and you can count on them to be honest and candid with you, even when you don't want to hear it.

My support structure consists of two tiers:

Tier #1: Your Core Support Team

If you are married or in a long-term relationship, ideally your spouse or partner will be your number-one supporter. I say "ideally" because this isn't always the case.

If your partner is resisting your efforts in this journey, then it will be tougher for you. There's no other way to say it. You can still succeed, but if you're coming up against a roadblock, then this may be an issue you need to deal with now. By no means let it stop you. I've heard many stories of dissenting men finally coming around... from women who refused to let their partner get in the way. Sometimes a little profit or cash flow is all it takes.

I guess the question to ask yourself is: "Is my partner an asset or a liability?" On one side of the coin, your partner can be your best ally and your strongest supporter. On the other, a liability or albatross around your neck.

Create Your Support Group

Another ideal scene is to bring together two, three, or four women who are embarking on a similar journey. There is something powerful that happens when women get together with the purpose of encouraging one another to go for that shot at their dreams. It is especially effective if the group's focus is financial because then you not only give each other moral and emotional support, but you can study together and share your experiences. It becomes a powerful educational resource. This type of collaboration is priceless.

There are many existing investment organizations and groups that could also fill this role. You may want to sit in on several meetings to determine which one best suits you. This is different from a small group of women, but often these clubs or organizations can be safe havens for you to deal with the obstacles or problems you're facing.

My support team has changed throughout the years. When I first started out, it was pretty much Robert and my mom and dad. That was my team.

Today, my core support structure consists of a small group of women and men. It is actually smaller than it was a few years ago. I find that what works for me is to have just a few people, close people, who I know will be there when I need them and for whom I will do the same. I have a much larger investment team and business team around me, yet my go-to support team remains small.

The point is this: Without some sort of ongoing support structure in place, you will probably quit. Imagine the conversation if it's you all by yourself: "This is too hard. I don't have time. My brother is right—I'll lose my money. That's it—I'm done." It's easy to justify this to yourself. But imagine making those same comments to three good friends who want you to make it, who know you can do it, and who are good enough friends to not let you quit. That's the type of support group we're talking about.

The Three Keys to Longevity

Robert and I treated ourselves to the luxury of seven days at Canyon Ranch in Tucson, Arizona. Canyon Ranch is dedicated to, as they state in their brochures, "revitalizing your spirit and leading a healthier, more fulfilled life." We can all use a little of that. Canyon Ranch offers spa services, yoga and exercise classes, lectures, and delicious, healthy food. There was a lecture I read about that I especially wanted to attend called "Living Younger Longer," something else we women could all use. At 7:30 in the morning, I walked into the lecture room with my coffee and my healthy bran-and-oat muffin and met the speaker, Michael Hewitt, a PhD and expert in health-and-exercise physiology. In his talk, Michael explained that in a study done of centenarians, people who are 100 years old or older, there were three traits that they attributed to a long life.

Those traits are:

1. **Purpose**
   *They have the sense of being of value—to themselves
   and others.*

   A sense of purpose is the core reason why you want to reach
   your financial dream. It is something bigger than you and
   bigger than the money. Your purpose drives you to keep going,
   no matter what.

2. **Optimism**
   They have a bright and positive outlook on life.

   Optimistic people tend to have a strong sense of well-being
   and confidence. It's been said that "pessimistic people tend
   to be more accurate, but optimistic people live longer." That
   certainly was true in this centenarian study.

   That is why my sister, Wendy, will probably live to be 150. She
   came home after a week-long trip and walked into her house
   to see a sheet of water cascading down the wall in her living
   room. Where most people would become frantic—yelling and
   running around—she calmly assessed the situation and said, "I
   guess we need to call a plumber." And then added, "That wall
   needed to be painted anyway."

   Another time, Wendy was visiting her daughter who works
   in Hanoi, Vietnam. Her first day there, she had a surprising
   medical emergency and was told that the Hanoi hospital was
   not equipped for what she needed and that she must fly to
   Bangkok. She and her daughter flew to Thailand and received
   the treatment there. It was an incredible ordeal. When she
   told me about it over the phone, it was clear that she never
   panicked or was ever distressed. She simply did what she
   needed to do. After she got out of the hospital, I asked her how
   she had managed it. She replied, "Well, I figured I had never
   been to Bangkok before so we checked into the Four Seasons

Hotel, had a martini, and the next day we toured the city. It was wonderful!" Yes, Wendy will live a long life.

3. Resiliency
They possess the ability to recover from a setback.

Resiliency is how quickly you can deal with, and bounce back from, adversity. Of the three traits, this is the one that I believe determines which people will see success instead of failure. Donald Trump told me that the determinant to whether a person will succeed in business depends upon how she responds in tough times. Does she curl up in the fetal position, resolved to a life of failure? Or does she dust herself off, smile wisely, and get back to work, smarter from the experience?

Maya Angelou, a civil-rights activist, writer, and dancer, said it quite succinctly: "I love to see a young girl go out and grab the world by the lapels. Life's a bitch. You've got to go out there and kick ass."

These three traits would benefit all of us in all areas of our life… including the journey to our financial dreams.

Soul Surfer

You may have heard the story of the young female surfer, Bethany Hamilton, from the island of Kauai, Hawaii. In 2003, she carried her surfboard down to the beach, as she did so many mornings, and paddled out into the surf. She was already an accomplished competitive surfer at age 13 with great dreams ahead of her. But that morning was not like other mornings. In the surf with her was a 14-foot Tiger shark that quickly struck her and her board. As a result of the attack, she ended up having her right arm amputated.

How would you react to such a horrific turn of events? Your dreams of being a world-class surfer have vanished. You have to learn how to live in this world with one arm, learning again how to eat, write, and even brush your teeth. It's hard to imagine such an incredible setback.

Bethany responded with unbelievable determination, optimism, and resiliency. She immediately wanted to get back on her surfboard. One month later, she was riding the waves. In 2007 she realized her surfing dream and turned pro. Her strength of spirit inspired a movie entitled *Soul Surfer* about her ordeal–and her comeback.

A System for Setbacks

For many people, the shark attack would have been the excuse to quit. An excuse to quit not just on surfing, but to quit on life. But Bethany had optimism, a sense of purpose, and one huge dose of resiliency. (No more grumbling about lost luggage!)

Resiliency, the ability to recover from setbacks, should be at the core of your support structure. You create your own system that allows you to deal with the inevitable setbacks and stumbling blocks along your journey.

I have had some remarkable setbacks in my life—broke and homeless in 1985, lawsuits, bad partners, people stealing from me, people cheating me, mistakes that literally cost me millions, not to mention public humiliation. That, of course, does not include the hundreds of smaller mistakes and mishaps I've experienced. And here I am, still standing.

I have two things I say to myself whenever I'm hit with a disaster. First, I remind myself, "This too shall pass." The next thing I say is, "Something good will come from this." I cannot say I'm smiling when I repeat those words, but I say them until I actually believe them.

It is obvious that statement number one is true because every setback I've had is behind me and here I am, still standing. For my second mantra, that too has come to be true. The results of the setbacks have always made me, my marriage, or our company stronger and better because of them.

There is an English proverb that says:

A smooth sea never made a skillful mariner.

A setback may be a small mistake, a disappointment, a problem, or a failure. A mistake points out something I didn't know. The key is distilling the "something I didn't know" out of the mistake.

I hate mistakes and setbacks as much as anyone. But once I get over the initial yelling and screaming, then I step back and ask, "What do I need to learn from this?" Sometimes the answer is crystal clear, and other times it takes a while. I do know this, however: If I do not discover the lesson out of the setback, then that specific problem will occur again and again until I get the message.

In the world of investing, most people fear making a mistake. Why? Because the result is often a loss of money. Does anyone like losing money? No one I know. Yet, herein lies the dilemma. If you are so afraid of making a mistake or experiencing a setback that you do nothing, then two things happen:

1. You don't learn.
2. You make no money.

Please know you will make mistakes, and there will be setbacks. It's all part of the process. Instead of looking at them as devastating events that must be avoided at all costs, step back and see them as possible opportunities to learn, to grow, to be a more successful investor, and to make more money. If you get the lesson, you will be smarter.

Tier #2: Coaches and Mentors

Having a coach or a mentor—someone more experienced than you who can guide you, teach you, and on whom you can call when things go off course—can be a vital member of your support structure or team.

The terms *mentor* and *coach* are often used as one and the same. The slight distinction between the two is that a mentor is typically someone with more experience and success than you have in doing what it is you are doing. Think of a mentor as a trusted wise man or woman. A mentor guides you. A mentor will relate to what you are going through because they've probably been through it themselves.

A coach works with you towards a specific outcome. The training is more structured and defined. This is my goal, and I want to accomplish it by this time. A coach will hold you accountable to do specifically what you say you will do by when you say you will do it.

For example, I have coaches and mentors for many areas of my life. I have a fitness coach with whom I train three days a week when I am home in Phoenix. I go to him for a specific workout routine each day. I have investment mentors with a wealth of experience whom I call on when I have questions on a potential real estate investment or I want their opinion on the economy or strategies on financing certain investments. I have business mentors with whom I brainstorm on all sorts of business problems and possible opportunities.

I also have what I call my "spiritual coaches" who work with me to process through my thoughts, decisions, and emotions that are not empowering me. They help me focus on what I want in life. These coaches are extremely valuable because I work with them when I'm not achieving my goals, when I procrastinate, when I lose my motivation, or when I'm bored or angry or upset. These behaviors are not me. They are not where I want to be. I want to be happy, motivated, in action, and achieving my goals. This is why my spiritual coaches are an important part of my support team.

Mentors and coaches can be the difference between mediocrity and excellence. Professional golfers, the best of the best, have coaches to keep them at the top of their game. It's the amateurs and hackers who think they can do it on their own. It's the same with investing. Mentors and coaches can keep you on track whether you're having a winning day… or a "learning" day.

This Red Ball Is Heavy!

The reason I have coaches and mentors is because I like to win. I like to achieve my goals. In order to win, sometimes you have to do things that are uncomfortable, difficult, and even scary.

My coaches and mentors keep me on track, especially when things get uncomfortable. I know my weaknesses, and I get lazy at times. I have coaches and mentors because sometimes I need people to push me harder than I will push myself.

I was working out with my trainer, JR, at the gym the other day. JR said, "Kim, pick up the red ball for your next set of exercises." I walked across the gym, leaned over to pick up the ball, expecting it to be pretty light. I slowly stood up with the red ball, realizing it was a lot heavier than the blue or yellow ball I was used to. I hesitantly walked back to JR, red ball in hand.

"Okay," JR started, "I want you to do 40 lunges with the ball over your head. Next, do 20 sit-ups on the incline holding the red ball. And last, 20 squats with the ball." I gave him a questionable look and set off to do my lunges. After the lunges, the sit-ups, and the squats, I came back to JR huffing and puffing, but quite proud of my accomplishment and ready to move onto the next, and easier, exercise.

Instead, JR said, "Good job. Now give me two more sets."

"Two more sets?" I protested. "This red ball is heavy! And you want me to do this two more times?"

JR just smiled and then said, "Do you want me to take it easy on you? Are you paying me to hold your hand, or are you paying me for results? It's up to you."

I quietly walked away with my red ball and began my next set of lunges. That's when I realized that, in order to get results in anything, there are times you've got to reach for the red ball. So often, we (myself included) go for the lighter yellow or blue ball because it's easier and more comfortable. It's familiar, and it keeps us where we are and with what we know. But in order to get the results that we want, to be willing to do what it takes, we've got to stretch for the red ball.

So ask yourself: Where in your life are you taking it easy, and where are you reaching for the red ball?

Your Customized Support Structure

You will create the support structure that suits you best at the time. The system you start with may not be the same system you depend upon one year from now. The people and strategies you call upon may change as you become more experienced and more successful. This is a natural part of the process.

I cannot stress strongly enough the importance of building a support team for yourself to call upon when needed. Not having a solid support structure is probably the number-one reason why so many women quit along their financial-independence journey. When you meet those unexpected setbacks and mishaps along the way, you will get discouraged if you think you have to have all the answers and solve every problem yourself. There is an easier, more gracious, more stimulating, and more fun way to do this. It's all about setting yourself up to win, and win again, and win again.

CHAPTER 12

EXPECT UNEXPECTED TURBULENCE

To rise up and just deal with it takes...

The airplane you are on has reached its cruising altitude, and you are settled in with a new magazine and beverage. All of a sudden, you feel the plane jerk, and then jerk again. The captain's voice comes on over the speaker and announces, "Ladies and gentlemen, we are experiencing unexpected turbulence. Please take your seat, and fasten your seatbelt."

Turbulence in the air is something that occurs, whether you like it or not. It's not right or wrong. It's not good or bad. It is an occurrence of nature that just happens. It just is. As a passenger on the plane, there is not a lot you can do about turbulence. But the pilot, the person in control of your aircraft, has several things she can do. She can slightly alter course to find smoother air. She can decide to go right through it and make sure her passengers are prepared. Or, if the turbulence becomes a safety issue, she can choose to divert the plane to another city altogether.

In life, every one of us has our own personal turbulence to deal with. The difference between the up-in-the-clouds airplane turbulence and the turbulence in our everyday life is that, in our life, we are the pilot, not the passenger. We can do something about it, and that "something" is to simply deal with it.

Turbulence or Problems

Turbulence is frequently thought of as a problem, but turbulence and problems are not the same thing. Eckhart Tolle, in his book, *The Power of Now*, describes a problem this way: "'Problem' means that you are dwelling on a situation mentally without there being a true intention or possibility of taking action now, and that you are unconsciously making it part of your sense of self."

You and I are the ones who make something a problem. Tolle goes on to say, "The mind unconsciously loves problems because they give us an identity of sorts… [We carry] in our mind the insane burden of a hundred things that you will or may have to do in the future, instead of focusing your attention on the one thing that you can do now."

Here is a question Tolle asks to make his point: "Do you have a problem now?" At this very moment, not tomorrow or in 10 minutes, but *right now* do you have a problem? Unless your house is on fire, you just slipped and broke your toe, or someone is robbing you at gunpoint, for example, every problem you currently think you have are problems in your mind that may or may not ever happen.

> *"My biggest growth has been sitting with things that are uncomfortable and dealing with them."*
> – Hilary Swank

What's the point? The point is that problems do not exist, except in our minds. A problem, according to Tolle's definition, is something we dwell on mentally.

So if problems do not exist, then what does? Tolle says, "There are no problems. Only situations to be dealt with now or… accepted… until they change or can be dealt with."

I call these situations *turbulence*. Turbulence is a given. It occurs repeatedly in everyone's life. The question is: Do you deal with it, or dwell on it?

When a pilot experiences turbulence, she must take action at that moment to deal with it. She cannot say, "Oh, I don't want to tackle this now. I'll handle the turbulence later." Yet, many of us do just that.

We experience turbulence that could be dealt with immediately, and we'd be finished with it. But instead, we put it off because we don't want to confront it in the moment. That's when we create a problem for ourselves. It could be as simple as not wanting to make a phone call we need to make. Instead of taking action now, we put it off, think about it, lose sleep over it, and after going through all that headache and worry, we still have to make the phone call.

Donald Trump was being interviewed by a female reporter shortly after he had pulled himself out of a $900-million debacle. The reporter asked him, "During that time when the banks were demanding millions from you, were you worried?"

He looked at her as if she were speaking Chinese and replied, "Worry? What good is worry? You either take action, or you don't."

Donald definitely had a situation that was causing turbulence, but instead of worrying about it, dwelling upon everything that could go wrong, instead of turning it into a problem for himself, he took action and dealt with the turbulence.

When you are cruising along and suddenly experience some unexpected turbulence, ask yourself, "What can I do about this *now*?" If there is something you can do about it now, then do it. If there is nothing you can do about it in that moment, then accept that and take the necessary action when you can. It may look at times as if other people are causing us problems and worry when, in reality, we may be creating it ourselves.

Turbulence in Investing

There is no way possible for you to become financially secure and independent without experiencing turbulence. The trouble for so many of us is that we don't deal with the turbulence when it first appears, and we create problems for ourselves because of fear, confusion, or lack of knowledge. Achieving your financial dreams takes confronting your turbulence head-on, in the moment, and not allowing it to turn into a lingering unresolved problem.

Here are two stories of people facing financial turbulence:

Jerry and Debbie were adamant in their belief that saving money was the best way to build towards their retirement. After a couple of years watching their savings account earn them almost zero interest and with increasing prices bumping up their monthly living expenses, they decided to look for new answers. Becoming rental property landlords did not excite this couple, and they had not had success in the stock market. You might have guessed that they had extremely little financial education and knowledge.

An acquaintance, well versed in precious metals, suggested they consider taking a percentage of their savings to buy silver. She explained that silver is a consumable product which is used in such things as computers, cell phones, light bulbs, automobiles, water purification, solar cells, and batteries. With emerging countries requiring more building and infrastructure, the demand for silver will most likely increase. "At $17 per ounce, this could be a good place to move your cash into," she added.

For Jerry and Debbie, this conversation created turbulence. What this person said made sense, but they weren't sure if she was accurate. "What if we lose our savings?" they asked themselves. "We don't even know where to buy silver." They thought… and thought… and thought.

The question they should have immediately asked themselves was, "Where can I learn more about silver as an investment? Whom can I ask to find out where to buy silver?" From those two questions alone, they could have taken immediate action.

What did they do instead? They said to themselves, "I don't know what to do. I don't know if what this person is saying is true. If I buy silver from the wrong place, I might get ripped off." They went from slight turbulence (unanswered questions in their minds) to a problem they created for themselves, which was repeated over and over again in their minds.

The final result? They did nothing. Not only did they not do anything, but they created such a problem for themselves that, one year later, they are still talking about whether or not they should buy silver. In that one year, the price of silver increased from $17 per ounce to $48 per ounce.

Ashley owned a 10-unit apartment building. One afternoon she got a call from a tenant who was complaining about her air-conditioning unit that was not cooling properly. This apartment building was in Las Vegas, and summer was just a few months away. Temperatures would soon be in the 100s. Because Ashley had not set aside a reserve account for emergency repairs, she was short of money to repair the unit or buy a new one. Ashley was encountering turbulence.

Instead of asking, "What can I do right now to resolve this matter?" Ashley called the tenant and told him she was working on it, although she had no immediate plan to solve the air-conditioning issue. At that moment, she turned turbulence, something to be dealt with now, into a problem. She kept that newly formed problem running in her head. She'd wake up in the middle of the night thinking about it.

Eventually, the tenant moved out. He demanded Ashley reimburse him for the past two-months' rent, and he reported her to the Better Business Bureau. If turbulence is not dealt with right away, it grows worse—guaranteed.

How to Deal with Turbulence—Now

You've been hit with turbulence of some form and degree. What do you do?

First, take a deep breath.

Second, ask yourself, "What happened?" What exactly is the turbulence you're dealing with?

Third, ask these questions:

- What can I do *now*?

- Who can I call *now* who knows more about this than I do?

- What information do I need and where can I find it *now*?

Fourth, of the various options you have, decide which action you will take now. Then ACT!

Asking these questions and acting immediately accomplish two things:

1. It puts you in action, which puts you in control.
2. It avoids creating a problem, and useless worry, for you to continually dwell upon.

Note: If, because of circumstances, you cannot act now, decide what action you will take at the first moment available.

Different Levels of Turbulence

We all experience varying degrees of turbulence in our lives. They range from:

- Bumps in the road which slow us down, to
- Flat tires that can stop us in our tracks, to
- Head-on collisions that require time and attention to heal, to
- Life-threatening, or perceived life-threatening, events that take tremendous spirit and courage to get through.

It is interesting to see that one woman's head-on collision may be another woman's bump in the road. A woman who has experienced very little turbulence in her life may see a broken toe as a major negative life event, where another woman who has been through many ups and downs may consider it as a simple scratch along the way.

Be aware that the size of your task, your mission, and your goal is directly proportional to the magnitude of your turbulence. The bigger your goal, the greater the turbulence you will likely experience.

And the size of your success is directly proportional to the magnitude of turbulence you can handle. Why?

Turbulence Happens Because You're Shaking Up Your World

When you decide to change your world, especially your financial world, then resistance rears its ugly head. Resistance is a form of turbulence, and it can prevent us from doing what we need to do. According to Steven Pressfield, author of *The War of Art*, resistance appears when we commit to "any act that rejects immediate gratification in favor of long-term growth, health, or integrity"—in other words, long-term positive change, which is exactly what you are doing in your personal journey to reach your financial dreams. Just know that turbulence and resistance are simply part of the process. They are just something to be dealt with.

Word of warning: When you commit to improving yourself, making your life better, and actively going after change, you will shake up the worlds of those closest to you if they are resistant to change.

Be the kind of woman that, when your feet hit the floor each morning, the devil says, "Oh crap. She's up!"

Those who don't like change may feel very uncomfortable, sometimes threatened, when they see someone close to them actively doing things to improve their life. What is really happening is that your action is reminding them of what they are not doing. You are moving forward, and they are not. This creates tension and stress within them. So the resistance you may experience from those close to you really has nothing to do with you, and everything to do with them.

So all I can say to you is: Shake up your world! Rock your world! Go ahead, and make those around you uncomfortable. You're actually doing them a favor. Meet turbulence head-on. Deal with it, and move on. Yes, it really is *rising time!*

CHAPTER 13

FIGURE-ATIVELY SPEAKING

To rise to your financial genius takes...

I think we women have been brainwashed since grade school to believe that we are not good with numbers. Whether it was obvious or subtle, the message teachers drummed into our heads was that boys excel in math and science and girls excel in reading and writing. We now know that that type of thinking is BS—"blue sky." On top of it, what a crime for any teacher to tell a student that she is not good at something. Ideas like that only breed doubt and lack of confidence and kill the creativity and genius every child is born with.

Money is a life skill. The fact that it is not taught in most schools today tells you something about how our schools are failing our children. Money and finance are about numbers. The numbers are simply our scorecard. They tell us how well we are managing our household, running our business or career, and investing our money. Some of us love working with numbers. Others... not so much.

The bottom line is, if you intend to be financially fit and reach your financial dreams, then you've got to become very comfortable with the numbers. If you can add, subtract, multiply, and divide, then numbers can be your new best friend along this journey. It's no more complicated than that.

The First Step

No more saying:

- "My eyes glaze over when I look at all the numbers."
- "My husband handles all of our finances."
- "I leave the financials up to my financial planner."
- "I'm just not good with numbers."

If you truly believe any of those statements or have similar thoughts in your head, then you will never attain your financial wants in life. In order to get to where you want to be, you must develop a healthy attitude towards the numbers.

I do not follow one religion, yet I do remember the phrase from the Bible: *And the word became flesh*. I interpret that to mean that whatever you think and say becomes real. If you have the thought that money is bad, the rich are evil, or that the poor are more spiritual than the rich, then those thoughts, whether they are conscious or part of your subconscious, will override your attempt to become financially independent. Why? Because often your subconscious thoughts about money will be in direct conflict with your goals. Your subconscious thoughts will override your conscious ones.

There was a very colorful and non-traditional religious gentleman named Reverend Ike who preached what he called "positive self-image psychology." He preached about wealth and money in the healthiest of ways. He would say things such as, "The best thing you can do for the poor is not to be one of them!" "It's not the love of money that is the root of all evil; it is the *lack* of money." And when it came to your attitude about money, he quoted this Irish proverb: "Money swore an oath that nobody who did not love her should ever have her."

Reverend Ike believed that what you say is precisely what you get. "People use their big mouths to talk money away from them. You can talk money into your life, or you can talk money out of your life." "Never say money is hard to get. Money will hear you, and that's just what she'll be."

And the same is true of numbers. Instead of thinking that numbers are confusing, difficult, and boring, ask yourself, "What if the numbers were creative and fascinating?"

The Mystery of Numbers

Once you've rid yourself of any unsupportive or negative thoughts about numbers, math, finances, and money, it's time to embrace numbers and the power they offer.

What are the numbers? They are the P/E (price/earnings) ratio of a stock. They are the NOI (net operating income) of a real estate property or business. They are the ROI (return on investment) of any investment. If any of these words sounds foreign to you, then look up their meanings and define them. As one of my teachers says, "If you can't define it, then you can't have it." So if you can't calculate, or define, the cash flow of an investment, then you can't have the cash flow. All we are doing in these next few chapters is defining the numbers so you can have them.

> *If you can't define it,*
> *then you can't have it.*

Note: One of the keys to learning is vocabulary. It's been discovered that if you're reading a book or an article and you notice that you're getting sleepy or you find you've re-read the same paragraph several times, then you have probably gone past a word you do not understand. At that point, go back to where you were fully attentive, continue to read from there, and you will find the word that is foreign to you. Once you find it, then look it up and define it. The same can occur when listening to a lecture or a talk.

For many of us, the numbers of investing are a mystery. They may appear intimidating and mind-numbing, but in reality, the numbers are not a mystery, but just the opposite. The numbers are our clues for solving the mystery.

Every investment is a story in itself. Every time someone approaches you to invest money in his or her particular investment, whatever it may be, they will tell you the story.

- "This company has just discovered the cure for cancer and will be coming out with its new wonder product in five months. The stock will explode!"

- "This 24-unit apartment building is where the growth in Texas is moving. Boeing aircraft company is opening a new plant there next year so the demand for rentals will be extremely high."

- "My partner and I have created a new clothing line geared for women at colleges and universities. We've been in the fashion world for 25 years. So far, 30 of the major universities have picked up our line. We have verbal agreements that that number will double in the next six months."

Every investment has a story. Where people get into trouble is when they act upon the story only, without getting to the facts that the numbers tell. The numbers may tell the same story or a different story. It's up to you to uncover the true story, to solve the mystery.

Numbers As Clues

A number by itself means nothing. I never see a number from an investment analysis as a number. Instead, I look at the numbers as clues. The numbers do not exist to confuse you. They exist to give you clues. Consider every investment you are pursuing as a mystery to be solved. The numbers are clues to guide you to discovering the truth about, not "whodunit," but "what-is-it." What is the investment? How is it really performing? How can we expect it to perform in the future?

Going back to our "Miracle" cartoon, this is the way many investment pitches are made. They show you the pretty brochures. They give you lots of facts about the industry—not the specific company, city, or property. Ken McElroy—our investment partner, Rich Dad Advisor, and author of the book, *The ABCs of Real Estate Investing*—was laughing with me one day as we looked at this very thick prospectus, or offering, of an investment deal. As we read through it, it told us nothing about the past performance, yet there were too-good-to-be-true projections on how the property would perform in the future. That's when we remembered the rule: *The bigger the brochure, the worse the deal.*

"I THINK YOU SHOULD BE MORE EXPLICIT HERE IN STEP TWO."

If the offering is not clear and concise, then chances are, the investment is anything but great. Don't baffle me with your BS (blue sky).

If it is a good deal, then:

- Show me the numbers—past operating numbers, as well as the worst- and best-case scenario of future numbers.
- Explain why and how this investment will increase in value in the future.
- Give me the expected rate of return on the money I invest in this investment.

Imagine you are told a story like this: "For the past two years, my business sold $5,000 worth of product. My projection for this next year, with your investment money, is that we will sell $100,000 worth of product!"

At that point, you have only one question to ask, "How?" Anyone knows you do not go from $5,000 to $100,000 without a strong plan in place. If she can't show you how she will get there, then the $100,000 prediction is meaningless.

A number standing alone means nothing. The number 10 has no meaning. But if the number 10 were the number of vacant units in a 20-unit apartment building, now the number means something and raises the question: Why? What causes this building to be 50% vacant? Now the mystery begins to unravel.

The number 1,000 means nothing. Yet, if the 1,000 were the number of dollars a small business was losing every month, then that would raise the question from any potential investor: Why? And the mystery starts to unfold.

The purpose of the numbers is for you to identify the red flags, the possible inconsistencies, of what you are being told. The numbers help you discover what the facts really are and raise the question: Why? Don't look at the numbers of an investment as just a bunch of numbers. Look at the numbers as pieces of the story, or clues of the mystery, to be solved.

Untangling the Numbers

Let's say you are considering the purchase of a rental duplex. The seller tells you that the property has very low operating expenses. That sounds like a good thing. You review last year's numbers and see that the owner has indeed spent very little on maintenance and repairs for this duplex. It raises a question (could be a clue) in your mind, so you dig a little deeper. The owner is telling you part of the truth. Yes, it's true his expenses to maintain the property were very low. Upon further inspection, however, what he did not tell you is that, because he has spent so little to maintain the property, there are many repairs that need to be done to the building to keep it operating. His maintenance-and-repair expenses are low, but yours, especially when you first buy it, will be very high.

Note: That is not to say you do not purchase the property, but you now have better information as to whether this will be a good investment for you or not.

The numbers are just as important if you are purchasing shares of stock in a publicly traded company. Most people buy and sell stocks based upon rumors, tips, and current news. When you buy shares of stock in a company, you own a piece of that company. If you are going to invest in a company, wouldn't you want to review its past performance numbers and future projections, just as you would a privately held company?

Warren Buffett, who knows a little about the stock market, chooses stocks solely on the basis of their overall potential as a company. He looks at each company as a whole. When Buffett invests in a company, he isn't concerned with the ups and downs of the market's price per share. He is concerned with how well that company, as a business, can make money.

The more comfortable you become through practice and experience at understanding the numbers of any investment, the greater success you will have as an investor. As you will see, there is much more to the numbers than just digits on a page. Let's continue to untangle the mystery of numbers.

CHAPTER 14

TAKE THE "NUMB" OUT OF THE NUMBERS

To rise up to the Rich Woman in you takes...

The numbers of an investment are anything but boring, if you know what to look for. The numbers are the life blood of an investment. They are alive. They paint a picture of what was, and what is. By creatively playing with numbers, you can paint the picture of what will be.

What Numbers Are We Talking About?

It's just not as complicated as people make it out to be. In the world of money, there are three financial statements:

- Income Statement
- Balance Sheet
- Statement of Cash Flow

We've already talked about the Income Statement: a record of the Income and Expenses for a specific time period—month, quarter, or year.

We also discussed the Balance Sheet: a register of the Assets and Liabilities.

The Statement of Cash Flow shows you the cash coming in, the cash going out, and the remaining cash at the end of a specific time period.

We've also seen the difference between Capital Gains and Cash Flow. Therein lie most of the numbers you will need.

To simplify it further regarding these three financial statements, the main areas to focus on when analyzing an investment are these four items:

1. Income
2. Expenses
3. Debt (Liabilities)
4. ROI (Return On Investment)

1, 2, 3

Whether you are looking at investing in a friend's private business, the stock shares of a publicly traded company, or a rental property, it is not much more complicated than understanding the first three items:

1. Income
2. Expenses
3. Debt

These three items cover the Income Statement and the Liabilities column of the Balance Sheet. (We'll examine ROI in a later chapter.)

A side note: The assets that the entity owns may or may not be a factor in the investment. When it comes to the Asset column, the assets I'm most interested in are the assets that *I* own.

Income

The question to ask is: Where is the potential to increase the income?

For a business, is the company expanding into new markets? Is there a new product being launched?

For an apartment building, can we add washer/dryers to each of the apartment units and increase the rent? Can we raise the rents? Can we charge a premium for units overlooking the pool area?

In other words, where is the upside for expanding the income?

Expenses

Any amateur can cut expenses. That is not necessarily the best action to take. Instead, ask the question: How can money be spent most effectively to improve the value of the property or company? For example, a company may decide to cut all salaries in half to save money, but if the result is that the entire staff quits, then that is not the best solution regarding expenses. Increasing the money allocated to the marketing department for the launch of a revolutionary new product may be a good use of expenses to increase the overall value of a company. Spending money on carpet, paint, landscaping, and lighting to update a rental property in order to increase the rents may make perfect sense for your bottom line.

It's the same with your personal expenses. The non-thinking "expert" will tell you to cut your expenses when, in reality, it may make more sense to spend more money on assets that increase the value of your asset column and generate additional cash flow.

Debt

Most financially uneducated people view debt as a four-letter word. We have been conditioned that all debt is bad. We've been taught to fear debt. But not all debt is bad. There is good debt too. Getting into good debt will most likely be part of your plan to financial independence.

Debt becomes good or bad based on how the money is used. If the borrowed money is simply spent on consumption—a vacation, jewelry, or shoes that you charge on your credit cards—then that is bad debt. The car loan that you write a check for each month is bad debt.

Debt becomes good or bad depending on who pays for it. Bad debt is debt that you pay for out of your own pocket. Good debt is debt that someone else pays for you. Our tax strategist, Tom Wheelwright, borrowed money to grow his business when he began his accounting practice. That debt was paid back out of the positive cash flow of his business. When you purchase a rental property, you will most likely have a mortgage or loan on the property. If you manage the property well, then the rent from the tenant pays the monthly mortgage payment. That is good debt.

> *Debt service is often your greatest expense and can be the difference between positive or negative cash flow.*

In 1973, Robert took a real estate investing course in Hawaii. He began looking for rental properties in Hawaii that would give him positive cash flow. He was amazed at the resistance he received from the real estate agents he approached. "You cannot find those kinds of deals in Hawaii. Hawaii is too expensive," they told him. These were real estate *agents*, not real estate *investors*. Robert persisted and finally found a broker who knew exactly what he was talking about and who had cash-flowing rental properties to show him.

Robert flew to Maui where the properties were located, steps away from beautiful sandy beaches. The condominiums were selling for only $18,000 each. Remember, this was 1973. Robert went through one of the properties, reviewed the numbers, and was told he needed a down payment of 10 percent, or $1800, to purchase the property. What did he do? He pulled out his credit card and charged the $1,800 to his Visa card. Now most credit-card debt people accumulate is bad debt—dinner at trendy restaurants, new tires for your car, or a new lamp for the living room. In this case, Robert's credit-card debt was good debt because every month the income from that rental property paid for the debt and the expenses of the property.

When borrowing money to purchase an asset, such as a business or a real estate property, the question to ask yourself is: How can I get the best financing terms possible? Financing terms include things such as the interest rate, the length or term of the loan, the cost of the loan, and penalties for paying off the loan early. Debt service is often your greatest expense and can be the difference between positive or negative cash flow.

The Numbers Tell a Story

Here are two "stories" with the numbers from a rental property and the numbers from a business.

Numbers from a Rental Property

Here are two rental properties similar in size. One is a 10-unit apartment building and the other has 12 units. They are located in the same area of town. Review the two properties. Based solely on the few numbers you see in the income column, which one looks more appealing from an investment standpoint?

Property #1	Income	Property #2	Income
Gross income	$6,000	Gross income	$7,800
Laundry	$125	Laundry	$80
Late fees	$0	Late fees	$100
Net Income	$6,005	Net Income	$5,640
Price	$550,000	Price	$744,000
# of units	10	# of units	12
Vacancy	2%	Vacancy	30%

Remember that the numbers give you clues. Comparing the income portion from Property #1 and Property #2, what do you see when you look at the numbers? Do any of the numbers raise a question for you? If so, which ones and why?

Choose which property seems like the better deal for you. Spend a moment reviewing these numbers. Do you see a story forming in the numbers?

Now review some of the expenses from both properties:

Property #1	Expenses	Property #2	Expenses
Electricity	$1,700	Electricity	$300
Water	$800	Water	$400
Manager	$900	Manager	$300
Painting	$30	Painting	$280
Carpet cleaning	$20	Carpet cleaning	$100

Do any red flags appear when you compare the expenses between Property #1 and Property #2? What questions come up on either property? Looking at the expenses of these properties, do you favor one over the other?

Here are the clues I see in these numbers:

Income

Vacancy rate

A vacancy rate is the percentage of all units that are not rented. Property #1 has a 2% vacancy rate which means that 98% of the units are rented or occupied. Property #2 has a 30% vacancy rate which means that only 70% of the units are rented or occupied. It appears that a 2% vacancy rate is better than a 30% vacancy rate. But is it?

This is where the questions come up, and the story begins to appear. Could a vacancy rate of 2% mean that the units are rented because the rents are too low, or under market? Maybe there is an opportunity to raise the rents and increase the income. That is simply a matter of comparing the current rents of Property #1 with the rents to other similar apartments in the area.

Property #2 has a high vacancy rate. How could that be a good thing? What if you were able to rent those units and greatly decrease the vacancy rate? What would that do to your income? The value of your property is directly related to the income of the property. If you can increase the income, then you increase the overall value.

Late fees

A late fee is an additional amount paid by the tenant for not paying rent on time. Property #1 has no late fees, which means that all the tenants are paying on time. Property #2 has $100 in late fees. That equates to four tenants ($25 per tenant) paying late rents. What does this tell you?

It tells me that in this property, not only are 30% of the units empty, but those that are rented are occupied by less-than-great tenants. A great tenant is one that keeps up the apartment, rarely complains, and pays rent on time. At this point, is one property looking a bit better than the other?

Expenses

Electricity

The electricity expense of Property #1 is extremely high compared to Property #2. What does this mean? It may mean that the unit is master-metered, which means that there is one meter for the entire building, and the landlord, or owner, pays for all the electricity. A high expense like that could severely cut into your cash flow. If the landlord pays all the electricity, then the opportunity is to hire a professional company that has the systems and experience to charge the electricity back to the tenants. That would significantly reduce the electricity expense.

Water

The water expense of Property #1 is double that of Property #2. This could mean a number of things. It may mean that there is a water leak. It could also denote that the property underwent a massive landscape renovation, and that it is a one-time expense for just one or two month, which could greatly increase the value of the property.

Paint and carpet cleaning

A high painting and carpet-cleaning expense signifies turnover, tenant move-outs, and move-ins. Turnover is a big expense. It appears that Property #2 has a good deal of turnover which raises a red flag. Why all the turnovers?

Manager's salary

Property #1 pays their manager $900 per month. Property #2 pays only $300 per month. Obviously, Property #2 got the better deal there. Really? Consider what this manager is doing, or not doing. You have high vacancy, tenants are not paying their rent on time, and there is a lot of turnover. Is it possible that you get what you pay for?

Synopsis

So, which of these properties is the better deal?

The answer is… it depends. It depends upon the answers you uncover to the questions that the numbers raised.

Property #1 may be a good deal, especially if the rents are below the marketplace rents and the units can each be monitored to pay their own electricity. On the other hand, Property #2 may be the diamond in the rough if you can solve the problems of high vacancy, less-than-great tenants, and turnover. Property #2 is a case of a poorly managed property. If you bring in good property management and turn that property around, you may end up with a nice healthy cash-flowing property. Numbers raise the questions to solve the mystery of "what-is-it." Once you solve the mystery of what it is, then it's up to you to determine if it makes financial sense to take it to what it can be.

Numbers from a Business

Below are two beverage companies operating in the same city. They sell beverages to hotels and resorts. The owners are looking for investors to grow their business. They approach you for investment money. Take a moment and review the abridged numbers. Comparing the income and expenses, what questions are you asking yourself? Do you see any warning signs? What do you like about what you see? Between the two businesses, which one appears to be the better business to pursue?

Monthly Profit and Loss (P & L)	Business #1	Business #2
Revenue	$100,000	$115,000
# of distribution customers	6	2
Operating Expenses		
Salaries and wages	$40,000 (3 employees)	$45,000 (5 employees)
Vehicle	$3,000	$3,000
Office rent	$1,000	$2,500
Travel and entertainment	$5,000	$2,500
Miscellaneous	$2,000	$3,000
Total Expenses	**$51,000**	**$56,000**
Net Operating Income (NOI)	$49,000	$59,000
Office upgrade/remodel (one-time expense)	$4,000	$1,000

Here are the highlights of the story these numbers tell:

Net operating income
Both scenarios indicate a high profit potential. Their net operating income (NOI = income minus expenses) is about 50% of their revenue.

Sales revenue
Business #2 has slightly more revenue, but they only have two customers. One red flag: What happens to the revenue of business #2 should they lose one, or 50%, of their customers? Is business #2 targeting the larger customers? If so, by bringing in just one more customer, they can greatly, and quickly, increase their revenue. Business #1 has six customers so it has less risk in terms of customer loss.

Salaries and wages
Business #2 has slightly lower wages for its five employees. Business #1 pays higher wages for its three employees, but it has more risk of a disruption of operations should one employee leave. Since business #1 is paying higher wages, it may also be more costly to add an additional employee.

Office rent
Business #1 has less rent expense and a more modest office. Their offices will require a one-time upfront upgrade of $4,000. Since salespeople call on customers at the hotels, is an office upgrade necessary at this point? Is that really the best use of the investors' money? Business #2 has a more upscale office that requires less upfront upgrade expense, if an upgrade is deemed necessary.

Travel and entertainment
Business #1 pays twice as much in travel and entertainment. Are they spending lavishly in this area, or are the salespeople making more sales calls and doing more beverage promotions to attract new business? Note that business #1 has six customers versus two customers for business #2.

Miscellaneous
The question for the miscellaneous category always is: What's in it?
Do the miscellaneous expenses increase as the number of employees
and customers increase?

One further question
Are there other competitors in this market? If yes, then how do
business #1 and business #2 set themselves apart from their
competitors? If they are the only two players in this field, then what
is the likelihood of new competitors coming in?

Embracing the Numbers

In just those few numbers above, the mystery begins to unravel,
and the story starts to unfold. This is the value of understanding
and embracing the numbers. All you want to do is separate fiction
from non-fiction.

DEBT IS NOT A FOUR-LETTER WORD

To rise beyond secure to wealthy takes...

I t's called *bad* debt for a reason. It's bad! We lose sleep over the amount of debt we accumulate on our credit cards, our cars, and our home. I know the feeling.

Robert and I once had a tremendous amount of bad debt. Some was from being broke and charging as much as we could on our credit cards just to survive. More bad debt came from an early business venture of Robert's gone south. It's a horrible feeling to wake up in the middle of the night, worrying how we will make our next house payment or wondering which expense I may have to give up next. It sucks. It caused conflict within me because I kept telling myself, "This shouldn't be happening to me!" It also caused stress between Robert and me. Robert and I are living proof that the number-one thing couples fight about is money.

For those of you who are struggling with bad debt, I do have a solution. This is not meant as a commercial plug, but as a tool for you to use, if you so choose.

When Robert and I were facing hundreds of thousands of dollars of bad debt, I went looking for answers. I ran into the same advice everywhere I turned.

The advice was:

- Pay off the debt or credit card with the highest interest rate first.
- Pay a little more every month on every debt you have.
- Cut your monthly expenses.

I had done some of that, but I was still in just as much debt as when I started. Then I came across a formula that rang true for me. I jumped on the get-out-of-bad-debt plan and started. This is a nine-step program that Robert and I put into an audio program called *How We Got Out of Bad Debt*. Here are a few highlights:

- I stopped paying off a little bit more on each debt. That didn't work. I paid the minimum on all bad debts except the one I was focused on paying off first.

- I did not pay off the debt with the highest interest rate first. I first paid off the debt with the least amount owed. Why? Because I wanted a win early on to prove that I could do this.

- I did not do anything differently regarding my expenses, like reducing expenses or cutting up my credit cards. The only one thing I had to do differently was come up with an extra $100 per month. Now if you can't do that, which any woman can, then your chance for financial freedom is slim.

As I said, it's a nine-step program, and it worked for Robert and me. Most people can eliminate their bad debt within five to eight years. So if you're fighting against a wall of bad debt, then this program is something to consider.

Thinking Good Debt Is Bad Debt

All money that you borrow is not bad debt. It is what you do with the money that you borrow that makes all the difference. Understanding and acquiring good debt is an advantage that the financially educated have over the financially illiterate.

Yet some women resist this concept because they have been convinced for years and years that all debt is bad.

Overcoming the Fear of Debt

SCORE (Service Corps Of Retired Executives) is a wonderful organization supporting small business owners. This story ran on SCORE.org in 2010 and was written by my friend, Rieva Lesonsky.

If you're like many women I know, you may be cautious when it comes to money. Call it "Bag-Lady Syndrome"—that irrational fear that lots of us have that, somehow, we're going to end up penniless (no matter how hefty our bank accounts currently are). That attitude invariably carries over to our businesses.

In today's economy, of course, a frugal approach to business might seem like a necessity. And to some degree, that's true. But there comes a point when being frugal really means you're being penny-wise and pound-foolish—and for many women business owners, it's hard to tell when you've crossed that line.

Consider the case of Andrea Herrera. Herrera suffered from an affliction common among women entrepreneurs: fear of debt. She had grown her 10-year-old catering company to $650,000 in sales, but her reluctance to take out a loan was hindering further growth.

A mentoring organization finally convinced Herrera it was time to bite the bullet. Three years after she obtained a loan, her company projects sales of $1.3 million and boasts big clients including Oprah Winfrey's Harpo Productions. With new employees handling duties she used to juggle, Herrera has time for long-range planning so her business can grow even more.

Andrea thought of expenses as liabilities, rather than as opportunities to grow her business. The loan she acquired was debt that made her money, not cost her money. That is good debt.

Here's another story from Donna Serpiello, a woman who learned to overcome fear.

My husband and I married 27 years ago. I was 18, and he was 25. Not having any money to purchase a home of our own and not wanting to throw our money away on rent, we were offered the opportunity to live with my parents so we could save our money. Three years later, we were still living with mom and dad… and we had two kids and a third on the way. Plus, we still had no money in the bank to purchase that home.

My brother, who is a lawyer and a real estate investor, told me of a duplex that was for sale. He suggested that we try to buy it and then consider our options. We could stay with my parents and collect the rent from both units of the duplex. Or, we could live in one unit and rent out the other so we would have a place of our own.

Since we didn't have any money, I really felt it was a waste of time to look at the property, but my dad and brother insisted that we look first, and figure out the details later.

I remember the day we went to look at the property. My dad and brother came along. We all went through the property and came out with a variety of opinions. Mine was, "Forget it. It needs too much work."

My father replied, "You're buying it! You can't buy four walls for that price." The price was $20,000. My brother agreed.

My husband was unsure because the place needed so much work. We decided to go ahead and buy it. So now the issue was how to come up with the money for the down payment.

After looking at various options, we felt the best solution was to borrow a larger amount of money from the mortgage company than we originally planned so we could use the extra for the down payment. Before we knew it, we were proud owners of this falling-down duplex.

We lived with my parents as my husband remodeled the two units to make it suitable for renting. Each week after getting our paychecks, we fixed something else. Little by little, it got completed.

We moved into one unit and rented out the other. The rental income we received paid for the entire duplex, including the mortgage payment. We lived in the duplex for approximately three years.

We then purchased a second property for our personal residence. It scared me to purchase the second one simply because we would now be responsible for two mortgages. My brother again convinced me to try it. His advice? "The duplex already pays for itself with just one tenant. The second tenant will help you pay for your second mortgage."

But of course I worried about all the what-ifs. "What if it's not rented? What if the tenants don't pay? What if, what if, what if...?"

Finally my brother said, "Do it. If you find it's too difficult, you can always sell." I think he knew that once I took the plunge, I would learn to deal with the what-ifs.

As the years passed, the income from our duplex increased. It was paying for itself and quite a bit more. All the years we had the duplex, my husband did most of the repairs so it became a burden for him. This was part of the reason for wanting to sell the duplex. We also wanted to make another move since it was now 20 years later.

We thought it would be a GREAT idea to put all the profit from the sale of the duplex down on the new house. After all, doesn't that seem to make sense? It would reduce our mortgage and make our mortgage payment less. I consulted my brother once again. He suggested we keep both properties, rent them out, and let them pay for the third property we were about to purchase. Fear once again interfered and this time caused me not to listen to him. We decided to sell the duplex anyhow. It seemed like the right thing to do at the time. Well, that is until I read Rich Dad Poor Dad *and* Rich Woman.

When we sold our duplex, we realized roughly an $80,000 profit. We began looking for our new home. Why not? We had all this money for the down payment. Great idea, right? Wrong. For over three years, we searched for a home. Over those three years, little by little, the profit we were saving began to decline until it completely disappeared.

So I learned that your money sitting in the bank doesn't work for you. And it's okay to sell an investment if you reinvest the profit intelligently. We could have purchased a personal residence and a rental property with the profit we made. Or we could have kept the duplex that paid for itself and also gave us a substantial monthly cash flow. There were many options. I just failed to see them at the time. Fear was the culprit. In reality, I could have had both properties free and clear bringing in a *monthly cash flow of approximately $2,300 that could have paid for the third property.*

But I can't look back. I can only learn from the mistakes. That's why we kept our second property and made it an investment rental property. It has no mortgage so the monthly rent is all cash flow.

Am I financially free? No, not yet. I still have more to learn, but I am on my way!

Donna was paralyzed with the fear of debt. It terrified her to have two mortgages, even though those mortgages were putting money in her pocket—$2,300 per month, to be exact. I applaud her. The lights went on, she got the lesson, and today she is much smarter because of the action she took. That was indeed a rising-time moment for Donna. Well done.

CHAPTER 16

THE
INVESTOR'S PRIZE

To rise to your reward of personal sovereignty takes...

A n investor has one primary focus. It is the most important number for most investors. That number is ROI or Return On Investment. If you invest X number of dollars, pesos, euros, or yen, how much money will X make, or return, to you? It's a simple calculation:

$$ROI = \frac{\textbf{Annual investment income (cash flow)}}{\textbf{Cash invested}}$$

The amount of money earned is called *cash flow*. It is also referred to as the *yield*, because it shows what the investment yields or produces. For example, you invest $1,000 in a stock that pays you an *annual* dividend of $40. Your return on investment is 4%. ($40 / $1,000 = 0.04 = 4%)

You put $10,000 cash as a down payment to purchase a $50,000 rental property. At the end of the *year*, you have a positive cash flow of $1,500. Your ROI is 15%. ($1,500 / $10,000 = 0.15 = 15%) This is also called a *cash-on-cash return*.

To me, the cash-on-cash return is the most important number because it tells you exactly what your invested money is earning. In other words, it tells you how hard your money is working for you

These two examples of stock dividends and rental property are cash-flow investments. But ROI also applies to capital-gains investments. For example, you purchase a share of stock for $20 per share. The stock price goes to $30. After fees and expenses are deducted, your profit or yield is $5. Your ROI is $5 / $20 = 0.25 = 25%.

You may also hear the term *Internal Rate of Return* (IRR) which is a bit more complicated. IRR takes into account the present value of money. The present value of money is the idea that $1 today is worth more than $1 in one year. IRR also assumes that the cash flow or yields you are earning are all reinvested immediately and are reinvested at the same rate of return (which is rarely, if ever, the case). One calculation for IRR is:

$$0 = - outlay + DCF_1 / (1 + r)^1 + DCF_2 / (1 + r)^2 + ... + DCF_n / (1 + r)^n$$

And this equation is precisely why I do *not* use IRR as a measure for my money. This is why I prefer to use a cash-on-cash return on investment. If you want to understand the internal rate of return more fully, then you may want to research it online. Knock yourself out

Caution: When someone is pitching you on investing in their deal, be sure to define if the return on investment they are stating is a cash-on-cash return or an internal rate of return. They are very different when it comes to your bottom line.

What Is a Good ROI?

It depends. It depends upon the type of investment. It depends upon the economy. It depends upon your financial intelligence.

Back in 1979 and 1980, I remember my parents talking about the rate of return they were getting on their bank's certificates of deposit (CDs). It seemed normal at the time, but their rate was 18%. Who wouldn't like an 18% return on a CD today? What I found really interesting though was when the savings-and-loan crisis hit in the 1980s. The bank retracted the 18% interest rate and basically cancelled the outstanding CDs. (If an *individual* had done that, lawsuits would have followed!)

With little financial intelligence, you can typically expect a low return on your investments. Why? Because you won't know what to look for in investments that generate higher returns and will probably end up in investments or savings plans that offer low yields. This is why financial planners recommend mutual funds, CDs, and savings to people with little money know-how. This is also why so many people get taken in when they are promised too-good-to-be-true returns on investments they know nothing about. To obtain and sustain a high rate of return takes financial education and experience. There is no secret sauce, no magic pill. It takes putting in the time and effort to study, research, and then take action.

There's One Born Every Minute

Karen and I have been friends for years. She called and told me about an investment she was considering. She was going to invest $50,000, which was pretty much all the money she had saved over the years.

Karen explained to me over the phone, "I've been reading several financial books and have attended a couple of investment seminars. But I've been very nervous about actually investing my money. My solution has been to keep studying. I'm thinking that as long as I'm studying, I'm in the investment world. I just cannot pull the trigger. I am still single and just don't feel I know enough about finance.

"My two friends in California called me a few days ago, and they are all excited about this new investment they just got into. They told me that I am guaranteed to get 100 percent of my money back within the first six months. They said their friends are in it and a few celebrities too, and I need to decide quickly because it is only available until the end of the week."

The word "guaranteed" was a red flag for me, as was "get 100 percent of my money back within the first six months." It definitely sounded like a deal that was too good to be true. But you never know.

I asked Karen, "What specifically are these people investing in, and how can they guarantee you a 100-percent return in six months?"

She told me she didn't know but would find out. I pleaded with her not to go forward until she had the answers to those questions. I also didn't like the pressure to make such a big decision so quickly.

At the end of the week, Karen called me and said she was not going through with that investment. I felt relieved and suggested some other possible investments for her to research.

Fast-forward five months… I got an email from Karen which said: "I didn't tell you. After I told my friends I was not going to invest, they came back a week later and said, 'You are so lucky. You have another chance. They have extended the deadline for one more week. You can still get into this deal. We really think you should do it.' The peer pressure got to me so I invested my $50,000. Today, five months later, my money is gone. It was all a scam. I lost it all."

I was overseas at the time. Had I been home, I'd have run over to her house, grabbed her, disconnected the phone, locked her in her bedroom, and not let her out until I was convinced that an ounce or more of common sense had flowed into her. I had no pity or compassion. I was astonished and even angry with her. She knew better. She let her emotions and personal friendships take over. She also didn't do what she knew she had to do to check out this investment. She so wanted it to be true that she put her good judgment aside and rolled the dice. This is gambling at its best.

The moral of that story is: With little or no financial know-how, a deal that sounds too good to be true… is. The lower your financial education, the higher your risk.

Myth: Higher Returns Means Higher Risk

Have you ever been asked by a financial planner or stock broker, "What level of risk are you comfortable with? Are you conservative or aggressive when it comes to your investments?" That is the wrong question to ask.

I was talking with a friend of mine, a bright businesswoman. She said to me, "The reason I don't invest in what you invest in is because I am conservative when it comes to investing." She is not conservative. She is uneducated.

The financial planner should instead be asking, "Are you educated or uneducated when it comes to your investments?"

Saying you are "conservative" is just another way of saying "I'm uneducated. I'm scared. I don't know what to do, and I don't want to take the time to learn."

You see, the conventional wisdom of most financial planners is, "The higher the return, the higher the risk." This is simply not true. What is true is, "The lower your financial intelligence, the higher the risk," and "The higher your financial intelligence, the lower the risk."

The mistake so many people make is that they think the investment is risky. It's not the investment that's risky. It's the investor. Think about it. An investment is just an investment—whether it's a business, a property, a stock share, or a commodity. It's you, the investor, who determine if a specific investment is a good investment or bad investment for you. Not every investment you choose will be a good investment. No investor has a 100-percent track record of picking winners. Yet the more knowledge and experience you have, the better odds you have.

Look at it this way: Is a car going 25 miles per hour driven by an experienced driver risky? Probably not. Take that same car at the same speed driven by a heavily drunken driver, and that same car becomes a weapon. It's not the car; it's the driver. It's not the investment; it's the investor.

I don't like taking risks with my money. Nor does Robert. Nor do our close investor friends. We study, we research, we build up our experience. Have I taken risks? Yes, I've invested in stocks I knew virtually nothing about. I've stupidly turned my money over to a money manager and blindly followed his recommendations. I've even invested in a hedge-fund deal that I suspected was too good to be true... and it was.

Why do financial planners tell you that the higher the return, the higher the risk? Because they assume you know little to nothing about investing. With some financial education behind you, you will quickly know more than the financial planner. You probably already do.

Redefining Risk

Warren Buffett says of risk, "Risk is not knowing what you are doing." Again, the key word is *you*, not the investment.

A simple diagram from my friend Tom Wheelwright, tax strategist and investor, is this:

I define risk as: **R**eckless
                    Investing
                    Sans
                    Knowledge

My friend and stockbroker, Tom Weissenborn, offers these two rules when it comes to investing in stocks:

1. If you don't understand how the company makes money, then don't invest in it.
2. If it looks too good to be true, then it probably is.

What Appears Safe May Very Well Be Risky... Very Risky

What is safe in the Rich Woman world of investing may appear risky in many other people's worlds. Why? Because what the financial planners and "experts" define as safe, I define as ignorant... and very risky. What is risky in their world is not only safe, but sane in my world... if you know what you're doing.

Safe or risky? Those words need to be redefined when it comes to investing. Here are three places you can "invest" your money that typical financial advisers have advocated as safe.

1. Savings
2. Mutual funds
3. 401(k)s

Are these safe or risky? The typical financial planner will tell you they are safe. I say they are risky. Why?

Savings

With the dollar and other global currencies decreasing in value, your currency is worth less and will buy you less in the future. On top of that, the interest you are paid by the bank for your savings may earn you less than the fees and expenses you have to pay to keep your money in the bank. By saving money, in many cases, you are losing money. Would you call that a safe investment or a risky investment? An investment that consistently loses money is a liability.

Mutual Funds and 401(k) Plans

Mutual funds and 401(k) plans are basically the same thing. A mutual fund is simply a collection of stocks, bonds, and other similar securities. It could also be a company that pools the money collected from many investors and then invests those funds in stocks, bonds, and other similar paper assets.

A 401(k) is a retirement plan, often considered a retirement *savings* plan, set up by employers that allows employees to contribute a portion of their salary into this plan. A 401(k) plan invests the employee's contribution into mutual funds. Similar plans exist in other countries under other names such as a superannuation in Australia and New Zealand, an RRSP in Canada, a 401(k) in Japan, and a pension scheme in the United Kingdom.

So what's risky about mutual funds and 401(k) plans?

Many financial "experts" tell us mutual funds and 401(k)s are the answers to our prayers because: "If you are 20 years old today and you invest $1,000 into mutual funds or your 401(k) and you earn 8% per year, when you retire in 45 years at age 65, that $1,000 will grow to $140,000." Or at least that's the sales pitch.

Here is the reality on mutual funds. These facts do not come from me. They come from John Bogle. Who is he? Mr. Bogle is the founder of Vanguard, one of the world's largest mutual fund organizations, and the author of a book entitled *The Battle for the Soul of Capitalism.* He is now speaking out against the mutual fund companies because, as he says, they have gone from stewardship of your money to salesmanship. They are there to make money for themselves, not for you, the investor.

These are the facts from Mr. Bogle as he talks about the mutual funds' "tyranny of compounding costs":

> *Well, it's awesome. Let me give you a little longer-term example I use in my book of an individual who is 20 years old today starting to accumulate for retirement. That person has about 45 years to go before retirement—20 to 65—and then, if you believe the actuarial tables, another 20 years to go before death mercifully brings his or her life to a close. So that's 65 years of investing. If you invest $1,000 at the beginning of that time and earn 8 percent, that $1,000 will grow in that 65-year period to around $140,000.*

> *Now, the financial system—the mutual fund system, in this case—will take about 2.5 percentage points [in fees] out of that return, so you will have a gross return of 8 percent, a net return of 5.5 percent, and [in that 65-year period] your $1,000 will [instead] grow to approximately $30,000.*

$110,000 goes to the financial system, and $30,000 to you, the investor. Think about that. That means the financial system put up zero percent of the capital, took zero percent of the risk, and got almost 80 percent of the return. And you, the investor in this long time period, an investment lifetime, put up 100 percent of the capital, took 100 percent of the risk, and got only about 20 percent of the return. That is a financial system that is failing investors because of those costs [fees] of financial advice and brokerage, some hidden, some out in plain sight, that investors face today. So the system has to be fixed.

The mutual fund companies, the managers, the salespeople—they all make money whether you do or not. Most are not concerned with the actual performance of the fund. They are mainly concerned about their fees.

So the first question to ask yourself is, "Are mutual funds a good investment?" If you have no financial education and don't know where else to put your money, then mutual funds may make sense for you. If, on the other hand, you have some financial savvy, then it's pretty likely that you can find an investment that will give you a better return for your money.

The second question to ask is, "Are mutual funds safe?" Talk to anyone in the past few years who has had their entire life savings in mutual funds and has lost 30, 40, or 50 percent in this economic crisis.

One big factor of safety is the word "control." Financial education reduces your risk because it gives you, the investor, more control over what you are investing in. Putting your money into a mutual fund is no different than blindly turning it over to financial advisers and letting them decide what they want to do with it, with no input or guidance from you. Is that safe? That's as risky as it gets.

Risky versus Safe

In the world of investing, there are no investments that are 100 percent guaranteed. There is no investment that is absolutely safe (safe meaning "free from losses"). There is no risk-free investment. When you invest your money, you will win and you will lose. That is a guarantee. Yet there certainly are things you can do to reduce the risk and increase the safety.

In summary, what is risky and what is safer?

Risky	*Safe... er*
Having no financial education.	Getting financially educated.
Blindly turning your money over to a financial planner or adviser.	Actively investing your money and gaining hands-on experience.
Not understanding the investment and the returns on the investment.	Understanding the investment and the returns on the investment.
Putting up the majority of the money and the risk and letting others walk away with the majority of returns.	Putting up the majority of the money and the risk and getting the majority of the returns.
Having no control in your investments.	Having control in your investments.
Depending heavily on a financial adviser.	Becoming your own financial adviser.

CHAPTER 17

A DIFFERENT STATE OF MIND

To rise to your entrepreneur within takes...

E ntrepreneurs think differently than other people. If you're an entrepreneur, you know what I mean. If you're not an entrepreneur, then simply look at entrepreneurs such as Steve Jobs (Apple computers), Henry Ford (Ford Motors), Mary Kay Ash (Mary Kay Cosmetics), or Anita Roddick (the Body Shop). Without knowing them, you have to admit that, to accomplish what they have accomplished, they obviously had to think differently than the average person.

Every Investment Is a Business

Robert and I were having dinner with Dave Ramsey, a very popular personal money-management proponent. He looked at us and asked, "Do you know what the difference is between the two of you and the rest of us teaching personal finance?" We shook our heads no. He said, "You two look at everything through the eyes of an entrepreneur, including your investments. You look at everything as a business."

Robert and I talked about Dave's comment on the drive home. He was right. We approach business, investing, our household, even our marriage, as a business.

What exactly does that mean? In the world of investing, it means that every investment is a business. Every investment has its own income statement and balance sheet. Every investment must have sales and marketing driving it. Every investment must be profitable to survive. Every investment must have a team behind it. Every investment must have a purpose for existing. These are the fundamentals of a successful business and the fundamentals of a successful investment.

"Yeah, but I'm just buying a few shares of stock. I don't need all those things," you may be saying to yourself. Perfect example. What does every stock represent? A share of stock is backed by a company. Does a company need sales and marketing, accurate financial statements, a strong management team, a purpose or mission, and a good revenue stream to succeed throughout the years? Of course it does. Yet how many people, when they buy a share of stock in a company, do their homework and research the fundamentals of the company they are investing in? Very few. But I can tell you that Warren Buffett does.

The Rules of Every Investment

I have been an entrepreneur since 1984 when I started my first part-time business with no money and no experience. It was "do or die" through trial and error. Through the eyes of an entrepreneur, here are the investment rules I live by:

- **The investment must put money in my pocket.**
  First, I look for cash flow. Second, I look for appreciation.

- **The investment must stand alone.**
  An investment cannot survive off the cash flow or funding of another investment.

- **I want to control the investment whenever possible.**
  In real estate and my businesses, I control the income, expenses, and debt.

With investments such as stocks, privately held businesses, and commodities where I don't control these things, I do my best to actively monitor and stay on top of what is happening.

Never stop looking at ways to improve the investment and increase its value or the value it returns to you.

- **Every investment must have an exit strategy or exit options.** The rule is: *Know when you will sell before you buy.*

This may be based on price, date, certain market events, or personal events.

For example, Robert and I tend to hold onto our real estate investments and not sell. Yet, we know what it would take to sell. In 2006 when the real estate market was at its peak, we were offered an extremely high price for one of our apartment buildings that was operating at maximum cash flow for that property. We sold that property and moved the profit into a larger apartment building that gave us a much higher return on investment.

Many people got into trouble with stocks and flipping real estate (buying a property and quickly selling it for a profit) when the market began reaching new heights. People thought that stock prices and real estate prices would keep going up and up. When the markets turned, they got trapped. They got caught up in the emotion of the rising markets and had no exit strategy as to when they would sell.

An Exit Strategy Is Your Friend

Having and executing an exit strategy gives you more control.

Stocks

When investing in stocks, you want to have a strategy for:

- when you will sell if the stock does not move in your favor, and
- when you will sell and take profits when the stock *does* move in your favor.

One is called *a stop-loss order*, in which you determine at what price you will get out of the stock should the price begin to fall. You can give the direction to your broker or trust yourself to click the "sell" button when the stock reaches the stop-loss point you've selected.

The second is called *a take-profits order*. It's the same concept, but this is the price at which you will sell if the stock increases to a pre-determined price. Then you take your profits.

The stop-loss order and the take-profits order are, in many cases, insurance policies against you and your emotions. How often have you heard someone say, "I should have gotten out of that stock earlier."? It's easy to get caught up in the emotion of a stock shooting upward or plummeting downward. The stop-loss order and the take-profits order are two examples of exit strategies you can use with stocks.

Real Estate

A Scottsdale, Arizona, developer had purchased a 330-unit apartment building and was converting those apartments into individual condominiums to sell. Robert and I, along with an investment partner, agreed to purchase the 10 units he had renovated and was using as models to show prospective buyers. We agreed to lease those 10 units back to him in exchange for a monthly cash flow on each unit. The agreement was that the developer would continue to lease the units from us for three years or until 300 condos were sold, whichever came first. This was at the height of the real estate boom so, instead of taking three years to sell 300 condos, the developer sold them all in just 10 months.

Going into this deal, Robert and I had two exit strategies laid out. Once the leases were up, we would either continue to rent the units to other tenants or, depending upon where the market was at the time, we would sell the units and move the proceeds into a newly purchased apartment building. Up until this point, we had never seen the units except in pictures. Since the property was only 30 minutes from our home, we drove to the condos so we could decide which strategy we would use now that our units would no longer be leased by the developer.

As we walked through our units, the reality of what was happening in this real estate market and with this property hit us. Standing in the kitchen of the second unit, we turned to each other and simultaneously said, "We're selling!"

Why? Because it was clear to us the market was heading out of control. These were small apartments that rented for $800 to $1,000 per month. They had been upgraded, mostly cosmetically, and were now on the market in Scottsdale for $400,000. This may not sound like a lot but, at the time, that was an outrageous price for such a small unit in Scottsdale. We knew these prices could not be sustained for long and we had better get out now while we could. Still standing in our unit, we called our good friend and investment partner, Ken, and said, "We've got some money to move into an apartment building. What are you working on?" He laughed and said, "Your timing is perfect. I'm working on a new property as we speak."

We followed through with our exit strategy and sold the 10 condos rather quickly. We then moved the proceeds into a 288-unit apartment building that continues to give us a healthy monthly cash flow. (FYI, the real estate boom came to an end 18 months later.)

Every Person Has a Business

In *Rich Dad Poor Dad*, Robert wrote a chapter entitled "Mind Your Own Business." The business he was referring to was your asset column.

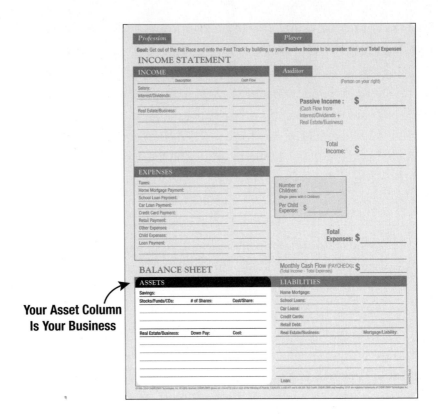

Your Asset Column Is Your Business

He said this about the financial statement:

The *Income* column is *you working for someone else* (the owner of your business).

The *Expense* column is *you working for the government* because your number-one expense is taxes.

The *Liability* column is *you working for the bank* because the bank makes money by loaning you money for such things as your BMW loan, your credit-card debt, and your home loan.

The *Asset* column is *your money working for you.* The asset column is your business because this is your future.

Most of us have been taught all our lives to mind our income column—our salaries, wages, and hourly fees—instead of minding our asset column, our real business.

How to Think Like an Entrepreneur

If you're like me, I was taught that the way to make money was to get a job. I was programmed to be an employee. The problem is that I am not good at being an employee. At my first job right out of college, I was fired by my boss after nine months. Others in the company saw my potential, and they hired me back. This time it took only six months before I was fired again. It wasn't for lack of ambition or brains. I just had a very hard time being told what to do and following so many rules. Yes, my parents raised an independently spirited child.

When I met Robert five years later, he asked me on our first date, "What do you want to do with your life?"

I instantly said, "I want my own business!" And three months later I did.

So I did not remain an employee for long. It's clear that there is a difference between the mentality, or thinking, of a serial employee versus a serial entrepreneur. In order to *mind your own business*, you do not have to quit your job and become an entrepreneur. But you do need to learn how to think like one.

It's All a State of Mind

We are products of our environments. People, our surroundings, and the values we live by all influence who we become and how we think. The mindset of a long-time employee is different from the mindset of a staunch entrepreneur. One is not better than the other. One is not right or wrong. The thinking is simply different. Here are a few distinctions between the two:

The Employee
- Values the security and guarantee of a steady paycheck over the uncertainty of greater wealth,
- Prefers a job with few problems,
- Dreadfully fears making a mistake,
- Strives for a higher paycheck and job promotions,
- Values time on the job over results.

The Entrepreneur

- Operates without a safety net. She knows there is no guarantee of a paycheck and may work for years without paying herself.

- Is a problem-solver. That is how she gets paid.

- Looks for new answers and new challenges. She's always learning.

- Is willing to make mistakes. It's how she learns.

- Is driven by passion and purpose. The goal is the mission.

- Knows that results are what counts, no matter how much or how little time it takes.

How It Plays Out in Real-Life Investing

Bringing an employee mentality into the world of investing can lead to two hindrances if you're not aware of them. First, if you value safety and security, you can easily be drawn to those investments that are deemed "safe" by traditional financial planners, such as certificates of deposit (CDs), savings accounts, money market funds, and mutual funds. *Safe* is very much like *conservative*. It means these investments are for the uneducated, scared investor who doesn't know what to do and won't take the time to learn. This is where the investor seeking security and safety will be directed.

The second, and more destructive, trait of an employee mentality is the fear of making a mistake. Even when we were in kindergarten, we were told, "Don't make a mistake!" "Don't color outside the lines." "Don't run. You might fall." In school we were rewarded for *not* making mistakes and punished when we did. It's no wonder that when we leave school, we forget what we loved as a child because we've been programmed for years to not take a risk because we might fail. We might, God forbid, *make a mistake*.

The truth is that mistakes are often our greatest teacher. It is how human beings are designed to learn. As Buckminster Fuller said, "Most children are *degeniused* by the love and fear of their parents—that they might make a mistake." In the world of investing, mistakes are part of the game and what lead to success. No investor can call it 100 percent of the time, but we can get smarter with our money with every investment.

This employee mentality can limit an investor's success, and it's certainly not limited to the working employee. Whether you are an employee, unemployed, or an entrepreneur, the key is to think like an entrepreneur when investing. To be a successful investor and get returns beyond the ordinary, you cannot do what the average person is doing. You have to think differently.

It's not difficult to adopt a more entrepreneurial mindset. From the previous entrepreneur list, let's just focus on three traits:

1. **Understand your mission and purpose.**
   My friend, Kim Snider, a successful investor and outstanding educator, always asks her clients, "What is your money's higher purpose?"

   What is the mission for you and your money? What do putting your money to work and minding your own business help you to achieve in your life? As you pursue your financial goals, always keep your mission and purpose at the forefront.

2. **Remember that results are what count.**
   You can talk, you can plan, you can research, you can keep very busy and put in a lot of time, but at the end of the day, the question to answer is: *How much money did my money make me?* In the world of investing, the bottom line is everything. And results require *action*. This is why, at some point, if you haven't already, you've got to pull the trigger. You've got to get in the game. You've got to put some money on the line.

   When investing, your focus must be on results, on the bottom line. We have a saying in our company: *What you focus on expands.* If you focus on the return on your investment, then your returns over time will most likely increase.

3. **Always keep learning.**
   Looking for new answers and new challenges? It's simple. The smarter you are with your money, the better your success. The learning never ends because the markets are always changing. And they are more volatile today than ever. A new economy is

emerging, and what that will look like, only time will tell. Yet it's clear that to be financially secure today takes new thinking, new ideas, and new education.

If you assume that the old economy is coming back or that what worked for you in the past will work again in the future, then chances are, you will find yourself in a financial struggle. If, on the other hand, you actively pursue your financial education and look for new answers, then you will start to see opportunity where others see doom and gloom. It's all about thinking differently about your money.

When it comes to you and your money, it makes no difference if you are an employee, an entrepreneur, a stay-at-home mom, or a full-time student. What matters is the mindset you bring to your business—your asset column. When it comes to your asset column, every one of you is a business owner. Now it's just a matter of thinking like one.

CHAPTER 18

A RECIPE FOR RAISING CAPITAL

To rise up to an abundance of opportunities takes...

You have an opportunity to purchase an old, but classic, 10-room boutique hotel that is about to go into foreclosure. But there's something missing. Could it be the—cash? Raising capital is also known as OPM—Other People's Money. It's a must-do in the world of investing.

You have a small business you want to start or you have an existing business you want to grow, yet you need an injection of money to take you to that next level. You call a few people you know outside the company as potential investors, but how do you persuade them to invest in you and your business?

A woman you've met on several occasions approaches you to invest in a privately run wind-energy company that has been in operation for five years. What do you need to know in order to decide if this investment is right for you?

Whether you are being asked to invest money or you are the person doing the asking, there are four questions you need to ask when being pitched a deal, and four answers you need to have ready when you're the one selling.

Only Lazy People Use Their Own Money

Many people only look to their own wallets and bank accounts to fund their businesses and their investments. I did, until a dear friend and mentor Frank, now 91, said to me, "Kim, you know that only lazy people use their own money."

Very confused, I said to Frank, "No, no, no, Frank. I work really hard to make the money, and then I invest it."

He laughed at me and countered, "Wouldn't it take more thinking and more creativity to use someone else's money instead of your own?"

My mind fought with that idea until I finally realized Frank was absolutely right. It was easy to use my own money to buy an asset, but I'd have to learn new skills and strategies to persuade someone else to part with his or her hard-earned money to put into my investment.

It's no secret that money today to invest in business or property has become tighter and tighter with current lenders. The traditional lenders are requiring you to jump through more and more hoops, plus they are requiring larger down payments and stricter terms. Many private lenders and investors are more cautious and have raised their standards as well. What's a woman to do?

It's Just Common Sense

Raising capital is actually not the mystery that many make it out to be. More than anything, it's good common business sense that will prevail. It's often said that the key to raising capital is a person's ability to sell. Selling is a crucial skill for any entrepreneur or investor. When it comes to raising capital, the question is, "What are you selling?" In other words, what is the lender or investor looking for?

The key to raising money comes down to four factors. If you can show a prospective lender or investor that you have command over these four main pieces of the puzzle, then selling will not be an issue, and you will attract more money than you thought possible.

The first time I raised money for my business, I wasn't aware of these four gems, so much of my sales pitch to prospective investors was based on sheer determination. The "sell" was much more difficult because:

- I didn't know what the investor was looking for, and
- I relied solely on my persuasion skills and friendships instead of sound business sense.

Even though it was difficult, Robert and I were still able to raise a quarter of a million dollars among 10 investors. And in the end, every investor got their initial investment back and made an excellent return on their money.

The process I follow today, whether I'm the one raising the money or people want to raise money from me, is much more efficient and leads to more effective results.

The Overall "Want" of a Lender or Investor

The what-I-want umbrella covering any deal that investors are considering to put their hard-earned money into is that they want a healthy return on their investment. They want a good ROI. If I give you X dollars, then how much money will I get back? That's the overall want of an investor. Understanding that, then here are the four points that will back you up and give confidence to a lender or investor that a strong return on their investment is possible.

Note: When I refer to a lender or investor, I am referring to either a traditional bank, a lending institution, a private organization, or an individual. The same criteria apply, no matter whom you are approaching for capital.

Music to an Investor's Ear

A presentation need not be long or complex. It will differ, depending on the business or investment involved. Often when a "pitch" is short and concise, it reflects that the presenters are confident in knowing what the investor wants and secure in knowing that they can deliver it.

Here are the four key factors a lender or investor wants to know, and in the order given:

- Project
- Partners
- Financing
- Management

If you can clearly and confidently address each of these four issues when looking to raise capital, then the odds of securing financing are in your favor.

Project

What is the project the lender or investor is providing you capital for? If it's for your business, then what exactly is your business? What makes your business unique from others in your industry? And what is the advantage your business has that will build confidence in the investor that it will be successful?

If you are raising money for an investment, then what exactly is the investment, and what makes this investment so attractive that I should place my money in this one versus another investment?

It's easy to tell a prospective investor all the good things about a project. It speaks volumes when you explain the negatives of the project as well, and how you plan to overcome them. Keep it simple. Keep it concise. Keep it real.

Partners

Who are the key partners behind the project? Who is putting the deal together? What is the track record of the partners? What experience do they have?

Put yourself in the investor's shoes. For example, whose music project would you be more likely to invest in—Paul McCartney's or Mike Tyson's? Would you put your money behind Oprah Winfrey or Lindsey Lohan to launch a chain of private entrepreneurship schools?

It's not rocket science. It's common business sense. What experience do the partners bring to the table and, as an investor, am I comfortable with their level of expertise?

Financing

Show me the *real* numbers. This is obviously a bit trickier for a new start-up company since most of the revenue numbers will be projected, not actual historical numbers. This is where previous experience can overcome that obstacle. Show the investor, as accurately as you can, how the project, be it a business or an investment, will make money. Be realistic. As an investor, I do not want to see the best-case scenario. I want to see the most realistic numbers, including the problems and roadblocks ahead. Every business and investment project has problems. To pretend that yours won't have glitches makes you look like an amateur.

How much money are you raising in total? Where is the money coming from? Is the money being raised from private parties, traditional lenders, pension funds, or government programs? What are the terms of the money borrowed? For example, let's say I'm being approached for the down payment on an apartment building. I'm told the other 80 percent is coming from a top lending institution. What would be more attractive to me as an investor: borrowing the 80 percent at a lower interest rate that must be refinanced in two years, or getting the 80 percent at a slightly higher fixed rate for 25 years? The first option presents more unknowns down the road (Will the interest rates be higher or lower in two years?) while the second scenario has fewer surprises.

How are you going to use the money being raised? What are the funds being allocated to?

One hint: If it's ever suggested that some of the money raised will be used to pay a salary to the owner of the business or the finder of the deal, then my door is closed. If you want a paycheck, go get a job.

And of course, you must answer these two key questions for your potential investor:

1. How soon will I get my initial investment back?
2. What is the return on my money?

The bottom line is this: Are your financing structure and terms attractive to an investor?

Management

The historical saying is: "Money follows management." I agree with that. However, your case for attracting capital is much stronger when you address all four components, not just management.

Investors want to know who is running the day-to-day operations. This is key to the ongoing success of any venture. Just as we looked at the partners, what is the experience level of the management team? Who are they? What's their background? What makes them vital to the success of this project or business? How do they react under pressure?

If you are starting your own business or if you're raising money to grow your existing business, then the partners and the management team may be the same people. That's not a problem at all if there are experience and expertise in the team that an investor feels confident in.

When it comes to commercial or residential rental properties, management is key. It is the day-to-day operations of an office building, a retail strip mall, a single-family house, or an apartment building that will make or break your bottom line.

I highly recommend reading *The ABCs of Property Management* by Ken McElroy if you own or plan on owning rental real estate.

How It Plays Out in Real Life

Let me give you a real-life example of how this formula works.

Robert and I were approached by a friend of ours about an investment opportunity. We knew this gentleman personally on a social level but had done no business dealings with him. He and his two partners are very well respected in the business community.

Here is what he told us for each of the four key factors:

Project

This is the investment. It is an Arizona landmark resort. Built in 1926, it was Phoenix's first resort. The resort includes three regulation 18-hole golf courses. This investment also includes two 18-hole golf courses from another Arizona landmark resort, the second built in Phoenix. Both properties were under the same ownership, and they both have gone into foreclosure. We are certain we can purchase them for about 25 percent of what the previous owner put into the property.

Partners

My two partners and I are purchasing this investment. This is the 54th venture we've done together. Here is a list of those projects and the results. You know one of my partners, Mr. XYZ. (Mr. XYZ is a business celebrity in the United States and, with his two partners, their reputation and track record are phenomenal.) We've been actively searching for three years for a great project, and we feel this is the one.

Financing

We are raising 10 percent of the purchase price from only a few private investors as a down payment. Two pension funds are putting up X number of dollars, and the bank who has foreclosed on the property is financing the rest of it. You can conservatively expect a return of X percent on your investment, and you should have all your money back within three to four years.

Management

As to the management, (At this point he drops a 4-inch binder on the table that falls with a thud.) this is the company that will be managing the hotel. They also operate the ABC and MNO resorts. (He then drops a second 4-inch binder on the table.) This is the company that will manage the golf courses. Here is a listing of the other golf courses they manage. We've checked out both of these companies thoroughly. Feel free to do your own due diligence on them.

That's the investment. What do you think?

What We Thought

It took us all of five minutes to say, "Count us in." Here is the beauty of our friend's approach. This is a multimillion-dollar venture. He could have gone into all sorts of graphs, figures, projections, and data. He could have spent hours telling us about what a great deal this was. Instead, he took all of 10 minutes, answered the four key questions, and five minutes later we had a deal.

Raising capital does not have to be a laborious, long, drawn-out affair. What you want as the investor and what your investor wants from you are simply good:

1. Projects
2. Partners
3. Financing
4. Management

If you can keep it to the four key points and give your investor or lender the confidence that you can deliver what you say you can, then money will flow to you.

One last point: *You'd better deliver!*

GOOD PARTNERS = GOOD DEALS

To rise to a more rewarding life takes...

I have a saying, "Business would be easy if it weren't for people." I say that jokingly because, when you have a great partner—be it in business, investing, marriage, or friendship—life is so much sweeter.

Good partners are worth their weight in gold. Robert, of course, is my number-one partner in everything. We are business partners, investing partners, marriage partners, and play partners. Is it always peaceful and happy? Far from it. No true partnership is. If the partnership does not allow space for one partner to disagree, to speak her or his mind, and to question the other partner's ideas, then it's not a real partnership. As I've said to Robert on occasion, "I am your partner, not your employee."

To me, good investment partners and good business partners have aligned values. They are generous. The goal is that everyone in the deal prospers. And they are people I enjoy being around. If I don't want to go out to dinner with someone, why would I want to go into a business deal with them?

An associate of Donald Trump once wrote, "You can't do a good deal with a bad partner." That is so true. No matter how good the project is, if you have a partner who is unethical, greedy, and uncaring, then that deal is doomed for disaster. A bad partner can break the deal. A good partner can make the deal.

A good partner is priceless. I am very fortunate to have very good partners around me today.

Frank's Two Rules on Partners

My 91-year-old mentor, Frank, taught me two invaluable lessons about choosing partners wisely. He said, *"Rule number one is: Never take on a partner who needs money."* He explained to me that if a prospective partner's number-one goal is to put more money in her pocket, then she will make and support decisions to make her money immediately versus doing what's best for the investment or the business. And if her primary purpose is to make money for herself, then we are not aligned from the start.

Frank told me, *"Rule number two is: Never give equity to a person whose services you can buy in the marketplace."* Let's say you have a duplex and, between your full-time job, your two kids, and assisting your aging mother, you decide to hire someone else to manage the property.

Your girlfriend says to you, "Instead of paying an outside company to do it, I'll do it for 10 percent of the deal." You now have a choice:

1. Keep 100 percent of the property equity for yourself (since you put 100 percent of your time and money into acquiring it), and pay a monthly fee for a property-management service.

2. Give up 10 percent equity of your duplex instead of paying the monthly fee. By granting equity (a percentage of the property) to someone else, that person is now your partner. It's a good guess that they are offering you their services because they have no money to put into the deal, thereby violating Frank's rule number one. Also, by giving away 10 percent of your cash flow and 10 percent of the profit when you sell, this option may end up costing you a lot more in the long run.

My Greatest Mistake

The question has been raised to me several times, "What's the greatest investment mistake you've ever made?" I've made many, but as I sorted through the myriad of blunders and mishaps, I found one common thread among them all. My greatest mistakes, or learnings, occurred when I did not trust myself. It may have been driven by fear or by wanting the too-good-to-be-true story to come true. I have done it with specific investment deals, and I've lost the deals as a result. I've also done it with partners.

The Hedge Fund

Years ago, Robert and I attended a weekend seminar on stock trading in North Carolina. While there, we met Stewart who founded and operates a hedge fund. A hedge fund is a private investment fund that uses investment strategies to allow the fund to make money in the ups and downs of the markets. Hedge funds are unregulated.

We spent three days with Stewart and discussed his fund. Several knowledgeable investors we knew were investing with him and telling us about the incredible returns they were receiving. We were interested—so interested, in fact, that we made a special trip to his firm in Florida to do our due diligence on his company.

This man claimed to have designed a unique and confidential trading system that was at the core of his success. We met his executive team, the traders, the secretary, and the receptionist. He had just refurbished and moved into very plush offices. I made a mental note of his high overhead. It all appeared to be as we were told.

That night, he and some members of his executive team took us out to dinner at an upscale local steakhouse. We were enjoying our evening. After several glasses of wine, Stewart and his cohorts turned into the most obnoxious, rude, womanizing, and embarrassing people I've ever been around. It was like Jekyll and Hyde. Diners seated around us literally got up and walked out because of their crude remarks and antics. At that, I should have walked out too, but I didn't.

The next morning, I justified the entire evening in my head that maybe this was just a fluke. Maybe this man was just letting off some steam. "Can I really judge a person's character from one incident?" I asked myself.

So why didn't I trust my gut at that point? It came down to greed. The returns on his investments were far beyond the averages. People I spoke with who were investing with him sang his praises. I could certainly overlook this one flaw if it meant I'd make a lot of money. I rationalized it all.

So Robert and I did invest money with this gentleman. The statements we received did show beautiful returns—on paper. We were about to invest more money into this hedge fund when Robert brought home a copy of a well-known investment newspaper. On the front cover was our friend, Mr. Hedge Fund, sitting in a beach chair on the beach with the headline: "Would You Trust This Man with Your Money?"

At first, I was shocked. Then I began defending the guy, "It's probably a disgruntled employee wanting to get even. This will all prove to be a lie."

It did turn out to be a lie. His lie. This man conned his investors out of millions of dollars. He spent their money on a new house, new boat, country-club memberships, new office digs, etc., etc., etc. The bottom line: This man is now in prison for many years. The investors may get about 10 percent of their money back.

The lesson for me? Had I trusted my gut at that defining moment at dinner, I never would have joined Stewart as an investment partner. I learned from then on to trust my gut, my intuition, my instinct. Because of that event, I decided that I will only have partners with whom I want to go to dinner .

Friends and Partners

Mel Jenner from Melbourne, Australia, learned her own lesson from a partner-gone-bad experience. Here is her story.

This story happened back in 1998, and to date, has been the most profound "Aha" moment for me in my investing life.

To give you a little background, my husband and I have a steel fabrication business in the Clare Valley in South Australia. When we went into the business, it was not a great stretch for me to be involved, as my father designed and fabricated stainless steel wine tanks and built wineries. As a child, I spent time with him in the workshop, visiting winery sites, and was very comfortable around steel. But I had absolutely no idea of what it meant to own a business. In the beginning, I would say that it owned us.

Our business had grown exponentially over time, and to accommodate this, we needed to expand our site. The site that we worked from was leased with a large portion of vacant land. So we arranged to build another workshop space with the landlord, who was also a friend. We had legal documents drawn up, and a valuation of the property was done before the new workshop was built and then seven days after the workshop was completed. The percentage difference in the valuation gave us the value of our investment should at any time the property be placed on the market, and the legal contract was drawn up to reflect this.

The landlord's marriage broke down, and so it came that the property was to be sold. As we had provided for all of this, I was not worried about the outcome of the sale. We had invested $30,000 to build the shed and on the current valuation, our investment was now worth $75,000.

But the landlord was not going to pay that. As he was a friend, we had discussed this project from the beginning with him, and he knew that it had cost us $30,000. This was all that he was offering. This friend, whom we had known for many years, showed us his true colors and his psychosis around money. It didn't seem to matter how many times we referred to the document, he was not going to pay.

In honesty, I also showed my emotions around money also. I was just in disbelief that this was happening. For one thing, I couldn't believe that this person was not of his word. It grated against everything that I was brought up to believe in. I also couldn't bring myself to take it further through the legal system due to our friendship. Secondly, I felt that this friendship was now conditional and had a price on it. Thirdly, I just could not move on. The sale had come to a stalemate, and we were sending faxes to each other that were getting no closer to a solution. The whole situation had become all-consuming to me, and I spent all of my time trying to claim what was rightfully ours, or what I thought was ours. I was so bogged down in what was right and wrong!

One morning, as I was complaining again to my husband about it, he just looked at me and said quietly, "Mel, just let it go. We will make far more than that when you can move on from this." Well, to say that the penny dropped was an understatement. The conversations that had been happening in my head and taking up all of my headspace just ceased. The silence was deafening for me. I grabbed the documentation, signed off on it, and the settlement occurred. I also was able to function again. I don't even remember if I had fed our daughter through the time that all of this was happening!

Today, I am most grateful for this "friend's" action, as the lessons in this were enormous for me. I was able to let go of so many of my emotions surrounding money. I would not say that they are gone completely, but I am much more present to them and able to correct them if they appear again. If I begin to let the emotions get in the way, I walk away and sleep on it for a night. Also, I have become very attentive to the partners that I go into business with. I do spend time choosing partners and being completely transparent with them on what the investment is. It's like a marriage. You come to it with an attitude of learning and being flexible, winning and pushing on through things even when it gets uncomfortable. I also spend time and money on good legal agreements, and I call my lawyers when I need their expertise. I have lawyers on my team that support me in our businesses. I don't try to do it all by myself. And with each experience, I am able to stand back and almost watch as if I am a third party, to analyze what was learned. It was a great wake-up call for me to just get on with it. In hindsight, the lesson for me was a small price to pay.

Not long after this, we purchased our own property with the workshop that we wanted. There were many offices and tenancies that came with this property. And so, off I went to learn my Commercial Real Estate Management. It is just exciting because the learning never ends.

Trust Your Gut

Mel talks about not letting her emotions get in the way of her decisions. Here's a story when my emotions led the way, with my gut screaming at me the whole time!

My cell phone rang. It was Robert. I was in Hawaii at the time, and he was in Phoenix. He said, "I'm here with Ryan, and we've been talking about the Thompson Center. We have an idea how it can work. All I ask is that you keep an open mind."

"Keep an open mind" was not a good way to start a conversation. What Robert was really saying was, "You're not going to like this idea at all."

Ryan is our commercial broker and friend. The Thompson Center is a small retail center with shops and restaurants that is directly adjacent to a larger property that Robert and I own. Our property is one of our best-performing assets with an incredibly strong cash flow. It puts a good deal of money in our pockets every month. We have had our eye on this retail center for six years, patiently waiting for that moment when the owner would be willing to sell. That moment had come.

I took a deep breath and asked, "What's the idea?"

"Well," he hesitated, "in order to make this work, we'll have to give up the cash flow on our existing property next door." I stopped breathing. Robert went on, "The cash flow from our property will have to fund the retail center." Now the voice in my head was screaming, my gut was going crazy, and my heart was pounding.

All I could get out was, "Give up our cash flow?"

"I knew you weren't going to like that part," he replied. His next words were music to my ears. "Look, I'm going overseas tomorrow. You take a look at this and see if this is a deal we want to do or not." I finally exhaled.

I lost sleep for the next two nights running numbers and different scenarios in my head. "There must be a way to make this deal work," I kept telling myself.

Three days later, I was back in Phoenix, meeting with Ryan and a possible lender. They laid out the details of their proposal. After hearing their pitch, I repeated back to them the terms they had just presented. "In order to buy this property, I have to give up all the cash flow from my property next door to fund the retail center. Oh, and I have to come up with a $3-million down payment. Oh, and you want to put both properties under one loan, thereby increasing the debt on my existing property by several million dollars. Do I have that right?" They nodded yes.

My head was spinning. I do not like risk when it comes to my money. I have three back-up plans for my existing property in case things go wrong. I do my best to take as much risk as possible *out* of investments. Including both properties in one loan meant that if the retail center did not perform in the future, then, not only do we risk losing the retail center, but we also put our best-performing asset at risk as well. This violated one of my main rules.

"The retail center must stand alone. It cannot depend upon our existing property for funding. The retail center must have its own loan." Ryan and the lender were not optimistic when they left.

On top of all that, there was a time constraint. I was leaving the country in three days. My due diligence, which typically takes me two to three weeks, would now have to be completed in three days.

I continued asking myself, "How can we make this work?" I wanted this property. It seemed obvious that the retail center would only add value to our property. The location was perfect. Yes, I was emotionally attached. I was so attached I was even willing to pay a premium to get it. And I was confused. I was getting conflicting facts and opinions about the retail center.

Finally, the lights went on. I wised up and realized there were some smart people I should consult regarding this type of property. I asked myself, "Who knows more about this than I do?" Two names immediately popped into my head.

First, I contacted Tom, our tax strategist and a real estate investor. Tom has been a trusted advisor and business partner over the years. I emailed him the details of this deal. He called me back right away. "Kim, I know why you're struggling with this deal," he told me.

"Why?" I asked.

"Because this is not your kind of deal. This actually goes against how you invest." He went on, "I know you want this center, but it will not cash flow given the numbers. You will have to feed it every month, and that's with 100 percent occupancy. You're going against what you know works."

I felt a bit of relief knowing the conflict I was feeling was somewhat justified.

Next I got on the phone with our Phoenix business partner, Mel. Mel is one of our partners on the Arizona resort and golf courses investment. He and his partners have built sports arenas, owned major sports teams, and have been involved in all kinds of real estate ventures. He is, without a doubt, one of the smartest people I know in real estate acquisitions and operations. I explained the situation and the short deadline. "I'll meet you for lunch tomorrow," he said.

Mel and I spent three hours reviewing this property. "Here is my conclusion," he told me. "The bottom line is that this property is several million dollars overpriced. Drop your offer price by four million, and then you'll be in the ballpark." I knew the seller would not go for that. But then Mel said something that caught me by surprise. He said, "You know, Kim, you do not need this property."

"I know," I replied, "but it will increase the value of our existing property."

"Who told you that?" he asked. "The time and cost to develop this may not be worth it. It may make more sense—financially, mentally, and emotionally—to just work with the property you own. It's a much bigger property and the location is just as good. In my opinion, this retail center is not that important for you to own."

Wow. I never even considered not owning this center. I was too attached to the opportunity to ever let that thought enter my mind.

That afternoon Ryan, the owner of the retail center, and I met. We discussed several options and at the end of the meeting, we mutually agreed that a deal would not happen at this time. Sometimes you have to know when to walk away from a deal, especially one you are emotionally attached to. I felt relieved, not because I was not doing the deal, but because, in the last three days, we—my partners and I—came up with the correct, non-emotional, and strictly business decision.

As I said earlier, you can't do a good deal with a bad partner. Well, I ended up not doing a deal because I have great partners.

PART THREE
APPLY

BRINGING IT ALL TOGETHER

CHAPTER 20

FOUR ASSETS ARE BETTER THAN ONE

To rise up to be a well-rounded investor takes...

F irst of all, be true to yourself. Which investments are you most interested in? One way you know when you really enjoy something is recognizing those moments when you get lost in what you're doing. My photography teacher gets lost in Photoshop enhancing his photos. He told me, "Last night right before going to bed, I decided to touch up one of my photos. I figured it would take me about 15 minutes. I couldn't believe it when I looked at my watch and over two hours had passed. I was just so into it."

When was the last time that happened to you? That's a sure sign of being completely in sync with what you love. I find myself in that state whenever I'm analyzing the numbers of a property. (Yes, I know that behavior borders on nerdy.) I get so engrossed with the story that evolves from the numbers that I lose all track of time. That clearly does not happen to me when I program the radio in my Range Rover. If I can't figure it out in three minutes, I lose patience and turn it over to someone else.

As you are acquiring your knowledge about the various assets and investments available, some will definitely capture your interest and others will not. Pay attention to those areas where you naturally want to spend more time.

In Part Three of *It's Rising Time!* you'll meet some incredible, passionate women who have found their niche and who share with you what it *really* took for them to go for their financial prize. They have some entertaining rising-time moments. They are learning and putting into practice much of the attitude and philosophy of *It's Rising Time!* across multiple asset classes.

There's More to Investing Than Stocks and Bonds

Most investors, perhaps as many as 95 percent, invest in stocks, bonds, and mutual funds—otherwise known as paper assets. Most of the major financial magazines focus on paper assets. The advertisers of these publications are also linked to the world of paper assets—companies such as Merrill Lynch, eTrade, and Prudential.

Most all of the financial television shows target the stock market. Several have the ticker tape running or stock prices popping up throughout the programs. Even the top morning news shows such as *TODAY, Good Morning America*, and *The Early Show* mention what's happening in the stock market in their news reports.

As I searched online for the words "types of investments" the other day, I found these comments from various websites on page one of my search:

- *Overall, there are three different kinds of investments. These include stocks, bonds, and cash.* (*Cash* here refers to money-market funds or certificates of deposit.)

- *It's important to understand your options. There are three main types of investments: stocks, bonds, cash equivalent. You can invest in any or all three investment types directly or indirectly by buying mutual funds. You may also want to consider an individual retirement account (IRA) or annuity, both of which can offer tax-deferred investment savings.*

- *Tax Implications of Different Types of Investments* The site lists six types of investments: stocks, stock splits, employee stock options, mutual funds, bonds, and day-traders of stocks and securities.

- *Investing 101—Types of investments*
  *There are many ways to invest your money. To decide which
  investment vehicles are suitable for you, you need to know
  their characteristics.*

They go on to list the four investments available:

1. Stocks
2. Bonds
3. Mutual funds
4. Alternative investments: stock options, stock futures,
   FOREX (foreign exchange), gold, real estate, etc.

After stocks, bonds, and mutual funds, everything else gets lumped
into "alternative investments." Here's what they say about alternative
investments: "There are numerous alternative vehicles, which represent
the most complicated types of securities and investing strategies. The
good news is that you probably don't need to worry about alternative
investments at the start of your investing career. They are generally
high-risk/high-reward securities that are much more speculative than
plain old stocks and bonds."

And that is just page one of my search!

There are so many other types of investments other than stocks,
bonds, mutual funds, money-market accounts, and certificates of
deposit. I would argue that mutual funds, money markets, and CDs
are not investments at all. They are savings plans—and not very good
ones at that.

I love the website that states that alternative investments "represent
the most complicated types of securities and investing strategies." They
are basically saying, "Don't bother. You won't understand it." As you
can see from several of the stories you've read, many women *do* get it.
And in this section of *It's Rising Time!* you'll learn about even more.

I have nothing against paper assets. I have girlfriends who make a
lot of money in the world of paper assets, including paper assets that
generate cash flow. My gripe is towards the financial "experts" who

lead the public to believe that stocks, bonds, and mutual funds are the only safe way to go, and everything else is so very risky. Without any financial intelligence, people believe the "experts" and stop thinking for themselves.

Diversifying Across Asset Classes

We've talked about being true to yourself and discovering what is of interest to you. If you're not interested in something, then you are probably not going to pay much attention to it. The same holds true for assets to invest in. It's crucial you choose the asset that best suits you—your personality, your values, and your lifestyle. Each asset class has pros and cons. Some require more time and effort than others. When an "expert" calls something risky or complicated, what they really mean is that the investment requires some education and attention. It may also mean that the "expert" is not knowledgeable himself and so it is risky and complicated to him. The assumption is that people want the quickest and easiest option. Many people do. That is why 95 percent of investors are in paper assets. They are the easiest to get into and the quickest to get out of.

Diversification is a term heard again and again. "Make sure you are diversified in your portfolio," the financial advisers will preach. The question is: What is their definition of diversification? When most financial planners and advisers tell you to have a diversified portfolio, they are usually referring just to your stock portfolio. Diversification to them means investing across the various stock sectors, such as large cap, small cap, blended, blue chip, high tech, or alternative energy.

To truly be diversified means to diversify, not just within paper assets, but across all asset classes. I started investing in rental real estate. Today Robert and I are invested in all asset classes. Each asset class reacts to the markets differently, and each asset within each class may respond differently as well. Putting all your money in one basket, called paper, may not reward you with the financial security you desire.

The following are the four *primary* asset classes. There are many, many more types of assets you can invest in.

Business

You can invest in your own business by using your own money, raising money from private individuals, or borrowing money from a traditional lender. The purpose of the money you invest, no matter where it comes from, is to work and generate a return back to you, the business, and your investors and/or lender.

You may also choose to invest in someone else's private business or company. The business and the owners may or may not be familiar to you. Make sure you do your due diligence which means—make sure you do your homework and research and analyze:

- The project (the business itself),
- The partners,
- The financing, and
- The business and management team.

My friend, Emilie, recently invested in a privately owned business that manufactures and markets women's licensed brand merchandise. She shares the reasons she invested in this company—and the results.

I decided to invest in this company for a number of reasons.

First, I believed in the project and the product and was willing to learn the financials. I hired a coach/adviser, an entrepreneur who built and sold a successful tech business and is also a CPA. He worked with me weekly via Skype sessions over a period of three months. We reviewed the business plan at length and many of the discussions were hard-hitting questions that exposed my risk. I was willing to take this financial risk. What I learned is that risk goes beyond the financial. Risk also involves health, relationships, and your general outlook on life.

Secondly, I felt I could make a difference. I have industry experience across a broad spectrum of business and, following my Kolbe score, push myself to the limits of production. After investing capital and working one and a half years of early mornings, evenings, and all weekends, I resigned my position as COO at the request of the partner. She requested my resignation when I refused to provide personal tax records that I believed would serve as an additional financial guarantee on the lease of warehouse space in her home town. We were already in arrears with an existing fulfillment service in California. Her claim was that my action supposedly appeared to new investors that I was "not engaged" in the business. (Early in the start-up, and with just a minority interest, I foolishly signed a personal guarantee on an SBA loan for the company, a mistake I was not about to repeat.)

My third reason was that I had a strong previous working experience with the founder. Our dynamic and balance was, at that time, a positive one. My error in using this judgment was that, even though I had witnessed a positive performance within the walls of a growing and prosperous corporation, I was not prepared for how this partner would act under the stress of personal financial difficulties. Nor did I expect to witness what is, strictly in my opinion, a character flaw when it came to facing the truth about the financial difficulties. I was not raised on the notion that "everything will be okay." Hearing these words without the positive action to back them up was unnerving, to say the least.

The fourth reason is that one of the primary investors in the new company is a world-class authority in a closely related business. A former CEO of a billion-dollar company which he helped to build, he now plays an active role on the board today. My confidence in the future of the company is based on the ongoing guidance offered by this person.

I have my life back. I am still an owner in the company, which has potential if the right investors take over key management decisions. I never intended to buy myself a full-time job and can now move forward with new investing ideas. I am backed by the mistakes I learned and the support of my friends and family.

Real Estate

There are two reasons to invest in real estate—for cash flow from rental properties and for capital gains when you buy and sell (flip) properties. I invest primarily in rental real estate because cash flow fits my formula for financial independence. You decide which works best for you.

There are all sorts of investment real estate: single family, duplex, triplex, apartment buildings, office buildings, retail strip malls and shopping centers, and industrial properties such as warehouses, hotels and mobile-home parks.

One of the biggest benefits of real estate is the concept of leverage. Leverage is the ability to use OPM, Other People's Money, to purchase the asset. A property that is highly leveraged means there is a lot of debt on the property compared to equity. (Equity means the current market value minus the debt.) A property that has a debt of 90 percent (which means the owners and investors put down 10 percent) is more highly leveraged than a property that borrowed 70 percent and put 30 percent cash into it. The higher the debt on the property, the lower the cash flow. The lower the debt, the higher the cash flow.

You'll read stories of how other women invested in real estate with little or no money down. If you can buy your own home, your personal residence, then you can certainly buy investment properties too.

Paper Assets

Paper assets include things such as stocks, bonds, mutual funds, and retirement accounts. You can invest in stock options, stock futures, and foreign exchange. Paper assets include REITs (real estate investment trusts) which are funds that only invest in real estate. Paper assets also include ETFs (exchange-traded funds). There are too-numerous-to-count paper vehicles you can invest in.

Paper assets are typically capital-gains investments. However, stock dividends are taxed as cash flow.

Commodities

Commodities are metals such as gold, silver, and copper; food such as grains, corn, coffee, and sugar; and raw materials such as oil, gas, and cotton.

The price of commodities is typically driven by supply and demand. If there is a bumper year of corn, then prices are low since the supply of corn is high. If, on the other hand, there is a shortage of corn due to a drought and unfavorable weather conditions, then the price of corn will be high.

You can buy commodities such as gold and silver at your local precious-metals dealer. Or you can buy what are called future contracts of any commodity through the futures exchanges.

Commodities are generally a capital-gains (or loss) asset.

Other Assets

You can invest in just about anything you can dream up in your mind. People have invested in individual hotel rooms, prisons, parking garages and a single-car park space, windmills, zoos, and even a public toilet. If you can dream it, then most likely someone will invest in it.

Kristi Adams from Santa Maria, California, started with absolutely nothing and ended up investing in all of the four major asset classes. She truly is a diversified investor. Her story is inspiring.

> *I grew up n a poor household and put myself through college. Right before graduation, my dad sat me down for the "What are you going to do with the rest of your life?" speech. I told him I was going to apply for a commission in the United States Air Force. This plan seemed to make sense to my father since he and his father had both retired from the Army Air Corps, the predecessor to the Air Force. After a few hours, he announced in his wonderful Southern drawl, "Girl, you know I been thinking 'bout it, and there's two places that are always hiring: the circus and the military. I figure this is a lot better than the circus." I chose this path because of the safety and security of a military paycheck, healthcare, and retirement. My family supported me. They were happy that I had landed a well-paying, safe, secure job. My original plan was to do my 20 years and start collecting a retirement pension at age 43. Not a bad plan, right? Not so fast…*
>
> *I was in the Air Force less than two years before I experienced the first round of what the Air Force calls "downsizing" or "force shaping." Personnel are ranked from top to bottom, and a certain percentage of the bottom is cut. Even though I survived that round of cuts, that was my wake-up call.*

Becoming financially free is a process, just like losing 20 pounds might be. You don't decide to lose weight and wake up the next day chiseled and fit. You must work to get there. So I set about putting my own process in motion.

To design my process, the first thing I did was buy a $1.99 notebook that I titled "My Goal Book." I wrote out a one-year plan. It was very specific, not with generic flowery phrases like "I want to be rich," but with specific detailed objectives.

Some of my first goals were to have at least one ounce of physical gold, learn how to buy a property, and set up an LLC (limited liability company). I also estimated how long it would take for me to be financially free (my timeline is 12 years) and set important milestones. For example, at the 25 percent mark of three years, I planned on at least 25 percent of my paycheck coming in from passive income.

Hands down, the most important part is that I TOOK ACTION even while I was reading! I bought one ounce of physical gold and 13 ounces of silver. I was now an investor and in the game.

I told anyone who would listen that I was going to buy cash-flowing real estate. Every single day someone would ask me if I had bought anything yet. I told people in order to keep me moving forward and push past that fear. You know that voice, the one that is screaming at you asking, "What ARE you doing? You aren't smart enough to do this! Get out while you can! Run for the hills!" Action will shut that voice up.

Simultaneously, I also began taking an accounting class to learn how to read financial statements and create them. People taunted me and asked, "Who do you think you are? Donald Trump?"

My reply, "No, but I'm going to be."

I figured if I could invest smartly across some major asset classes, the markets could go up, down, or sideways in any one market, but the likelihood of all the markets going down for all the asset classes was pretty slim.

I invested in real estate, precious metals, and very specific stocks in a company that I had researched well. I did not risk any more money that I could afford to lose. I positioned myself to do well in each category so that when the market started moving, I had assets to move with it. The housing market crashed, people needed a place to live, and what did I have? Class C residential real estate. When the Middle East turmoil began, my Exxon Mobil stock went through the roof. President Obama stressed innovation and global competitiveness at his meetings with Jeffrey Immelt, the CEO of General Electric. When my GE stock doubled, I realized their jingle is true: They do bring good things to life!

I knew that if I kept investing long enough, there would be a day when I could walk away from the military because I would no longer need their retirement plan. When the Air Force offered a voluntary separation package to entice more personnel to leave before it would be forced to cut, I took it. I converted it into silver.

I know that, due to inflation, silver is increasing in purchasing power and can very soon be converted into more cash-flowing real estate. However, if the madness some are predicting happens in 2012 and the dollar crashes too, I am positioned to survive and thrive.

My formula is:

Financial education + Courage + Action = RESULTS!

I repeat that formula in one asset class. Then I repeat it in another asset class. I will keep repeating it until I am as rich as I want to be.

CHAPTER 21

GOOD DEAL TO GREAT DEAL

To rise beyond good to spectacular takes...

U pside is music to an investor's ears. What is *upside*? It is what you can do to increase the value of an asset. Upside is what makes a prospective investment especially attractive to an investor. Upside is the opportunity to significantly increase the income or the value of an investment in the future. It is in the upside where the greatest profits and returns are made.

The upside of a poorly managed apartment building could be to increase revenue by replacing non-paying tenants with on-time-paying tenants. The upside potential of a pharmaceutical company's stock would be the announcement of a medical breakthrough. The upside of gold would be that the government is continuing to print money. The downside would be if the government stops printing money. (This probably won't happen any time soon.) Robert and I invested in a solar-energy company because they had a revolutionary technology for minimizing the size of those obnoxious solar panels—great upside potential. Unfortunately, two other private companies were working on the same technology!

Finding a solidly performing investment is great, but finding an investment where you see the opportunity to increase value with an outstanding upside is what gets the adrenalin flowing.

She Who Solves the Problem Wins

The upside is often found in problems. Think about the great entrepreneurs. Most entrepreneurs begin their business because they've come across a problem in their lives and thought of a solution. Mothers are a great example of this. Just recently I heard about the mother of a two-year-old boy. She wanted to give him water out of the small water bottles you buy in the store, but he had trouble maneuvering the bottle. He always ended up spilling the water all over his shirt and pants. This woman invented a "sippy cup-like" top that screws onto the top of water bottles. At first she created this just for her son, but then other mothers saw it and asked her for one. Next thing you know, she's in business, just from solving a simple problem.

Steve Jobs solved the problem of individuals not having access to personal computers. Henry Ford made auto transportation available to the masses. Anita Roddick solved the problem of chemicals in skin-care products and launched the Body Shop internationally offering natural lotions and cleansers. Mary Kay Ash was one of the first women to provide business ownership to women throughout the world via Mary Kay cosmetics.

It is the same with investing. She who can find an investment with a problem and solve the problem wins. Many investors shy away from problem investments, but it is in the problem where the profit lies. Look no further than our current economic situation. There are problems galore, and more to come. What if you were able to invest in the first company to solve the problem of finding the alternative to oil and gas? What if someone created a viable and scalable solution to inexpensive housing in third-world countries? What if you were the first to invent delicious zero-calorie chocolate truffles? Do you think investors would be lining up?

Finding the Upside

Landlords of rental property want to give their tenants what they want. To be successful in any business, it's crucial that you find out what your customer wants and deliver it. For years the number-one thing renters wanted was safety. They want to live in a place they feel is safe. Owners and property managers provide safety with security gates and good lighting at night throughout the entire property. Studies show that trimming the shrubbery in front of windows and doors and places where burglars can hide creates a safer environment. Safety is a major factor in the rental housing industry.

For the first time, however, studies now show that safety comes in second in importance for tenants. The leading "want" of residents today is washers and dryers in the apartments. Maybe it stems from the safety people feel or don't feel in community laundry rooms. Or maybe people just value the convenience of not having to go back and forth to the laundry room. For whatever reason, people like it a lot when you, the owner, can provide in-unit washers and dryers.

One of the simplest upside potentials for several of the apartment buildings that Robert and I have invested in with our partners, Ken McElroy and Ross McCallister, is to add washers and dryers to the units in the buildings we purchase. There is an upfront cost, but the advantage is that it increases the NOI (net operating income = gross income minus expenses). The value of an investment property is derived from its NOI. The higher the NOI, the more valuable the property. Whenever you can increase the income of a property, you increase the overall value of that property. The simple task of putting washers and dryers in the apartments allows us to charge additional rent. This may equate to only $50 per unit, but if you have 200 units, that increases the income by $10,000 per month or $120,000 per year. If you had a 10-unit apartment building, a $50-per-unit rent increase would increase your income by $500 per month, or $6,000 per year. That one step alone increases the value of your property.

Additional Sources of Revenue

Mel and his two partners acquired a classic historical resort in Arizona. These three individuals are experts at seeing and developing the upside potential of an investment. Mel and his partners at one time owned major sports teams in Arizona and developed sports arenas and other key properties. Because this resort had gone into bankruptcy, many needed repairs were ignored, and there was much to be done to restore it to its original elegance.

Robert and I attended the grand re-opening of the resort after a good deal of the renovation had been done. As Mel walked us through the property, he explained their strategy and thought-process for upgrading the resort. One of the key approaches they took was to look at every square foot of the property and ask themselves: Where are the opportunities to generate income? For example, there was a small intimate sitting area near the "library room." As a sitting area, this location yielded no revenue. But as a relaxed private dining area set apart from the restaurant, they could serve dinner for 12 people twice a night—a brand new revenue stream for the resort. They took this approach throughout the entire property, including the newly built water park where you can rent a private cabana with television, room service, and a massage, or send the kids to day camp or out for ice cream at the new ice-cream bar. Every square foot, every unused space, became a potential source for added revenue.

Claudia Schmidt has an amazing story to tell. She began with a piece of real estate and, because she solved her own problems, she created an incredible opportunity for herself.

When I was 20 years old, I moved from Canada to Mexico. I not only learned Spanish (my original goal), but I met my wonderful husband. Together we embarked on this journey.

The government granted a small piece of land to my husband, on the condition that he build on it by a certain deadline or else he would have to return it to the government. So, we started building.

We didn't make a lot of money. So every day after work, we started digging the ground ourselves by hand with picks and shovels. Four years passed. We had been working non-stop on the house, little by little, day after day. We finally finished after five years and started renting out the three levels of the house.

To attract tenants, I was targeting people particularly in Mexico, the United States, and Canada. Of course, these people speak different languages: Spanish, French, and English. Most websites only offer one or two languages so trying to find websites that I could afford and that would cater to the languages my prospective tenants spoke, was very time-consuming and frustrating.

Even tenants in Quebec City that I spoke to complained that they couldn't find enough websites in French to search for rentals in Mexico for their holidays.

Therefore, since I love the web, I had the idea to build my own website to help myself and others advertise their rentals. I finally decided on the name "RentingInternational.com" so that anybody, anywhere could list their rentals for free and in multiple languages.

Originally, I just thought it would be about real estate rentals. But one day, I got an email from a car rental company asking if they could advertise their cars for rent too, and that's when another idea sparked. I thought, "RentingInternational.com" could actually mean any type of rental. So I decided to create categories for all types of rentals, including car rentals, real estate rentals, boat rentals, plane rentals, tool rentals, and much more.

Then I got more emails from people and companies asking if they could sell things on my website too. That's when I realized there was a whole business-to-business side where suppliers or manufacturers could sell their products to rental companies, who in turn rent their cars, houses, equipment, and so on to renters. I thought this would be another great addition to my website to help complete the supply chain.

So again, just like building the house little by little, day after day, I started to build my website, RentingInternational.com, after work and on weekends. It's been six years now, and my biggest mistake was hiring developers that didn't have the experience, which is why their rates were so low. It cost me more in the long run because I had to redo the website three times over.

The upside was that, because I had to get so involved in my website's development, my knowledge and passion grew. I learned so much that I made a career out of it.

Our next goal is to save for a house in Canada and continue expanding our real estate portfolio to live financially independent on the rental incomes. We will also continue to grow our website, RentingInternational.com, to support fellow rental owners and entrepreneurs reach their financial goals too.

Tapping into Your Creativity

Investing is actually a very creative process. You have to look at things differently to what's obvious. That takes right-brain thinking. Looking at ways to create upside in a property or business takes ingenuity. It's a fun process because, as you look at the problems of a potential investment, you can come up with every crazy solution possible because you have nothing to lose. If, in the end, you do not come up with one or more solutions to the problem then, guess what? You don't have to purchase the investment. This process also forces you to seek out new answers and experts you may have never explored.

Think Outside the Box

Donald Trump invited Robert and me to visit him at his golf course in Los Angeles named Trump National Golf Club. As Mr. Trump was giving us a personal tour of the gorgeous oceanfront golf club, he stopped in front of the main ballroom and said, "I've got to tell you a story." Some of the greatest lessons I've learned from Donald Trump and other successful investors and business people are through their personal stories.

The story began with a problem: The main ballroom at Trump National had seating for a maximum of 150 people, so they could not compete with other venues for requests for parties larger than that number. The folks at Trump National began looking for a solution. The most apparent answer was to add an addition onto the existing ballroom. The bids started coming in. When the final numbers were tallied, the total cost of the addition, including additional chairs and tables, came to an estimated $3 million. The project would probably take six to nine months to complete. $3 million and nine months is a lot of money and time.

One evening Donald was walking past a large party in the ballroom. He paused for a moment to observe the celebration, thinking about the problem of how to expand the ballroom to accommodate more people. He noticed an older woman struggling to get out of her chair. The ballroom chairs were very nice, but they were big and heavy. They were awkward to maneuver. That's when the idea struck Donald. Instead of building an addition onto the ballroom, why not get smaller chairs?

The next day his team started researching this idea. The final result? They found smaller attractive chairs that increased the seating capacity from 150 to just over 250 people. On top of that, they were able to sell the existing large chairs for more money than the new chairs cost! Trump National increased the capacity of their ballroom so they could now handle parties of up to 250 guests. Instead of costing Mr. Trump $3 million, he actually made money on the deal. Now that is putting your creativity to work while adding considerable value to your property.

The Ultimate Upside

What is the number-one thing an investor wants? She wants a return on her investment, or ROI. What is the ultimate ROI? Some people would answer that the ultimate ROI is 100 percent. If you invest $1,000 and that investment generates $1,000, then that, many would say, is the ultimate return. But what if your $1,000 returns $2,000 or $3,000 to you? Then you would have a 200 percent or 300 percent return. So what is the ultimate return on investment an investor would want? You invest $1,000 and that investment returns $1,000 to you. You have now gotten back exactly what you invested. You are now playing with what is called free money. You have none of your own money in the deal. You haven't sold the investment, be it a rental property, a stock dividend, or a vending machine. You have simply accumulated, in cash flow, the amount you invested. So at this point, you have your original investment back, you still own the asset, and it is still cash-flowing to you. What would you call a return like that? I'd call that an infinite return. If you received $100 per month in cash flow, then the annual calculation would look like this:

$1,200 ($100 x 12 months) ÷ 0 (since you have no money invested) = ∞

An Infinite-Return Example

Robert and I, along with our investment partners Ken and Ross, purchased a 252-unit apartment building. Robert and I invested $1 million. The building was 30 percent vacant. Over two years, Ken and Ross and their team improved the value of the property by reducing the vacancy rate to 2 percent, installing washers and dryers in every unit, and doing necessary repairs and maintenance to improve the overall look and feel of the property. As a result, in two years the value of the property increased from $11 million to $15 million. On the original $11 million purchase price, we put down $2 million and took out a loan for $9 million. When the property appraised at $15 million, the bank was willing to lend us 80 percent of the appraised value (80 percent of $15 million = $12 million). This is called *loan to value*. With the newly refinanced loan of $12 million, we paid off the original loan of $9 million, the investors got back their original down payment of $2 million plus split the additional $1 million. At this point in the deal:

1. We have been earning a monthly cash flow on this property for the last two years.
2. We have all of our original investment back, plus a portion of the additional $1 million.
3. We still have the same percentage of ownership in the property.
4. We still receive a monthly cash flow from the property.

That is what I mean by an infinite return on investment!

Rowena Rabino from London, England, is a remarkable woman and an incredible role model for women all across the globe.

I am a 38-year-old Filipino citizen. I am a single mom and work as a housekeeper abroad in London.

I never thought it would be possible to become financially free from my situation. I started thinking about saving money after I had problems with my visa. Because I was sending all of my salary back home, I never thought about what would happen if I couldn't work anymore. I started doing the budget and sending only the required amount of money. I gave instructions to my sister to find a house or land for sale in the Philippines. I was lucky in 2005. One of our neighbors sold their house to us for just 120,000 pesos ($3000). It was a tiny house, but my dad converted it into two flats. It was rented straight away. Today it gives us 1500 pesos a month per flat. In three and a half years, I had my original cash investment returned to me through the cash flow from the rentals. I now have the house, and I reinvested the cash flow. We now have 19 units being rented.

I want to share my story, especially to all overseas workers who are working hard and choosing to be away from their families and home. You will love and appreciate your hard work more when you start investing part of your salary because, not only are you helping your family, but you are also securing your future and freeing yourself financially.

I'm so happy! I am still learning and enjoying the progress of my journey.

Now that is the ultimate upside!

BUSINESS

CHAPTER 22

GETTING STARTED...
IN BUSINESS

To rise up as a brilliant business investor takes…

T he former editor-in-chief of *Cosmopolitan* magazine, Helen Gurley Brown, said, "Nearly every glamorous, wealthy, successful career woman you might envy now started out as some kind of schlep." In other words, we all have to start somewhere.

You can look at business from several different vantage points:

- as a business owner in your own business you work in,
- as an investor in someone else's business, or
- as an inventor, writer, or product creator who produces their masterpiece one time, but sells it again and again.

Whichever path or paths you take, getting started can be relatively simple.

The Internet has opened up a whole new world to budding and seasoned entrepreneurs and inventors. Apple has changed the playing field with its introduction of apps (applications). If you know that world of technology, build an app that people want and offer it to the world.

The publishing world has been revolutionized by eBooks. A couple of friends were experimenting with how to publish an eBook themselves. They did a lot of research and learned the step-by-step process. In order to see if their process worked, they actually wrote a 20-page booklet on how to publish an eBook and offered it for sale online. From this "experiment," they now make about $200 per month from the sale of their eBook. These two friends took their knowledge and turned it into an asset. Getting into business can be that easy.

Marilyn's weak spot was designer handbags. Most of her luxury spending was on the latest Louis Vuitton, Armani, Prada, or Gucci purses. Her friends would occasionally ask her if she could borrow them. Jokingly, one day her best friend said, "You would make a fortune from just renting out your fancy handbags." The lights went on. Today Marilyn makes a healthy profit every month from her small boutique of rental handbags. She has since expanded into other designer rental items as well. It's as simple as a Prada purse.

The network marketing or direct selling industry is becoming more and more popular these days. You choose the company, sell their products, and invite others to join the company. Not only do you make money from the products you sell, but you also receive a percentage from the product sales of those you brought into the company, also known as passive income. The beauty of direct selling is that the company provides the business systems as well as the education to be successful. Choose the company that best suits you— one that is aligned with your goals and values and, most importantly, is committed to building you into a successful entrepreneur.

You may even have some liabilities that you can turn into assets. For example, a very successful music producer attended a three-hour talk that Robert and I presented. He immediately went back to his company and called a meeting. "What things do we have that cost us money (liabilities) that could make us money (assets)?" he asked his team. What they had were two SUVs (sports utility vehicles) that they purchased for company use. Their bright idea was to start an executive car service and offer their cars for hire to their well-to-do clientele and associates. These two vehicles are now putting money into their pocket every month, instead of taking money out.

Getting started in business simply begins with an idea. We all have ideas. It's just a matter of rising to the occasion and putting that idea into practice.

The next few chapters are real-life stories from women who took their ideas and, without knowing just how they were going to get there, brought their ideas to life.

The Pros of Owning Your Own Business

- **Control**
  You have full control. You control the income, expenses, and debt.

- **Leverage of OPM (Other People's Money)**
  If you choose to raise money for your business, you can fund the start-up or growth with investors' money.

  If you are investing in someone else's private company, then you are the OPM.

- **Leverage of OPT (Other People's Time)**
  Eventually OPT can replace your time completely.
  If you are working in someone else's business, then you are the OPT.

- **Unlimited revenue**
  There is no limit to how much revenue you and your company can make.

- **Tax advantages**
  Most of the tax law, in most countries, is geared towards reducing the taxes of business owners. Almost all business expenses are deductible, meaning you deduct them against the revenue which reduces the company's taxable income.

  If you are investing in someone's private business the losses from the business are deductible against income from other passive business or real estate investments. Gains often are subject to the lower long-term capital-gains rates.

- **Flexible hours**
  You set your own hours.

- **Freedom to express yourself**
  A business can support you in being true to you. You can fully express who you are and what you stand for through your business.

- **Home-based business**
  Include your children. What a great education for them!

The Cons of Owning Your Own Business

- **Difficult**
  Operating a business is the most difficult of the four asset classes to get into and to sustain.

  If you are thinking of investing in a private business, this is a major factor to consider and is why the track record of those operating and growing the business is so important.

- **High failure rate**
  Nine out of ten businesses fail within the first five years.

- **Many hours**
  Lots of hours are required. This will not be a 9-5 job.

- **No guarantee**
  There is no guaranteed or steady paycheck.

- **People**
  You must deal with and manage people—employees, clients, consultants, etc.

  This includes their various personalities, moods, and all their quirks. Unless this is your strong suit, this could be stressful.

CHAPTER 23

RUFFLES
TO RICHES

Kim Babjak's Story

Kim Babjak just makes you feel good being around her. She makes you laugh, is full of energy, and is a champion for women making it in business and money. Kim started with very little money, a smattering of business knowledge, and no experience. She faced plenty of obstacles and kept going where other women would have quit. She is a brilliant role model of what it really takes to excel in business.

— Kim Kiyosaki

E ver since I was a little girl, I dreamed of being an inventor. I would make and design little projects that I would build and use. I wanted to invent so many things that most of the time I would have half-built, half-thought-up projects lying all over my bedroom. Year after year these things and ideas would come and go, with little hope they would be fruitful beyond my bedroom walls. My father was the inventor in our family and my inventive side was established at a very early age. I owe it all to him.

In the early 1970s, I lived in a middle-class neighborhood in Phoenix, Arizona. Back then, all fathers on our block had a workshop that they would escape to on the weekends. They would build birdhouses, doll cradles, and other fun stuff for kids to enjoy. Most of the neighborhood workshops were quiet, clean, and moderately organized. My father's was very different. It was loud, messy, and very busy.

I would spend countless hours with him at his patent attorney's office, just tinkering with all the inventors' gadgets. I loved every moment of it, and it defiantly gave me the insight to think very independently about the ideas I had and about creating products that would help me.

I firmly believe that every idea is a good idea, no matter what. However, every idea is not commercially feasible or saleable. I know that a good idea, a lot of hard work, and strong persistence can help you achieve anything you desire.

I have spent the last ten years building my business, KimCo, from the ground up. I started with three things: a borrowed $1000, the support of my loving husband Bill, and a strong determination to succeed.

Prior to making the decision to start my own company, we were faced with the possibility that my husband could be laid off from the large airline where he worked. That was a scary time, and I felt the urgent need to do something to contribute to our family finances. I was, and still am, a stay-at-home mom and love doing that. However, we were facing the harsh reality that I would need to start doing something to produce income.

Since I dropped out of school in the 10th grade, it was very challenging for me to find and maintain adequate employment. I also suffer from AADD, Adult Attention Deficit Disorder, which causes many challenges for me. I struggle every day to stay focused. Knowing the issues I was faced with, I knew I was not going to be able to find a high-paying job, but I also knew that I needed to help out my family. So I did the only thing I thought I could do at that time. I got a job at McDonald's.

I was working as a McDonald's cashier, after being promoted from the French-fry job, when an old classmate of mine came in. She said to me, with her hand on her hip, "I thought you would turn out to be the successful one from school, not flipping burgers for the rest of your life." I was extremely humiliated, and I knew at that very moment that this was definitely not what I wanted out of life for my family or myself. In retrospect, my classmate did me a huge favor that day. She made me take a look at my life and the purpose for why I was put on this earth. I knew I was meant for greater things.

Since I have always invented things, it made sense to expand on that strength as my starting point. I had an idea for a product that I might be able to turn into a business. I developed a zip-on/zip-off interchangeable bed skirt. I designed it because I needed a solution for a problem I was having, which could not be solved with a product that was already on the market.

The problem was, I could not remove my bed skirt all by myself. I, like several other people I know, have a large mattress that probably weighs at least 300 pounds. The only way I could remove my existing bed skirt successfully, without injuring myself, I had to enlist the strength of at least three of the neighbor gals, or wait for the weekend when my husband was home. Every time I asked him for help he would comment, "Can't you find a better way to do this?" Right at that point, I thought, "Yes, I can. And I will." That was the pivotal moment in my life when I knew I needed to take that problem and develop an easier solution.

I pulled that ugly, old, dirty skirt off and went feverishly to work. I found a company that could supply me with a really long zipper. My new product, Zip-A-Ruffle, was born. I perfected the product, found suppliers who could make it for me, then took it to QVC (a home shopping TV broadcast) for a test on national television. That was over 10 years ago, and it's still selling today on QVC.

Today, I own a very successful multi-faceted product development company that offers a wide range of consulting in the areas of consumer product and business development. KimCo LLC helps companies with product licensing, development, prototyping, manufacturing, and retail placement.

I am passionate in helping entrepreneurs with product design and development because, many years ago, I knew I had a good idea, the determination to help my family financially, and knew that no one was going to stop me.

Kim Babjak • Denver, Colorado • USA
www.kimbabjak.com

Kim Babjak, founder of KimCo LLC, is a mother of four, entrepreneur, inventor, author, and speaker. Despite only completing the 10th grade, she was resolute that employers and paychecks would not determine the course of her life.

KimCo LLC is a multi-faceted product-development company that offers a wide range of consulting in the areas of consumer product and business development. KimCo helps companies with product licensing, development, prototyping, manufacturing, and retail placement. With KimCo's vast retail buyer relationships, KimCo can assist with the product being placed into electronic retail like QVC, and big-box retail outlets like Walmart, Target, Home Depot, Costco, and many others. With over 20 years of combined retail experience and sourcing overseas, Kim Babjak and her team of professionals can help create successful product creation and placement.

Kim is known as "the go-to girl" for QVC and HSN and has shown that her expertise for selling product on TV can help clients reach millions of new customers. Kim has also teamed up with Stephen Key, the industry leader in product licensing, to help clients secure lucrative deals with companies like Disney, Crayola, and Lego.

Kim was recognized with a feature story in the August 2005 issue of *Entrepreneur* magazine. The feature story told of Kim's successful endeavor to bring her products to market through a Walmart local purchase program. In 2007, she received expansive exposure in the *Wall Street Journal* for her business savvy and experience.

Kim appears on national television regularly, writes a blog about "Mind to Market" product development on Startupnation.com, and contributes to many other business-related websites like InventRight. com. Kim is passionate about helping entrepreneurs with product design and development with her exclusive consulting services.

CHAPTER 24

CHOICES AND JOURNEYS

Lisa Lannon's Story

From police officer to social entrepreneur, Lisa's life has been anything but boring. Lisa is one of the most giving women I know. She is the perfect embodiment of "aspire, acquire, and apply." She goes for her dream, and it's a big dream. Her passion for learning is endless. And she puts what she learns into practice faster than anyone. Lisa is a dear friend and I thank her, not just for her story, but for her incredible encouragement to me and to women worldwide who are willing to go for their dreams.

– Kim Kiyosaki

My road to becoming a Rich Woman started with taking a stand for life. Kim often says that for some women, it takes an event—a wake-up call—before they make a change. I was no exception to the rule. I had a great job, made good money, and so did my husband. We didn't have much debt except our personal home. But I did have a wake-up call and finances were not, initially, a part of the wake-up call. It was a series of events that led me to my financial freedom.

My event slowly happened over the course of six years. I watched my husband spiral down the path of addiction. One day, I had enough. I decided to take a stand for me. I was going to give him a choice and, based upon his decision, I would either go down the path alone or he would go with me. But first he had to go to rehab.

I was claiming back the power that I had given away to his addiction and telling him he could either go to treatment or I would divorce him. Thankfully, he was ready and chose treatment.

The day he got out of treatment, we got Rich Dad's *Choose To Be Rich* series and I completely unplugged from the financial matrix. I realized that, even though I made good money, I was not really getting ahead. I was in the Rat Race and knew there was so much more out there.

I realized I had the choice of living my life working for someone else or choosing to change and have the freedom to do what I want. I had listened to and read other books before, but the Rich Dad and Rich Woman messages rang true with me. What Robert and Kim teach was powerful and inspiring.

Empowered by this new learning, we decided to open our own Addiction Healing Centers and enter the world of business and investing. We found a social problem (well, actually, we lived the social problem) and knew we could capitalize on it, provide a service to the community and give back. I knew I wanted to be a part of the solution and reunite families. If I could get my loved one back, I knew that others could as well. I had a strong "why" to be in this business and this space. Even though I didn't have a degree in the field, the plan was to hire the doctors, therapists, and staff we would need. My husband Josh and I would operate the business.

I knew there would be many challenges because we had many questions. Where would we build it, what rules and regulations did we have to follow, who was on the team, and where would we get the money to start this new venture? And… did I mention that I was pregnant with our first child? Working a full-time job, being pregnant, and starting a full-time business was challenging at times! And since I had never owned a business before, and neither one of us had experience in this field, we basically learned as we went and made many learning mistakes.

I am fortunate that my husband and I enjoy learning and growing together so to embark on this journey together made it a lot easier. And I considered it a win because we were in alignment on our path and goals. I wanted our children to grow up in a healing environment. Because our jobs at the time of start-up were a nightclub manager and law enforcement officer, the choice to do this for our growing family was easy.

One of our big challenges was our friends and family. We were told we "couldn't do that," or that it was "too risky." They asked, "Why would you leave your safe and secure jobs?" I knew in my heart that there was more to life than that and had found my purpose. The risk for me was the possibility of losing my husband to addiction again if he continued to work in the nightclubs. The choice was easy.

We were also faced with the challenge of no money. We basically had none and needed not only start-up capital, but the down payment for a property. Because we had never taken out more than car loans or a personal mortgage, this was also new territory for us. After many failed attempts at getting loans from banks, we were able to raise the money from a private investor. Another huge win!

We were young and inexperienced in the field, and it seemed that the odds were against us. But we were determined, and I knew if we continued to learn from the mistakes and failures we made, we'd only get better.

Our business plan to start the business really sucked! We went through many versions of it before the investor had faith in us. The overall plan was to have multiple centers and expand internationally. It was a big goal, but I knew we could do it. At times there was fear, the thought of failure, and the "what ifs" that come with uncharted territory… but because we were clear on where we wanted to go and what we wanted to build, we found the determination to continue boldly, even when obstacles crossed our path.

Journey Healing Centers opened its doors one year after my husband went to rehab. Our daughter was born the same month we acquired the first property. Today we have multiple centers in two states and are working on our expansion into Australia. I know any woman can accomplish financial freedom with determination, perseverance, a passion, and strong goals!

I have also started my own companies, my own investments outside of our business, and I continue to increase my financial IQ so I can grow stronger. For me, it did start with a wake-up call. I faced the possibility of losing my marriage and faced the challenge of taking care of myself again financially. I needed to move forward, not backwards and into the past. We now have a great marriage, wonderful kids, and a life filled with open doors and possibilities… all thanks to the choices we made in seeking out financial education.

Lisa Lannon • Salt Lake City, Utah • USA
www.JourneyRecoveryCenters.com

Lisa Lannon, is a Social Entrepreneur, Co-Founder of *Journey Healing Centers* and Founder of *Creative Land Development*. She oversees the property portfolio for JHC International and is involved in property identification for quality standards and expansion. Lisa also oversees the PR for JHC which has included feature pieces in national media such as *People* magazine, *USA Today*, MTV, PBS, and Fox News. Lisa continues to be involved in the global vision and management of JHC.

Lisa opened Journey Healing Centers' first facility in the state of Utah with her husband, Josh, in 2002. After being in law enforcement with the Las Vegas Police Department and dealing with addiction on a day-to-day basis, Lisa also found her passion in building businesses and providing a safe, world-class healing environment that assists people and families in sobriety and healing.

Lisa started investing professionally in real estate when she and Josh acquired the first JHC property. Since that time, Lisa has developed a keen eye for properties that fit in the JHC World-Class

Healing Model, where clients recover in comfort with dignity and respect. Lisa also invests in apartment complexes and commodities and is a mentor to women.

Lisa's background includes a bachelor's degree in Criminal Justice. She has worked for Citibank, Bellagio Casino, and the Las Vegas Police Department. She currently lives in Scottsdale, Arizona, with her husband and two children, Haley and Jake.

CHAPTER 25

A SELF-FULFILLING PROPHECY

Trinidad Apumayta's Story

Trinidad's story is an inspiring one. She could have quit, on herself and her children, many times. But she chose to persevere and has made her life a testimony to what anyone can become if they are willing to do what it takes.

The network-marketing, or direct-selling, industry is an asset that many women are discovering and flourishing in. In most cases, the business structure and systems, including a support system, are already in place with the purpose of supporting your success. It typically requires very little money to get started and can be done on a part-time or full-time basis. Trinidad is doing it very well.

— Kim Kiyosaki

I t is amazing to me when I think about the changes I have seen from one generation to the next. In less than two decades, my life has changed very dramatically. These recollections are most moving as I watch my son, carrying his backpack, on his way to college. He will graduate as an engineer in five years.

I remember when I was a very young and very poor little girl who sometimes, in her dreams, imagined her greatest desire would come true: she would be eating a piece of bread. Today, as a 38-year-old woman, I am someone who never thought she would be able to send her own sons to the university.

At age five, I was a tiny native shepherdess without a father. These conditions are common among excluded people in Peru. I lived on a farm in the middle of an internal conflict sparked by a bloody Maoist terrorist group: Sendero Luminoso. Now, 30 years later, having raised four children on my own, I watch my oldest son walk joyfully into his future. And I feel very happy about that.

In an attempt to escape from terrorism, I migrated with my mother and brothers to the nearby city of Huancayo. There I began work as a street vendor at the young age of eight. I never quit school and persevered until I graduated from high school.

I later travelled to Lima, the capital of Peru, to study nursing. I stayed with relatives and, once again, worked as a street vendor to earn money to advance my career. Unfortunately, one of my relatives stole all of my money.

I left my relatives' home and rented a room. I had to start over. I met a man, fell in love, and we got married. Together we sold clothing in a "mercadillo," a marketplace. In time, I learned how to get bank loans so I could invest in merchandise. Years later, my husband and I created a small clothing factory by securing, and promptly paying off, a bank loan.

These were busy years, raising four children and running a business. Yet another setback occurred when I got sick and my husband had to take control of the business. Because of bad management and a lack of knowledge and experience, he lost everything. One day when I returned home, I discovered that he had left me and taken all our belongings. I was left alone with four children, no money, and a bankrupt business.

I was devastated. I began to believe that all my projects and dreams were condemned to fail. It was my sons who brought me back to life. I knew I had to start from scratch again, but this time I took a different road. I was invited to be part of a Peruvian nutrition enterprise, FuXion

ProLife, a company that produces and markets nutraceutical products under a multilevel-marketing strategy.

In the beginning, I did not understand the meaning of network marketing. I only wanted to sell the products to feed my family, but I was required to attend meetings where I was asked to find FuXion ProLife affiliates to sell the products. At first, I thought it had to do with loans so I refused. At home, I looked into the mirror and said to myself, "You are not worth anything. You are a failure."

Despite these feelings, I continued to attend ProLife's meetings and was approached by an independent distributor. I started to sell the products (nutraceutical drinks, herbal teas, and protein shakes) directly to friends in order to create my own downline of distributors through relationship referrals. I received my first commission checks but was still discouraged and confused. Eventually, thanks to the ProLife Leadership School, I discovered I was a valuable person—and a great saleswoman.

I learned how to improve my internal communications. I began to understand how my low self-esteem was deceiving me to believe that my life was only failures. I started to appreciate the many goals I had accomplished throughout my life and began to recognize the many valuable lessons I had learned from my experiences.

Listening to Robert Kiyosaki at a ProLife conference, I understood how the business I was building was creating value. Kim Kiyosaki shared that my business was the way to build my future and a way to generate richness for myself without relying on a husband, family, job, or government aid.

I met ProLife's CEO, Álvaro Zúñiga Benavides, which was a key event in my life. He not only received me with a smile and encouraged me to pursue my dreams, but also conveyed high levels of energy and passion for the mission. I decided to stay close to the good energy he provided, something I had never received from a father, and to follow his example of passionate focus.

In time, I discovered that I was important to others as I helped them find the same values and business opportunities I had found. I have become the leader of a ProLife distribution network that continues to grow and support the expansion of the overall organization. At the same time, I am achieving higher monthly incomes. My average income is now higher than the salaries of doctors or engineers in Peru. I travel and receive recognition that has encouraged me and my network to grow together. I have learned from my mistakes. I have learned to forgive those who have hurt me in the past, to face my fears in order to overcome obstacles and negative beliefs, to improve my communication skills, and especially to help others find their way.

Before I found my business with ProLife, I was earning less than $100 dollars per month. Now my income is more than $5,000 per month. Just as important, I am helping others to follow the tested path of growth and success.

Today, I feel that I am a self-confident woman, a woman who believes that nothing is impossible. I know I am still only halfway through my journey, but my changed life has shown me that positive beliefs are self-fulfilling prophecies that are leading me to my financial freedom.

Trinidad Apumayta • Lima, Peru

A business owner and mother of four, Trinidad's life is a testimony to the power of perseverance and the life-changing role a mentor can play in one's life. Growing up in Peru, she faced more challenges than most and met them all with humility, patience, and a will to survive. She has used her affinity for business to build a means to support herself and her family and, in the process, become a strong and confident woman.

CHAPTER 26
SWEET INSPIRATION

Eileen Spitalny's Story

I met Eileen's brownies before I met Eileen. Fairytale Brownies are one of a kind, and so is Eileen. She is definitely a whatever-it-takes woman. How would I describe Eileen? She's persistent, knows what she wants, and is a joy to be around. She is generous with her time and with her knowledge, and I am honored to have her share her story with you.

— Kim Kiyosaki

Whom my business partner David Kravetz and I decided to create Fairytale Brownies, the one thing we knew for sure was that we wanted to bake the best brownies in the world. It was a simple goal—or so we thought. It was 1992, and we were just 25 years old. We knew next to nothing about owning our own business or baking brownies, and we didn't know our dream of baking the best brownies in the world meant starting a manufacturing and direct marketing company. We had no idea what we were getting ourselves into, and maybe that was best.

David and I met in kindergarten on the school playground in Phoenix, Arizona. I don't remember the initial play date or conversation, but it was enough fun to cultivate a lifelong friendship. I know one thing, our first get together definitely included a plate of his mom's brownies.

Her brownies were a behind-the-scenes part of our formative years. A plate of brownies always rested on her kitchen counter waiting to be devoured by everyone who walked by. As we grew older, David and I discovered that we made excellent partners on school projects. I visualized the big picture—the "where we're going with this"—and David knew exactly what formula was needed to make that vision materialize.

In high school, David and I talked about owning our own business together when "we grew up." I'd say, "I'm in charge of demand, and you're in charge of supply." It was a classic economics model that we eventually realized we wanted to make true with brownies as our product. We went our separate ways for college, but we were only an hour's flight away from each other. He went to Stanford and majored in mechanical engineering. I went to the University of Southern California and majored in business and Spanish.

During my days at USC I worked in the Entrepreneur Program. There, students had access to the Advisory Council and their real-world advice. It was in that program that I learned the importance of asking for expert help.

A few years later, both David and I graduated and joined the corporate world. I took a job with a Spanish television network in Phoenix. David went to work as an engineer for a large consumer packaging company in Cincinnati. We gained some professional training and "real-world" experience in management, marketing, processes, and HR and learned some good and bad skills to apply (or not apply).

I did well in my sales position, and David made a great engineer. But after almost six years I was still itching to be my own boss, to create something on my own. David was too. So without delay, David proposed to his girlfriend, moved back to Phoenix, and asked his mom for her brownie recipe. The recipe was free, and we were on our way.

I'd like to say that the first thing we did was jump in with both feet, rent a retail space, buy a mixer and an oven, and start baking brownies.

But it wasn't that dramatic. We were too pragmatic. The first thing we did was write our business plan. The second thing we did was save enough money for one year's worth of living expenses.

From there, while still employed, we started asking for advice. We showed our business plan to a friend who is a local manufacturing plant business owner. He said, "It looks great. But get rid of your credit card debt before going to the bank and asking for a loan." We took his advice, paid down our debts, and then went to the bank for a loan. We must have looked like eager kids with our business plan in hand, our college degrees, and our naïveté. The banker kept looking around the room as if expecting someone else—and he was! He was looking for our co-signer.

Needless to say, we didn't get a dime from the bank for our efforts that day, and in the end, our parents co-signed for us. But just one short year later, we got our first SBA loan. That got the parents off the paper, and from that point forward, David and I have been on our own as 50/50 partners.

That first year was one of sacrifice. And so were years two and three. One of our advisors told us to start thinking and acting like a Fortune 100 company if we ever wanted to be successful. "Be ready for where you're going before you get there," he said. It was great advice, but it meant paying ourselves very little, putting everything we had back into the business, and picturing ourselves right up there with Godiva Chocolates, Ben & Jerry's Ice Cream, and Harry & David.

At age 26, I cashed in my 401(k) so that my boyfriend (now my husband), Mike, and I could pay the rent. He was our baker at minimum wage, and David and I weren't getting paid so that we could put every dollar back into the business. I didn't even have health insurance. That wasn't smart.

Believe it or not, you can act like the "big guys" even when you don't have much money. Thinking like a Fortune 100 Company wasn't all dreaming. We started to create systems—systems we really didn't even need at the time—and processes too. For us, that meant product consistency.

We bought that first machine, our brownie-cutting machine, with a credit card with zero interest for six months. It was like free money! And we just rolled it over to another credit card offer, and so on and so on. The cutter helped with production because it guaranteed a consistent 3"x3" brownie. Not only did it speed up our process, but it also made our product look more legitimate.

In the beginning, consistency was there for our budding group of customers, but efficiency wasn't there for all of us behind the scenes. We had no baking experience, and it showed. We baked brownies at night in a friend's catering kitchen after working our day jobs. We baked a couple of pans then we'd sit outside and wait for them to cool. If they weren't perfect, we threw them away. To us, quality and product consistency were our customers' first impression. So, there was no room for error.

One thing we did know was that there had to be a better way to do what we were doing. So, once again, we asked for help. We asked anyone who would listen, and that included family, friends, neighbors, and local small business outreach services.

Beth, the daytime pastry chef at the catering kitchen we were using by night, steered us to an importer so that we could find the very best chocolate for our brownie recipe. She also told us we were going to make it—that she believed in us.

We were in over our heads, but we weren't willing to give up. Batch by batch, we experimented with chocolates from all over the world. I took plates marked "A" and "B" to my coworkers and clients at my day job and asked which brownies tasted better. I told them that my friend was thinking of starting a brownie company and needed some true opinions. They eventually realized my "friend" was me—and our "taster clients" later became loyal Fairytale Brownies customers.

It's hard to pinpoint one particular thing that was the toughest part of our first year. There were so many challenging moments that gave us opportunities to learn. Everything we did that year was new, and we had to make so many important decisions. That year, we learned we had a "fourth quarter" business that we had happened to start during the fourth quarter. We didn't know our business would naturally be seasonal and that we'd happened to start it "in season."

The fourth quarter is the busiest time of the year for gift giving. As a result, we were busy. But then our first summer arrived. As the thermometer climbed, our sales sank. We realized two things: We sold and shipped chocolate in Arizona. Not smart. Shipping chocolate brownies in 112-degree weather isn't good. Thankfully, the first problem was easy to solve using David's engineering know-how. We quickly learned about air packs, ice packs, and insulated boxes. But then came the second realization, we didn't really have anything to ship in our wonderfully insulated packaging. Apparently people don't buy many gifts in the summer.

A triumph came out of that summertime hardship. Here we were with more brownies than money, and because we had no money to advertise, we sent brownies to food editors at newspapers and magazines hoping that they would love Fairytale Brownies as much as we did. Amazingly, The *New York Times* wrote about us in their Dining section in June of that year! In the food world, that's like getting the golden ticket or winning the lottery. That article brought enough business to get us through the summer.

With more sales and an inefficient production system in place, we decided it was time to get a little baking consulting from a real baking pro. We found an expert who taught us a quicker baking procedure, which we loved. She also showed us ways to cut corners using different ingredients and skipping some baking steps. At first we thought this was great, but we soon realized that taking the cheaper route was not the direction for Fairytale Brownies. Our goal was (and is) to be the best-tasting and #1 brand of brownies in the world.

That was a big lesson for us. Expert advice is always valuable, but you don't have to take *all* of the advice you get. Today, I still ask for advice, and if more than one expert says the same thing, it's probably worthy of a try. The ultimate test? My gut instinct.

It wasn't long before we achieved a level of success that gave us the resources to market our brownies. You'd think that would have meant smooth sailing, but not so. One year, we ran out of brownies during our holiday season!

Even though we were primarily a mail order company, we always have a small storefront at our bakeries. People can walk in and buy family and corporate gifts, and we often get very big orders. Here was the problem: we had loose and very speculative inventory controls along with thousands of prepaid orders from our direct mail customers. We had to fill those orders before we could take new ones. So, right at the peak of the holidays, we had to limit the number of brownies we could sell in our store.

This was painful, particularly when our customers could look behind the counter and into our production facility and see brownies stacked everywhere.

In business, particularly when you're a hands-on entrepreneur, it's always one challenge or another. One day we arrived at the bakery to discover that someone had cut all the telephone wires by our back door. Not good for a mail order company. Another time our landlord forced us to move into a larger space. . The larger space was wonderful, but he made us move during our busiest time of year. We were wiped out physically and mentally. Then the landlord's movers dropped our mixer. That was the icing on the proverbial brownie! All these inconveniences were lessons in disguise. From that point forward, we got smarter about everything–including lease negotiations.

As an entrepreneur, you'll face challenges day after day. But when you own your own business, you're so passionate about what you do you somehow get through it all. You work 18-20 hours a day and don't mind because your passion keeps you going. Best of all, it's thrilling to see your creation grow before your eyes.

But other things can suffer during these exciting times. My weight went up and down in 10-pound increments. Sometimes you just forget to eat, and sometimes you eat too much—especially when you're making brownies.

Your family may never see you. Being an entrepreneur was my dream, not my husband's. The idea of owning my own business excited me, not him. But I was asking him to trust me even though I didn't know what I was doing. Thankfully, my husband supported my dream even when we had no idea what would happen next.

The good news is that a healthy, well-designed business can eventually provide the best of both worlds: the entrepreneurial thrill and the balance you and your loved ones need and deserve. For me, the freedom, flexibility, and successes of owning my own business far outweigh the trials and tribulations—and it's way better than working for someone else.

It's actually quite exhausting to recollect all these memories because I know how tired I was when they were happening. But interestingly, even while in the moment, the thought of quitting never once occurred to us. Maybe you feel the same way I do. Once you see your business and employees growing, you never want it to go away. You pour yourself into the business, overcome the challenges, and celebrate even the tiniest of successes. Each hurdle you overcome is a company success, a milestone. And in the process your business reaps the benefits and becomes that much stronger and valuable.

When David and I began our business, we wanted to create something special and memorable. In looking back, it seems we have… created a fairytale come true.

Eileen Spitalny • Phoenix, Arizona • USA
www.brownies.com

Eileen Spitalny, along with childhood friend and business partner, David Kravetz, turned a dream of entrepreneurship into Fairytale Brownies, a gourmet mail-order company that ships more than 3 million brownies and cookies a year. The company now has annual sales of more than $9.3 million and has been featured in *Edible Phoenix* and *Life & Style Weekly.*

Eileen is involved in Entrepreneurs' Organization, ASU Art Museum, Slow Food and Les Dames d'Escoffier International. She was named the USC Alumni Entrepreneur of the Year in 2002 and Arizona's Small Businessperson of the Year in 2006 bt the SBA. Eileen is also featured in the cookbook, *Cooking with Les Dames d'Escoffier: At Home with the Women Who Shape the Way We Eat and Drink.*

REAL ESTATE

GETTING STARTED... IN REAL ESTATE

To rise up as an outstanding real estate investor takes...

D onald Trump once said, "It's tangible, it's solid, it's beautiful, and it's artistic, from my standpoint. I just love real estate." I have to agree. Yet, even more than the real estate, I love the cash flow.

Every, and I repeat *every*, successful real estate investor I know, male or female, started very small. If you have or are invested in real estate, my guess is you started small as well. There is a lot to learn, which means mistakes will be made. It's all part of the process. But when starting out, it's a lot easier to make mistakes on smaller properties with smaller amounts of money instead of jumping into a big deal which could lead to costly mistakes.

When I speak of real estate, I am talking about rental real estate that produces a positive cash flow. That being said, one strategy women (and men) have used, if they want to accumulate the funds to put into a larger rental property is to buy and sell, for a profit we're assuming, until they have acquired the funds necessary to move into a positive cash-flowing rental building. *One note:* Buying and selling for a profit works when real estate is appreciating in price, not depreciating.

The term "real estate," when it comes to rental properties, covers a whole array of products, such as the single-family house, the duplex, the triplex, the apartment building, the single office building, the multiple office building, the retail store, the retail shopping center, the big boxes, the self-storage facility, the industrial warehouse, and the industrial park. There are other not-so-common forms of real estate as well.

Tenzin is my sister-in-law. She is a Buddhist nun with His Holiness the Dalai Lama. She never took a vow of poverty, as that is not required, but she does live quite the frugal lifestyle. Since a costly medical scare, she realized that money does have a role in her life, and she began her journey into money and investments. Her search led her to an inexpensive, relatively easy way to get into real estate. The "real estate" is mobile homes. Mobile homes are not common in many cities throughout the world. They are prefabricated or manufactured houses that technically can be transported. Many people who live in mobile homes place them in mobile home parks with other mobile home dwellers.

What Tenzin found is that she can buy a used mobile home for about $3,000 and receive a positive cash flow of about $200 per month. That is a very healthy return on her money. Tenzin also discovered that in California, where she lives, a mobile home is deemed a motor vehicle. She doesn't go through the whole real estate process of getting title for this home. She simply goes down to the Department of Motor Vehicles and picks up the title. Being a nun with many non-income-producing responsibilities, this is a viable solution for Tenzin as she begins growing her asset column.

Clinica Hernandez tells of another not-so-known type of real estate.

I found an investor—a woman!—and I asked to work for her, not for money, but to learn from her. I am happy to do the homework she gives me. In the process, I finally decided what type of investment I would pursue—billboards!

I had no idea about billboards. I always thought the city owned them. I learned that they are considered real estate. They are rentals without tenants!! Billboards are good income almost 100% of the time. When the economy is good, they are used. When the economy is bad, they are the lowest-cost advertising for companies. You can make $1000 - $5000 rent per side per month. None of that ever occurred to me. Now when I see billboards, I think money, money, money!

I remember walking down the street in downtown Los Angeles and seeing huge ads on the sides of buildings. The owners of these buildings created their own billboards. What was once a blank wall is now an income-producing space where companies advertise. Anywhere you can place an ad—the back of airplane seats, the windows of a car, or even a toilet stall—is real estate.

Turning a Liability Into an Asset

My friend, Mona, and her husband had always wanted to own a cabin in the mountains of Arizona. When the summer heat hits Phoenix, the mountains offer cool relief. They looked at various mountain towns and available properties and came upon a small cabin that would be a "cool" getaway.

They never liked the idea of taking on a mortgage that they had to pay for and, in their research, they found there was a shortage of rental properties in the area. They weren't the only ones in Phoenix looking for an escape from the heat! Problem solved. All they needed to do was put a lock on a closet in the cabin that became the "owners closet" where they could lock up their personal items, and they were in the vacation rental business. Mona and her husband took a property that was a liability—a mortgage that they had to pay—and turned it into an income-producing asset. There was even a unexpected bonus: They're not "snow people"… but they've learned that lots of people visit the Arizona mountains for winter skiing. Another opportunity—to generate income year 'round!

As Donald Trump said, real estate is "artistic." There is so much creativity in the world of property, be it a 20-unit office building or a bathroom cubicle. It's all in how you see it.

The Pros of Real Estate Investing

- **Leverage of OPM (Other People's Money)**
  You may pay 10%, 20%, 30% as a down payment, and a bank, lending institution, or private party provides the rest of the funding. You can own a $100,000 piece of property for just $10,000 or $20,000.

- **Cash flow**
  If bought and managed correctly there can be tremendous opportunities for a monthly profit, or cash flow.

- **Appreciation** *(an increase in the value of the property over time)*
  If the value of your property has gone up and you decide to sell, your profit is called appreciation. Cash flow and appreciation are two forms of revenue from rental properties.

- **Control**
  You have control over the income, expenses, and debt of your properties.

- **Not as subject to the fluctuations of the markets**
  A cash-flowing property is not subject to the daily ups and downs of the markets. It is typically a long-term play. A down real estate market can actually be the best time to buy.

- **Tax advantages**

  1. Depreciation: An annual deduction that is typically a percentage of the value of the property that you can write off as an expense against revenues.

  2. Tax credits are available for low-income housing, the rehabilitation of historical buildings, and certain other real estate investments. A tax credit is deducted directly from the tax you owe.

  3. In some countries, the gains from the sale of real estate can be postponed indefinitely as long as the proceeds are reinvested in other real estate.

- **Slow**
  You usually have time to do your homework, make comparisons, analyze the numbers, and make the best investment decision for you.

- **Experience in real estate ownership**
  If you can buy your home or personal residence, then you can get into investment real estate.

- **Home-based business**
  Include your children in each rental property you purchase. You can learn together!

The Cons of Real Estate Investing

- **Time lag**
  Offers, counters, appraisals, inspections, financing—they all take time.

- **Not liquid**
  Liquidity is the ability to convert an asset to cash. You cannot get in and out of real estate quickly. Where the lag or purchase process time in can be an advantage, it can also be a disadvantage if you need to sell quickly or buy in a hurry.

- **Difficult**
  Of the four asset classes, real estate is the second most difficult (after business). You must also deal with vacancies and bad tenants at times.

- **Time-consuming**
  It takes time to find a good deal. Properties must be managed on a daily basis.

CHAPTER 28

TURNING PROBLEMS
INTO PROFITS

Lesley Brice's Story

Lesley is the smartest woman I know in the world of property management. What makes her so brilliant? Every day she is managing thousands of apartment units. I'm sure she has seen or heard it all. Lesley is also a truly wonderful, down-to-earth woman. She is kind and thoughtful… but if you're late on your rent, you'll see a whole other side of Lesley Brice.

When it comes to property management, there is nothing better than real-world experience, because you just can't make this stuff up. The stories I have heard from rental owners and managers are better than any television show.

Lesley came to my rescue on an apartment building I owned, and thanks to her and her team, she turned one big liability into a very nicely performing asset.

— Kim Kiyosaki

Kim Shares One More Mistake... or Learning Experience

For 17 years, Robert and I have owned an 18-unit apartment building in a prime location in Scottsdale, Arizona. As I explained earlier, I like to buy and hold my properties. Since day one, I always oversaw the on-site manager and paid close attention to the income, expenses and, of course, the cash flow.

There was a point several years ago when, because of a complete overhaul of our financial education company, most of my time and attention was focused on that business. I took my attention off the management of this property. I assumed that, after all these years, it could pretty much run by itself. The property manager was the same woman who had managed the property from the beginning. "What could go wrong?" I asked myself. To stay in touch with the operation of this apartment building, I asked Teresa, a woman who worked with us, to be my liaison between the on-site manager, the maintenance man, our bookkeeper, and me. She had never managed a property, so what happened next had nothing to do with her capabilities or intellect. I was the stupid one.

Do you know when you feel something is out of whack, but you can't put your finger on it? Your gut is telling you one thing, but you have no proof to back up your feeling. Every month I reviewed the profit-and-loss statement and the cash-flow statement on this property. I noticed that expenses for repairs continued to increase. The explanation I received was that most of the units needed quite a bit of updating and the manager and maintenance man were doing that one unit at a time. What was driving me crazy was that our cash flow on this property went from a nice healthy return to a negative number that we had to feed every month. This broke my number-one rule of property investing. That I could not live with.

Finally, after many frustrating months, I asked Ken, our investment partner and owner of a very large and successful property management company, for his help. This property is only 18 units, too small for his company to handle, but as a favor, he jumped in. That was when I met Lesley. She took on the project with a vengeance. Here is what she found.

The on-site manager, who has been with us since we first owned the property, was getting older and she did not feel up to handling all of the everyday tasks that went along with managing the 18 units. She had turned most of the duties over to a new maintenance man, her son Pete. Her son had been unemployed up to that point.

Pete, it turns out, was overcharging us for just about every job he did. But that wasn't the biggest expense. When a tenant moved out, Pete would not look for a new tenant. Instead, he would use the empty unit as a storage unit. What was he storing, you ask? Items such as dishwashers, microwave ovens, handyman tools, and carpeting that he was charging to us to update the apartments. But he wasn't renovating the units with these items. No, he was buying them for himself, either to use in his own house or to sell for cash. No wonder there was no cash flow.

That is the cost of bad property management. I took my attention off managing the property, and it didn't take long for the income to go down, the expenses to go up, and the cash flow to disappear.

Lesley to the Rescue... Here's Lesley's Story

In 2008 Ken McElroy and I were approached by Kim to take over management of her mid-century, 18-unit apartment building in the heart of Scottsdale, Arizona, called Loloma Vista Apartments. She had purchased the property in 1995 and had hired on-site staff to oversee the operations. She was growing increasingly concerned that the property was not operating like she felt it should, and that she was having to feed it each month for operations to stay afloat. There was a high vacancy rate, even though the market didn't justify it, and the maintenance costs seemed out of control. We typically manage much larger buildings, but because of our great partnership with Robert and Kim, we of course agreed to help.

We learned that Kim was managing the property through a very long-term employee who was in charge of collecting rent, negotiating leases, and general upkeep and maintenance. For a long time, this formula worked and the investment was profitable. Over time, however, cash flow was eroding which led Kim to ask us for help.

Our approach started with financial analysis. Before stepping onto the property, we asked Kim to give us the operating statements and rent roll to review. We identified several items that quickly formed our initial plan of attack. This is what we found:

1. We recognized that revenue was the biggest problem. Economic losses were 36%, most of which related to vacancy rate with the remainder tied to rent discounts off each month's rent. With occupancy at 67%, this meant that six of the 18 units were vacant.

2. Operating expenses were also an issue. Payroll, utilities, and maintenance expenses were eating all profits to the point that the property would have to be 150% occupied in order to just break even. You may ask yourself, "Is this even possible?" Well, no—not unless you can build another nine occupied units!

3. Capital improvement expenses were astronomically high. Buried in the general ledger, we discovered high levels of replacement costs related to carpentry, flooring, and appliances.

4. We also performed a rent study, comparing rents at the Loloma Vista property with other competing apartments within a two-mile radius. We found that occupancy in the area was well above 90 percent, compared to 67 percent at Loloma Vista. Rents for like-age and like-size apartments were about the same as at Kim's property.

Armed with the forensic financial analysis and market data, we had a plan of items to review when we visited the site. Upon first blush, the site looked very good. The grounds were clean and well-manicured, and the pool was blue (always a good sign).

Our focus then turned to the biggest problem, which was vacancy. We walked through all the apartments and confirmed that there were six vacant units. Four of the six units were uninhabitable (or "down"), due to equipment storage and long-term maintenance issues. The other two were in the process of being renovated with wood flooring, new cabinets, granite countertops and new appliances—at the cost of a whopping $7,000 per unit!

Well, this certainly answered the "Why is occupancy so low?" and "Why are capital expenses so high?" questions. Not only were there no rent-ready apartments to lease, but the units were being over-improved. There was virtually no premium or upside return for the investment, since the renovated units were renting for the same price as their non-renovated peers.

Our inspections continued based on our next priority: operating expenses. We wanted to find out why payroll was way out of proportion for a property of this size. We discovered that the manager had hired her son as a maintenance technician. This resulted in twice the overhead that should be necessary to run an 18-unit building. We found tools, flooring materials, light fixtures, cabinets, and other items that had been purchased and stockpiled throughout the property.

We found significant HVAC (heating, ventilation, and air conditioning) and plumbing problems, including active plumbing leaks that drove utility expenses up. We discovered one of the "down" units had a plumbing leak in the concrete slab that could not be repaired. We were told that every time they attempted to fix it, another leak would pop up a few feet away. So they just shut the door and locked it—several years ago!

Needless to say, we stepped in to take over management of the asset. We brought in new part-time staff and took quick action to get all vacant units ready to rent without a major renovation, embracing the "vintage" lifestyle that comes with living in a historic area. We increased income 30 percent by filling up the property and maintaining a low vacancy rate. Ancillary revenue sources, such as utility billing, application fees, pet rent fees, and non-refundable administration fees generated additional revenue streams. Coupled with expense savings, the overall cash flow increased 350 percent. We continue to manage this asset today.

Now you may be asking yourself, "How does this happen to a building owned by Kim Kiyosaki?" The true answer is that it can happen to anyone. When operations run smoothly and profitably for a very long time, it's hard not to accept that things are as they should be. Kim did the brave thing by asking why, and she did the smart thing by hiring someone who may know more about property management than she does.

Lesley Brice • Glendale, Arizona • USA
mccompanies.com | mcresidential.com

Partner and President of MC Residential
Communities, Lesley Brice oversees property
management on both the corporate and property levels. Beginning her
real estate career more than 20 years ago, Lesley has extensive experience
in multi-family housing. She served in a wide variety of roles in real
estate development, investment, asset management, and condominium
conversion. Lesley is a visionary entrepreneur with a genuine sense of
ownership and pride for the properties she oversees.

Lesley began her career as a resident services agent at a very large
apartment community and worked her way through the ranks—gaining
expertise in leasing, and as a corporate housing agent, assistant manager,
manager, asset manager—to her current position of president of
MC Management.

She holds a Broker's license and sits on the Arizona Multi-housing
Association's (AMA) Board of Directors. She serves as Chair Elect on the
board's Executive Committee. As a leader in the Multi-housing industry,
Lesley believes in the value of education and provides challenging
opportunities to her employees. Lesley is an passionate educator and was
fortunate to be part of the inaugural Rich Woman forum in 2010 and
has spoken at several Rich Dad educational events. She has served as a
delegate to the National Apartment Association, a member of the Arizona
Commercial Real Estate Women (AZ CREW; www.arizonacrew.org), the
Scottsdale Area Association of Realtors (SAAR www.saaronline.com), and
the National Association of Realtors (NAR).

Lesley was a finalist for AMA's Property Supervisor of the Year, and
her properties and employees have been recognized as candidates and
finalists and winners of NAA and AMA Awards. She also is involved
in UMOM's Big Hearts for Little Hands campaign, working to end
homelessness in Arizona.

Lesley and her husband live in Glendale, Arizona with their three
children. In addition to spending time with her family, she enjoys outdoor
activities and in her spare time she loves cooking, reading and traveling.

CHAPTER 29

TAKING CALCULATED RISKS

Rita Khagram's Story

Rita's cultural upbringing was one in which men, not women, were brought up to be the business person and money-maker. Because she wanted more for herself, she rebelled against the traditional norms she was raised with and set out to make a difference, not just in her own life, but in the lives of those around her, especially her daughter. I asked Rita for her story because it beautifully illustrates the influence a mother has on her daughter's financial future.

— Kim Kiyosaki

I was born in Kenya, the third in a family of four children. My father first arrived on the shores of Kenya as a mere 13-year-old child from India, having no money and very little education. Yet within a few decades, the company he founded was thriving in four countries and employing several thousand people. His greatest successes though were as a father. He was our idol, someone that my siblings and I looked up to and admired.

While I was being raised, the sons were encouraged to take up a serious education, but the daughters were not seen as a force to reckon with in the business world. In a Hindu culture, the man was expected to solely provide for the family. This was something I was very sad about because I felt the women were not given the same opportunity.

While studying abroad, I met my husband, an intelligent man living in England, but not from a business background. My father was very concerned. I remember the words he uttered that day, "It's a tough world out there, especially with no money and being a girl in a new country. It's not for you."

I took it as a challenge, promising not only him, but myself, that I would be as successful as he was. Taking that step is still one of the biggest challenges that I have taken because, at the time, I thought it takes money to make money. I am an optician by profession, but I also engaged in several endeavors to set up a business since I assumed that would be the first stepping stone to achieve success. I managed to start one, although it was a small business. In spite of having a good job for a few years, I had no money and had to sell our car to put down the first deposit for an opticians' practice. I invested well over 60 hours a week in my business!

I love my daughter dearly. She is, without a doubt, one of the best things in my life, and I like to imagine that I strived so hard because I wanted the best for her. Time flew by while she was growing up, and the balance between work and spending time with my child was like a delicate see-saw that was tipping towards work. Before I realized it, she was in the wrong company and became a troubled teenager. She once told me, "How dare you tell me what to do! Who are you? All you worry about is your work." My heart sank. My husband was very supportive and believed in me.

That was the turning point. I had to find some kind of equilibrium. If only there were more hours in a day and an easier way to be successful!

I decided to sell my practices (I owned two by then), thinking that I'd find a part-time job that would give me more free time. Having no financial knowledge at the time, I made many mistakes, but I was always careful that I had enough money for her education, so I was content with our decision to take up a part-time job.

A few months later, I received a tax bill from the tax office claiming 60 percent of my money! My accountant hadn't given me the right advice. Because I had no financial background and did not know the right questions to ask, I fell into this deep rut. All that hard work, all those hours, all the years I'd lost out on my daughter growing up made me feel so vulnerable. I was hurt.

Yet I promised my daughter we'd still go off to India for a holiday. The poverty there really got to me, and I had one experience that changed my life. While visiting a temple in Mumbai, I saw two children—a three-year-old and five-year-old—holding hands, begging outside the temple walls because they weren't allowed in. I walked up, bent over, and looked into their innocent eyes. I could sense fear as I stuck my hand out to offer them some money. To my surprise, they refused it. They just wanted food, hot food, something I think everyone is entitled to. So I took them to a cafe (where they were not allowed in), and they waited patiently outside. I went in, and got a few hot dishes as take-outs.

Meanwhile, my husband was waiting outside on a very busy street and really wanted me to get into the taxi. I stepped out holding the food boxes, and two teenage boys ran past me and snatched the food! The next thing I remember was my husband pulling me into the cab. As I looked back through the window, I saw tears rolling down the cheeks of those two small children. That image is forever with me. I couldn't sleep for days and sometimes still think of them. I knew I had to do something to help them. It was no longer about me or my family. I needed to do more to help the impoverished.

I wanted to make more money and dedicate a portion of it to that cause. It was then that a very dear friend, Naftali, took me to a Rich Dad seminar after reading *Rich Dad Poor Dad* by Robert Kiyosaki, and we played the *CASHFLOW 101* game. All of these things made me realize that I needed to learn more if I was to achieve the success that was necessary.

My life journey took a positive turn as I started to learn about leverage and passive income. The first step was to refinance my property. My new mindset empowered me to make increasingly successful investments. Within the first three months of my financial education, I acquired six properties, all with a positive cash flow. It's all about learning to take calculated risks. Kim Kiyosaki was a great inspiration to me during this time.

Despite losing my father almost two years ago, I am glad he had the chance to see myself as I am now, an owner of a successful opticians' franchise with a wide property portfolio. He told me how proud he was of me for achieving so much despite my setbacks in life. All the hard work and sacrifice were well worth it.

My daughter Naiya is an inspiration to me as her intelligence is so evident as I relate to her now as a business partner. Together we set up a charity to help young children, and we both facilitate CASHFLOW Clubs in London to share with everyone this life-changing game.

Rita Khagram • London, England • UK

Born in Kenya, Rita and her daughter and business partner, Naiya, share the dream of business entrepreneurship and creating passive income. They've faced challenges and hardships together… and Rita is shaping future generations with the foundation that she and her daughter have built.

CHAPTER 30

PARTNERS IN LIFE, PARTNERS IN BUSINESS

Leanne Carling's and Anita Rodriguez's Stories

So many people say, "Yes, Kim. You can do that in Phoenix, but you can't do that where I live." Leanne lives in Glasgow, Scotland, and she is definitely doing it, and doing it well in Glasgow. Leanne embarked on her financial journey with her husband, Graeme. Building your financial future with your partner or spouse is the ideal, but is not always the easiest. In her story, Leanne expands upon what it really takes to do money with your partner.

— Kim Kiyosaki

I was born in Glasgow, Scotland, in 1980, a time when industry was booming. Margaret Thatcher was in power as the first female prime minister. My parents taught me to get a safe secure job with benefits—a job for life! They taught me that my house is my biggest asset, it's important to save, and don't acquire debt.

Going to school for me was to socialize with my friends. I didn't enjoy what I was being taught. My favorite subjects were sport and languages.

I left school at 16 and fell into my career with a distribution company capturing orders for a popular retail chain. I loved earning my own cash to buy and do things for myself. For the next 11 years, I moved from company to company, pursuing promotions from stock taker to stock control manager, managing my team and controlling my KPIs (Key Performance Indicators).

I enjoyed impending events, meeting deadlines, and solving problems, but I was always looking for something else. I was an independent young lady and purchased my first property at 18 years old.

In 2005, I met the love of my life, my soul mate, and my teacher/mentor. The unfair advantage that Graeme had over me was that he had read Rich Dad books and played the *CASHFLOW 101* game. My first gift from Graeme was Kim's book *Rich Woman*. I loved the book, and then read other Rich Dad books and started to play the game. My journey had begun.

For the next two years, we talked about freedom. While planning our financial freedom, we noted what our dream home would look like, and that we would be there within five years. In September 2007 when I was seven months pregnant, Graeme and I gave up our high-paying, safe, secure jobs to chase financial independence.

We started a property investment company. We would purchase properties and then rent them out to generate monthly cash flow. We had saved enough money to live for the next six months until January. After that, we would need the cash flow, or we would have to return to work.

We continually researched the property market and mortgage products, but time was ticking. January came and with it our first deal which generated £500 cash flow and enough capital to buy more time. Was I terrified? Yes. Did I make mistakes? Yes. Did I learn from them? Yes. Will I continue to make mistakes? Yes. Will I continue to learn from them? Yes.

In April, I was approached by a lady in her 70s who wanted to sell her house, rent it back, and release the inheritance for her children. Her reason for this was, her children had already started fighting over her money, and she wanted to decide what was done with it. After a visit to my home with a friend, she was prepared to sell her home to me, and advised her friend to do the same. He did! So we successfully purchased three properties by the end of April. We were on our way.

Graeme attended a Rich Dad conference, "How to Predict the Future," in October 2008. When he returned, he was on fire. He told me, "Leanne, we have to get involved with the Rich Dad team if we are going to grow to our full potential."

We were out of the Rat Race and financially free by the end of February 2009. We continue to purchase properties, changing and adapting with the market. Is this challenging? Yes, but with continuous education, it's exciting.

We traveled together to Scottsdale three times in 2009 for additional Rich Dad conferences and training. Everything we learned we put into practice. For instance, when we purchase a doodad (a luxury we want but don't need), we have an asset to support it. For example, when I turned 30, I purchased my dream Mercedes 4x4 using the income from one of our assets.

Every New Year, we use a program called PERT to plan for the coming year about which assets we will purchase along with various professional and personal goals. We review our goals every three months, holding each other accountable for goals we are behind on and celebrating all wins.

As we unpacked boxes in January 2010 in our new home, I came across a paper where we had described our dream house three years earlier. I could not wait to show Graeme. We had achieved a five-year goal in three years.

At one of the conferences we attended in 2009, "Art of the Deal," we learned about exchanges. We continually review what we learned, again putting it into practice. In July 2010, one month after our second child was born, we purchased our first business, using exchange and money we had generated from deals.

I know I would not be where I am today if I had not been prepared and took the opportunities that came my way. I will continue my financial education. Every property purchase and enquiry has a story, a lesson, and opens a new door. Success is not a destination. Success is a journey. And it is a journey I am delighted to be on.

Leanne Carling • Dundee, Scotland • UK

Leanne Carling, a 31-year-old real estate investor, business owner, and entrepreneur, lives in Dundee, Scotland, with her husband Graeme and their two children. Together they have built a substantial property portfolio and have both started and purchased successful businesses.

They are firm advocates of financial education and continue to focus on the growth of their companies and property portfolio. Both Leanne and Graeme are keen learners and teachers and travel the world in pursuit of financial education.

Anita Rodriguez's Story

> *Anita was a school administrator for many years in*
> *the U.S. public school system. Even though she worked*
> *in the school system, she was so disillusioned with it,*
> *that she homeschooled her four children. Anita has*
> *been a staunch advocate of getting financial education*
> *into the school system. No small feat. She became a*
> *life-long student of money and investing, and today*
> *she has the assets to prove it. If only we had educators*
> *like Anita running the school system!*
>
> *— Kim Kiyosaki*

At the time we discovered the Rich Dad messages, my husband and I were a pretty typical couple. We were working hard at our jobs, maxing out our retirement plans, and hoping that the stock market would cooperate and give us a decent return when we were ready to retire and withdraw the money.

Slowly but surely, as we received more financial education, our context was changed and expanded from the inside out. Instead of relying only on income from a job and hoping that the stock market would go up, we were learning to use leverage to acquire assets. Our asset of choice was single-family rental homes.

In addition to the wonderful feeling of having cash flow coming in each month from our real estate assets, one of the most gratifying lessons for me has been learning to overcome fear by taking action. We started investing slowly by taking small risks with small properties and have grown, through experience and education, to take larger and more educated risks.

One of those larger risks is now bidding on homes at foreclosure public auctions, also called trustee sales. It's a pretty intimidating process because we usually can't even see the inside of the house we're bidding on before we buy it. No inspection period, no backing out. An all-cash deal.

But the low prices at these auctions can be amazing if you do your homework, which can make it worth the risk. With our first auction purchase, we were able to buy a house that had cost over $200,000 a few years ago. We paid $40,000. When we turned the key and opened the front door to see what we actually bought, we were pleasantly surprised. Nothing major. Just a lot of painting and cleaning. Thankfully, that deal turned out very well and cash flows great. We then won bids on additional properties through these foreclosure auction sales.

One thing about it though—every house brings with it a different learning experience. You can never say, "I've arrived" or "I know it all" because each experience is so unique, and there's always something new to learn. In other words, it's a process.

On a recent purchase, we learned and experienced firsthand what the term "cash for keys" means. We bought a house at a foreclosure auction at a bargain price. Unfortunately, we discovered that the previous owner and his wife still lived there and were in no hurry to move out. They had not been paying the mortgage for over a year, and they seemed determined to milk everything they could out of this property before they were forced to leave.

We knew nothing about the eviction process or what the legal ramifications were. My husband, Al, started calling real estate lawyers, the police, and government agencies to research our options. We found out that we could go through the court system to evict them, but that can take one to two months. Even worse, angered homeowners can really damage the property before moving out. We had seen plenty of foreclosed properties, previously beautiful homes, with the kitchen cabinets missing, huge holes in the walls, and graffiti everywhere.

So we decided to do something we'd never done before. We decided to learn to negotiate with the foreclosed homeowners ourselves in order to evict them from their house. Actually, I should say that my husband was the one who was brave enough to take this on. It's definitely not my cup of tea.

After doing more research and due diligence on the legal requirements for eviction, Al went to the front door and rang the door bell with some real fear, not knowing what kind of response to expect from distressed homeowners who had just lost their home. We prayed for courage and grace before he went to the door.

After three separate meetings, Al and the previous owners were able to come to an amicable solution. He gained their trust without threatening them with the law and gave them time to clean the house and move to another property. Negotiations were completed in half the time it would have taken a constable through the court system.

Remember I mentioned the term "cash for keys"? Well, that's when the homeowners agree on a date to move out and promise to leave the property in good shape in return for an agreed-upon sum of money. (They get the *cash*, and the new owners get the *keys*.) We discovered that the standard "cash for keys" rate at the time was $2,000. But because of Al's negotiations, they accepted $800 and left the house in reasonably good condition with no damage (although they took the chandelier with them along with *every* light bulb, *every* battery from the smoke alarms, and *all* the refrigerator shelves and drawers)! Through this new experience, we learned about compassion as well as negotiation.

It was pretty stressful during those weeks of waiting and negotiating on dates, which appliances would stay and in what condition, and all the other details. Several times we wondered if we had made a mistake by doing it ourselves. Maybe we should have hired someone to do it for us. Now looking back, we're glad that we had that experience. As the Rich Dad credo says, we took "leaps of faith" and "did not allow fear to stop us."

Even with that fairly positive outcome, we don't intend to do another eviction if we can help it. However, our first-hand knowledge and success in doing so gives us insight, confidence, and power to do bigger and better things. We become stronger through the process of overcoming fear and taking action.

Anita Rodriguez • Phoenix, Arizona • USA

Anita Rodriguez is Director of Education at
The Rich Dad Company. She also invests in
foreclosure real estate with her husband Al through their business, Equity
Investment. With the recent housing crash, especially in the Phoenix
area, they give private investors a healthy return on their money while
purchasing foreclosure property at rock-bottom prices.

Anita has been involved in various avenues of education for much of
her life. She homeschooled her four children for fourteen years. Her two
sons were both accepted to West Point, the Naval Academy, and the Air
Force Academy. Both graduated from the U.S. Air Force Academy. Her
older daughter went on to earn a Masters degree in Quantitative Analysis.
Her younger daughter is a lawyer. After homeschooling, Anita entered
the public school system as a classroom teacher, and then as a high school
counselor and high school administrator.

After becoming disillusioned with many aspects of public education
and then discovering the Rich Dad message, she's now applying her
background knowledge to the world of financial education. Anita works
with the Rich Dad and Rich Woman teams to connect with those schools
and community organizations that are interested in teaching financial
education. Her passion is to share the Rich Dad/Rich Woman message
with others as she lives out those principles in her own life.

CHAPTER 31

PRACTICE MAKES PERFECT

Stacey Baker's Story

If you have ever said to yourself, "I can't do this because I don't have the money," then please read Stacey's story. Stacey, a Kiwi from New Zealand, was on welfare when she began her quest for financial independence. She did not buy into any excuse, even though it would have been easy for her to do. Instead she put her creativity to work and asked herself, "How can I do this?" Here is what she figured out.

— Kim Kiyosaki

I left school at the age of 16 in 1982 with no qualifications and what I felt were no real prospects. I worked various jobs, living pay packet to pay packet and spending intermittent periods on welfare, which I'm not too proud of. I despised living on that poverty line. My life more or less continued like that until the late 1990s when I picked up the book *Rich Dad Poor Dad*. After reading this book, my attitude towards money changed. I started to learn the vocabulary of money through playing the *CASHFLOW* board game. I was on welfare at the time and a single mother of a young son. I remember worrying about how I was going to pay the $10 for my son's kindergarten fee. Times were hard, but with my new insight and positive thinking, I started looking for opportunities. Like in the game of *CASHFLOW*, I knew there must be a way out of the Rat Race.

Long story short, I was sharing a small house with my friend who was a doctor working at the local GP (general practitioner) practice. She told me that the owner of the medical practice had made her an offer to purchase the practice from him. I would normally not have been interested in such a venture. However, because I had read *Rich Dad Poor Dad*, all I could see was an opportunity. After a few discussions and lots of thinking, together we put forward a proposal. After reviewing the financials of the business, Medical Assurance Society offered to loan us 25 percent of the total amount, and the owner financed the remaining 75 percent of the loan. The clinic was ours.

Suddenly I was thrust into the world of lawyers and accountants, a new world that was quite foreign to me. Purchasing that medical practice was a scary big step, but I am so glad I did it. Sometimes to succeed big, you have to take these scary steps, and I have never looked back or regretted my decision. We paid back all the loans in three years, and we never put any money down to purchase it.

However, for me, my main interest has always been in real estate. Through the purchase of the medical clinic, I now had the wherewithal to start investing in houses. After reading a few more books and going to seminars on buying rentals, I purchased two houses in 2002 and started renting them. Always the astute student (when learning something I was interested in), I put my learning into practice and managed to acquire them under value, which meant I was able to generate a positive cash flow from them. From the equity I had made from buying them under their value, I was then able to buy my third property in 2003, once again under value. This in turn helped me to buy two more houses in 2004. In 2006, I ended up doing major renovations on one as it had become a bit rundown, and I was intending to sell it. However, the tenants that had moved out before the renovation wanted to move back in when

I'd finished. Realizing that this particular house produced my largest cash flow, I kept it and the tenants moved back in. I then bought house number six in January 2007 and ended up living in it, as I now had numerous rental properties, yet was still renting myself.

In 2009 the recession hit the property market. With my ever-growing knowledge of the property market, I realized it was a good time to buy. I bought another four houses at bargain-basement prices, bringing my total rental properties to nine, all in Auckland. Not bad for a teenager who left school with no real prospects in sight.

I have slowly worked my way up with real estate. Even with the booms and slumps in the last 10 years, the value of my properties has continued to rise. The first few I purchased have already doubled in value. I still have shares in the medical clinic which continue to give me passive income. My investments allow me to live a lifestyle that I enjoy.

From that worrying day when I wondered if I could scrape together the $10 for my son's kindergarten, I am now able to afford him the very best private-school education. My passion for travel is fulfilled with annual trips to Europe and a hop across the ditch to Australia whenever I want to. I am a successful businesswoman who is still young enough to enjoy living the life I want with financial security and independence. I am the director of my own companies and have not worked for anyone else since 1998.

Stacey Baker • Auckland, New Zealand

Stacey Baker, a free spirit who grew up in South Auckland and now lives in North West Auckland, is in her forties and considers herself someone who had "no qualifications," but credits the success she has seen in her life to her hunger to pursue her financial education. She left high school to enter the work world and saw opportunities to stake a claim in the real estate rental market.

PAPER ASSETS

GETTING STARTED...
IN PAPER ASSETS

To rise up as a stunning paper asset investor takes...

Getting started in paper assets is very easy. Anyone today can go online and buy or sell a share of stock. Deciding what and when to buy and sell is where it gets tricky.

Stocks are only one form of hundreds of the paper assets available today. There is a term you may have heard: derivatives. It's a fancy word that is used often. What does it mean? The root word of *derivative* is *derive* which means "to come from something."

If you have ever made fresh orange juice, think of it this way. You slice an orange. You squeeze the juice out of the orange into a glass. The juice is a derivative of the orange.

A share of stock is a derivative of the company that issues it. A stock option, such as a put or a call, is a derivative of a stock. So a large part of getting started in paper assets is learning the vocabulary of the world of stocks, bonds, mutual funds, and all the derivatives included.

We talked earlier about being true to yourself. A big part of that is deciding which asset class is the best fit for you, your values, and what you want to accomplish.

It's obvious that I am a huge proponent of women getting financially educated, myself included. I knew nothing about the stock market so I did what, at the time, seemed like the smart thing to do, at least it's what everyone told me to do—find a stockbroker. I did. His name was Mark. I told Mark, "I have a little money to invest in stocks. What do you recommend?"

He said, "You can't go wrong with Coca-Cola. It's been on the upswing for the past three months."

Not knowing anything about Coca-Cola, other than I loved it as a kid, I said, "Okay, I'll buy $400 worth." Almost a year went by, and I was hearing some rumblings about the stock. Since I had bought it, the price had gone up modestly, and I was happy with my profit. I called up Mark and said, "Mark, I want to sell my shares of Coca-Cola."

"This is not the time to sell. You're getting out too early. Stay in it," he advised.

"No, I'm happy with the money I've made. I want to sell."

He continued his argument, growing more convincing as he made his case. Long story short, I did not sell. Weeks later, the stock price fell below where I bought it. I was angry. I was angry at Mark for talking me out of it, but even more angry at myself for not trusting my instinct. I called up Mark and said, with an attitude, "Sell!" I took a loss. I sold out of emotion. What else could be the reason I sold? I didn't know anything to start with. You see, I knew I didn't know, and now I knew he didn't know either. I declared I would never have anything to do with the stock market again!

Then, once I calmed down, I realized maybe I needed to learn about the stock market and then decide if it was a place I wanted to play.

As a result, I have taken stock-option courses and day-trading seminars. I've read books on the subject. I've been involved in taking a company from absolutely nothing to a publicly traded company. I am involved in another company as I write. I stay aware of what's happening in the world of stocks, bonds, and derivatives because it does affect so much of the world economy that I would be foolish not to.

Yet, in being true to myself, I know this is not a world where I choose to spend a lot of time. It does not ignite that spark in me or get my adrenalin flowing. That is why it's so important to have good and trusted advisers. I still want to participate in the game. I just don't want to be a star player. There are others who love it, who flourish in it, and who have found their passion in the world of paper assets.

Our stockbroker, Tom, has also become a dear friend. Why is he our stockbroker? For three reasons:

1. He *never* comes to us with a hot tip.

2. He thoroughly researches every recommendation he gives us. He will fly to visit a company's corporate offices and meet with the executives. He organized a dinner in Los Angeles and invited Robert and me and a few of his clients to meet with the founders of an alternative energy company he was considering as an investment. He wanted to give us, his clients, the opportunity to ask the founders the tough questions.

3. Tom has already invested in every single investment he suggests to us. He practices what he preaches.

Tom's two rules for investing in stocks are:

1. If you don't understand how the company makes money, then don't invest in that company.

2. If it looks too good to be true, then it probably is.

Tom is an educator, although he may not realize it, and my knowledge grows whenever I work with him.

The Pros of Paper Assets

- **Very liquid**
  Paper assets are quick to get into, and quick to get out of.

- **Easy entry**
  It does not take a lot of time or effort to begin investing in stocks, bonds, etc. (However, you still have to do your homework.)

- **Cash flow**

  Stocks that pay dividends can provide long-term cash flow. There are other paper vehicles that will deliver cash flow if you learn the strategy.

- **Tax advantages**

  The gains, or profits, for paper assets held longer than a year are taxed at the lower long-term capital-gains rates. Dividends are taxed at the lower long-term capital-gains rates as well.

- **Home-based business**

  Include your children in what you are investing in. They can learn along with you!

The Cons of Paper Assets

- **No control**

  You have no control over how the company makes money, spends money, or manages its debts and liabilities. (Unless, of course, it's your company that is offering shares to the public.)

- **Volatility**

  Stock prices can rise and fall dramatically, especially in uncertain economic times.

- **No leverage**

  For the average investor, they must pay 100% to own the asset. They cannot borrow money to purchase a mutual fund or shares of stock.

- **High fees and commissions**

  High fees and commissions are charged on the majority of trades, whether you are buying or selling.

Let me introduce you to a few magnificent women. These women are smart, driven, and passionate when it comes to the world of paper assets. They truly do flourish in this environment, and they have the success and track record to show for it.

CHAPTER 33

FOCUS ON THE FUNDAMENTALS

Donna Miller's Story

Donna is a fantastic educator in the world of paper assets. More than that, she is an educator of getting people, women especially, to push beyond where they themselves think they can go. Donna had a life-changing wake-up call that led her to question her future, specifically her financial future. What I love about Donna is that she is a brilliant investor and has a gift for inspiring women to action. Donna cares about those around her and wants them to win.

— Kim Kiyosaki

In 2002, my husband and I first started investing in the stock market. At the time, we thought we knew everything we needed to know about investing by watching the news and reading *The Wall Street Journal*. After all, how hard could it be? We opened an online brokerage account and accumulated one position of over 30,000 shares of a well-known retail stock using almost all our capital.

This was done without ever knowing what a stop loss was to mitigate risk, looking at a chart to understand the prevailing trend, or understanding the company's fundamentals condition. In short, the company was being blown down by the bearish trade winds, but rumors of a buyout kept our hopes alive. This investment was meant to be our retirement. All it needed to do was rise ten points. The rumor came and went, and so did the price of the stock. I felt completely helpless and paralyzed as we watched the stock price sink lower and lower each day.

My husband was convinced that all the stock needed was one more news item or rumor to make it go up so we could get out at break-even. Those items never materialized. Later, the stock was delisted and ultimately filed bankruptcy. We learned an invaluable lesson the hard way. It's easy to rationalize when you are down on a position. I now refer to it as the "hold-and-hope syndrome."

Deep down inside, I knew we could do this, but finally concluded that we needed an educational program. We researched various courses online and finally enrolled in Rich Dad's curriculum on paper assets, formerly known as "Teach Me to Trade." At first, I sat by my husband's side, not really participating. My thoughts were that I would let him do it, and I would just watch. My life was busy with work, children, and the everyday schedule. My role was a sounding board for my husband's decisions. Finally it dawned on me—what would I do if something ever happened to my husband? I pushed him aside and delved full force into the classes and stock market. Several years later, we came face to face with this exact scenario. He developed cancer twice and underwent several months of intense treatment.

There were many sacrifices along the way. One such instance was not taking family vacations for several years in a row. Instead, we dedicated this time to trading and being in front of the live market. Every free moment was spent reading, studying charts, and watching trading videos. Another fond memory involved our daughter's swim team. Daily practices and meets were long. I remember sitting there for hours, poring through market information, stopping only to watch her events.

Repetition was my key to making the knowledge stick, so diving headfirst was my only option. Learning the stock market takes perseverance, dedication, time and self-management. I often use the term "stick-to-itiveness" as the ability to hang in there when the going gets tough. It's easy to quit, but quitting wasn't a choice for me. Things worth having in life require an abundance of effort and energy.

I've instilled these same principles in my children. My son recently received his degree in aeronautical engineering and is a naval aviator. Currently, my daughter is a cadet attending the United States Air Force Academy. Children emulate what they see their parents do, and I am fortunate that they have the same drive and determination. They are both realizing their dreams and have bright futures ahead of them.

The stock market is perceived to be "a man's world." When I started, there weren't many women in trading but, to my surprise, I was told over and over by market veterans that women make better traders. The big question is why. In general, women are not ego driven and are better able to detach their emotions from an investment or trade.

In 2004, I became the only female mentor with Rich Dad's financial program on paper assets. One vivid memory occurred while conversing with a seasoned market veteran. We were discussing trades and market conditions. He stopped mid-sentence and said, "Wow, I am amazed. I didn't know that you knew how to trade! I thought you were here for your looks." From that point on, I gained his respect. Now I am known as one of the better technical analysts in the company.

Donna Miller • Louisville, Kentucky • USA

Donna has the unique perspective and experience of being an actual student of our company. In 2002, she began her journey taking classes. In recognition of her skills and abilities, she was selected as a mentor in 2004. She is the author of the FACT (Futures and Commodities Trading) course and teaches online classes and trading labs.

CHAPTER 34

BOUNCING BACK FROM BROKE

Kim Snider's Story

*The first time I met Kim Snider, I knew we would do
more together, and we have. Kim's philosophy is the same
as mine—invest for cash flow and expand your cash flow
to afford the lifestyle you desire. Kim applies this strategy
to paper assets, which was an eye-opener for me. She faced
a shocking financial situation at one point in her life that
would have defeated many women. For Kim, she got her
lesson, rebuilt, and now teaches people how to do what
she does. Kim is a kindred spirit, and I so thank her for
revealing an important part of her life to us.*

— Kim Kiyosaki

T oday I am an author and radio talk show host. I speak publicly on
the subject of saving and investing for retirement. I have taught my
cash-flow investment method to thousands of investors. But all of that came
later. Originally, I just had to solve this problem for myself: How do I make
sure I never find myself in this position again?

The "position" I am referring to is going from rich to flat broke in less than two years! Maybe some of you can relate. Twenty years ago, I went to work for a small computer-supplies wholesaler. At the time, they were doing about $36 million a year in sales. I was just a few years out of college and started as a clerk in the purchasing department.

Over time, I rose up through the ranks, ultimately reaching the level of senior management. With each promotion came additional responsibilities and pay. Some of that pay came in the form of stock options.

In January 1995, the company went public. By then, they were closing in on $500 million a year in sales and would soon reach a billion.

At the moment my employer's ticker symbol crossed the tape for the very first time, I suddenly had more money than most dream of having after a lifetime of work. I was 31 years old.

I knew nothing about investing or taking care of money. In fact, at the time the company went public, I was basically living paycheck to paycheck (albeit a fairly large one) just like everyone else.

I had gone to some of the finest schools our country has to offer. I had business law in high school, and I graduated from college with a degree in business. I took several classes in corporate finance. I could do double-entry accounting, tell you about supply-and-demand curves, program a computer, and read a novel in French. But nowhere along the way did anyone ever sit me down and explain the basics of personal finance or investing. Strange, isn't it?

So, having grown up on television commercials, I did the thing that seemed most reasonable. I went to one of those large brokerage firms and asked them what I should do with the money. They told me they had brokers who would be more than happy to manage that money on my behalf.

Cool! Problem solved. Abdicate responsibil... I mean, hire someone else to handle it.

Mind you, I didn't just pull a name out of a phone book. I got a recommendation from the lead underwriter on our public offering. My broker came highly recommended and worked for the parent company of the investment bank that took our company public. Without naming names, I'll just say that unless you have lived your whole life under a rock, you know the name of this firm.

In all fairness, I will be the first to admit that I didn't handle my side very well. I spent a lot of money on really dumb things. In fact, I quit my job and proceeded to have a really good time. That is what you do when you are young and foolish and feeling bulletproof. But you know what? The broker did his fair share of dumb things too.

I didn't understand what he was doing. Frankly, I didn't even *try* to understand what he was doing. After all, he was supposed to be the expert. Whatever he suggested, I agreed to. How could I not? I didn't have any facts to base a decision on, one way or the other. I was like a leaf floating along in the river, going wherever the current might take me. And where it took me was over the falls!

Less than two years later, I was dead broke. I had to admit to God and the world that I had screwed up the opportunity of a lifetime. That is a pretty bitter pill to swallow when you look at yourself in the mirror each morning.

I didn't have a penny to my name, I was in debt up to my eyeballs, and all my cool toys were repossessed. I sold my swanky high-rise condo at a terrible loss just to stay out of foreclosure. My credit was wrecked, and I had no job. I couldn't even afford to buy dog food for my dog.

The worst part about it was going to my own mother for a loan so I could eat. No, that wasn't quite the worst. The worst part was facing my father. That was pretty much the low point of my life.

It was also a catalyst. Because of that experience, I told myself, "*Never again* will I rely on someone else to take care of my money for me. If I lose it, so be it, but I have to be responsible for my own financial well-being."

So I started learning about money, and I started experimenting with investments. Sometimes I was successful; other times I was not. But what I found out was that the more I learned, the more I made. The more I learned, the more control I had. Instead of feeling hopeless and helpless when it came to money, I began to feel I had power over my financial situation. I was being accountable, and it was the best feeling in the whole world.

Today, 12 years later, my situation is dramatically different. Not only am I a good steward of my own money, but I also teach others how to do the same.

People often ask me why I feel so compelled to share my story and my lessons with other people. Why not just apply what I learned to my own life and be done with it?

First, my story points to the moral that if it can happen to a smart, young, up-and-coming business executive, imagine how most people must struggle with personal finance. But more importantly, I am proof that no matter how poorly you have handled money in the past, you can make a conscious decision to change it—and succeed.

Second, I believe that if you are smart, you will always learn from your mistakes. If you are truly blessed, you have the opportunity to take what you have learned the hard way and use it to help others. In fact, I believe there is a moral imperative to do so.

Third, the need for financial education today is reaching crisis levels. Studies indicate that our financial literacy isn't keeping pace with the demands being put upon us. This is especially true of women, minorities, young people, and the less educated.

When people ask me how I went from being broke to not being broke in 12 years, I tell them, "I decided to." That is the truth. Without commitment and determination, you probably won't get there because financial success requires making hard choices. Usually that means giving up what you want now for the opportunity to have something better down the road. That is hard, I know.

But think about the reward—financial success. My definition of financial success is "being able to do what you want, when you want, without having to worry about how to pay the bills." That, to me, is so worth the price.

Kim Snider • Dallas/Fort Worth, Texas • USA
www.KimSnider.com

Kim Snider is the Founder and President of Snider
Advisors, a SEC Registered Investment Advisor.
The firm manages approximately $90 million directly for clients, using
the Snider Investment Method®, and advises on an additional $320+
million managed by her extended family of Snider Investment Method
Workshop alumni.

Snider Advisors was honored as one of the fastest-growing, privately
held companies in the Dallas/Fort Worth area in 2006 by the Caruth
Institute for Entrepreneurship at SMU's Cox School of Business. In
2008 and 2009, the company was named to the Inc 5000 list of fastest-
growing, privately held companies in America. It ranked 34th among
businesses in Dallas/Fort Worth and 45th among financial-services firms.

In addition to her role in building and operating Snider Advisors,
Kim is an author and a speaker. Her first book, *How to Be the Family
CFO: Four Simple Steps to Put Your Financial House in Order* (Greenleaf),
hit bookstores October 1, 2008.

CHAPTER 35
TAKING STOCK
OF YOUR LIFE

Barbara Anderson's Story

*Barbara inspires me. I cannot keep up with her in her
research and knowledge of the world economy, future
predictions, and their impact on investments. Barbara,
elegantly and without the fanfare, gets things—an amazing
amount of things—done. She is a philanthropist and has
a passion for supporting young, often under-privileged,
women get a better shot at their dreams in life. Barbara
is a fabulous role model and is definitely a woman who
lives life being true to herself.*

— Kim Kiyosaki

M y path to investing began after my four children went off to
college. I had just separated from my husband of 24 years. He was
a brilliant businessman and started his own oil company two years after
we were married.

After realizing that I had no credit history and did not exist on any
financial records (other than as a supplementary on my ex-husband's
accounts), I applied for my own credit card. This was quickly denied, and I
found myself in my banker's office asking for help. He quickly arranged for

me to receive Visa and American Express cards, and they are still the only cards I carry. Today most women establish that kind of credit out of high school.

The first item on my list of "To-Dos" was a 30-day tax course. Then, as an avid reader, I started reading financial books and newspapers and attended informational seminars in my area. *Benjamin Graham*, my first financial read, was way over my head. Warren Buffett and some articles on Charles Munger came next. Then I hit upon the book *Buffettology*, followed by *The New Buffettology* by Mary Buffett, Warren's daughter-in-law, and David Clark. They both had a blueprint-type outline of the actions Warren Buffett took to determine a good company. Jim Rogers became one of my most interesting investors. He is known as the "Indiana Jones of Finance."

In 2000, I invested in my first major stock, Phillip Morris. At the time, this stock was trading at $5.07 a share because of all the litigation it was facing. I purchased 5,000 shares anyhow because my research showed that the company felt it would win all the cases except the one filed by several states. This was already factored into their plans. The company had many other products other than cigarettes. Phillip Morris did eventually lose the major litigation. They paid off the states in installments. California issued tobacco bonds at 8 percent, and I purchased some bonds and still have them today. Phillip Morris changed its name to Altria Group Inc. Altria ultimately spun off Phillip Morris to divest itself from the cigarette image, and my stock portfolio received 5,000 shares. Altria later spun off Kraft Foods Inc., and my stock portfolio received another 3,460 shares. All these shares pay dividends which, to this day, I continually reinvest.

In 2001, my ex-husband sold his company. We had split the company's stock in our divorce settlement so this became an immediate deemed disposition in Canada. I paid my taxes, moved to Phoenix, and took back my U.S. residency.

I was inundated with offers from firms who wanted to manage my assets. Instead, I took my time, kept up my research, and slowly started purchasing the stocks I wanted. I have never been sorry about this decision.

In 2002, I purchased shares in a number of companies. All but one of these paid dividends, and most are reinvested.

These stocks were purchased based on the *Buffettology* blue print that I follow. However, there was one I purchased in 2004 that did not quite fit. That stock was Apple. I spoke with my son-in-law. He thought I should buy Microsoft instead and wanted to know why I would buy Apple. I told him, "Every time I go into the Apple Store to buy something, I stand in a line five people wide and eight people deep." They have a much better system today. I never have figured out why Wall Street kept resisting Apple. Maybe it was because Wall Street people were all on PC computers.

A few of my stock selections were major disasters. It certainly taught me a good lesson. I had not done my due diligence on any of them, and two of them were hyped recommendations. ALWAYS follow your blue print. Stocks are like buses: There is always another one coming down the road. Lesson learned!

When I first started investing in stocks, my goal was to preserve capital and create growth. Thank goodness the tech stocks did not match my criteria. However, I did get hit in 2007 when I did not follow my instinct to take money out of the market and wait. It took me over two years to recover, but it gave me the opportunity to purchase physical gold and silver as a future hedge.

After my initial investments, I expanded my sights and started looking at other countries. There now is a large satellite on top of my roof that is just for the Deutsche Welle, a German international news broadcaster. Every other hour it broadcasts in English. This opened many doors and gave me a much broader perspective on what is going on in the world, which also impacts what is happening here. It is interesting to hear our news from another country's point of view, which is often quite different from what is presented here.

Finance is another passion of mine and has been for the last few years. I love the research. It is an ongoing journey about learning. I have been fortunate to take a couple of Forbes Cruises. They were wonderful learning experiences. I find Steve Forbes has very realistic views. I liked his book, *Flat Tax Revolution*, which outlines why he favors a flat tax. Several different speakers gave their perspectives on various facets of the financial world and, best of all, you are around a group of like-minded people.

Robert Kiyosaki gave one of the best seminars I ever attended in 2007. Richard Duncan (*The Dollar Crisis* and *The Corruption of Capitalism*) spoke for over two hours. Kim followed with an exceptional financial seminar for women. After these seminars, I more fully understood the Federal Reserve and why it was created, and how money is created and used in our banking system.

On July 31, 2011, a Sunday evening, I discussed with my broker about the stocks I wanted to sell the next day, Monday, the first of August. I wanted him to realize that, no matter what was going on in the market on Monday, I was being rational. I sold most of my stocks that Monday and plan to sit on the sidelines watching for a while. I cannot determine if our country is ultimately going to work together and do the right things. All my research indicates that what's coming up ahead is not good. I am going with my instincts this time and getting out of the way. Time will tell if that strategy will reap rewards.

I encourage the women I know to be passionate about life and the things you enjoy. Have fun, engage in your community, and give of yourself. Position yourself around good people and create a 100% team of supporters. It can't be a 50-50 team, as they say in marriage, or it won't work. Everyone has to give 100 percent in order to finish as a winner.

Barbara Anderson • Calgary, Alberta • Canada

After her four children were raised, and while living in Canada, Barbara became involved with the Sir Edmund Hillary Foundation and was on the Board of that foundation for several years. After moving to Phoenix in 2001 she had the opportunity to become involved with both of her: passions: Women and Education. The Fresh Start Women's Foundation has given me the opportunity to start a Scholarship Program, in honor of her mother, which gives women the opportunity to obtain an education. Teach for American has enabled her to sponsor teachers in the Phoenix area and help many young students in that community. Barbara enjoys music, golf, reading and traveling and has managed her finances for the last ten years.

COMMODITIES

GETTING STARTED...
IN COMMODITIES

To rise up as a magnificent commodities investor takes...

T here are many commodities that you can invest in.
They include:

- Agriculture (such as soybeans, wheat, milk, and cotton),
- Livestock (such as cattle and hogs),
- Energy (such as oil, natural gas, and ethanol),
- Precious metals (such as gold, silver, platinum, and palladium), and
- Industrial metals (such as copper, lead, zinc, and tin).

Commodities, along with the other asset classes, are a science unto themselves. In *It's Rising Time!* we like to keep it simple, so let's just focus on the few commodities many people are talking about today. That seems to be where the interest lies. For those of you who want a more thorough explanation of how the commodities markets operate, I'm sure there is a *Commodities for Dummies* book on the market. I'd start there.

Silver

Silver is a popular subject today. The public wasn't talking about silver years ago, but today the price of silver pops up on the TV screen throughout the financial news shows. What makes silver so attractive?

Silver is a consumable commodity. It is used in the manufacture of things such as computers, cell phones, televisions, light bulbs, cars, mirrors, medicine, and water purification. With the growth of emerging countries, the demand for silver is certain to increase exponentially, even as the supply is dwindling. As a result, for the first time in history, there is more gold available throughout the world than silver, approximately five times more. So it stands to reason that the price of silver should increase as the demand increases.

My First Silver Purchase

My first silver purchase was in 1985. Even though Robert and I had very little money at the time, we walked into a precious metal shop in La Jolla, California, and asked about the price of silver. At that time it was about six dollars per ounce. We took the plunge and purchased a 100-ounce silver bar.

When you have nothing, $600 is a lot of money. We walked home to our condo and hid the silver bar in our bedroom closet. We had made the decision that, instead of putting money into a savings account, we would splurge on a silver bar whenever we had accumulated enough money. We kept to this strategy for years.

In 1988 we were about to buy our first house. It would be our personal residence. We had been building our business for three years and did not have "regular jobs" or, more importantly to the banks, steady paychecks. Plus, we had a great deal of bad debt and a low credit score so it was nothing less than a miracle that we had finally gotten a loan approval on our new home. The broker, who was also the seller, said to me, "We have to move fast on this." I know *she* wanted to move fast on this because we told her we would give her the full purchase price she was asking if she could secure financing for us. "We are going to close on the house in two days," she informed me.

"Great!" I thought to myself. "I can't wait to move in."

Then she added, "So we will need the $24,000 down payment wired to the bank tomorrow."

"$24,000!" I screamed to myself. "Where am I going to get 24,000?" Robert was overseas and not accessible. All I told the broker was, "No problem. I'll have it there." I hung up the phone and my mind was racing. "Where in the world will I find that money in one day?"

And then the lights went on. I opened the door of our bedroom closet, and there sat our own little Fort Knox. I counted the silver bars and, yes, we could cover our $24,000 down payment. I filled up a paper grocery bag with as many bars as I could carry and walked three blocks to the coin shop to cash them in. By the fourth trip, my arms were pretty weary, but I kept going until I had the $24,000 to purchase our first home. Once the last bar was sold, I wired the funds to the bank, and Robert and I were homeowners. Silver was a very *precious* metal to me that time.

Gold

As the global economy worsens, the price of gold continues to rise. One reason for that is because gold has real value. As I write, a one-ounce gold coin can be exchanged for almost $1,900. As governments print more and more money, the value of that money is worth less and less. One dollar two years ago could buy you more than it can today. As the U.S. economy worsens, investors—individuals and foreign governments—lose confidence in the ability of the United States to pay back what they have borrowed. Investors are therefore hesitant to invest in dollars, which weakens the dollar even further.

Gold is a tangible asset that throughout history has held its value. Gold is real money. A dollar bill, a peso, or a euro is not real money. It is a currency. What's the difference? True money has value within itself, intrinsic value. A gold coin today can be cashed in for about $1,900 and buy goods and services anywhere in the world. *True money is always currency* because it can be used to purchase other items that have value. *Currency, however, is not always money* because it does not have value by itself. For example, pull a $20 bill or Euro note from your wallet. Do you think that piece of paper you are holding is really worth $20? No, the paper itself is probably worth about five cents. The only way a currency has value is because people have confidence in the government issuing the currency and a shared agreement that the currency is worth something. As that confidences wanes, so does its value.

As a hedge against a weakened currency and inflation, gold can be a good investment.

Oil and Gas

The price of oil and gas is a popular subject. Oil and gas prices affect so many parts of our lives—the cost of a gallon of gasoline for our car, the cost of an airplane ticket, and the cost of heating your house.

As an investment, I've found it very important to differentiate between the types of oil and gas properties you can invest in. The four main categories are:

1. **Producing**

   The drilling wells are currently producing oil and gas.

2. **Proved developed**

   The oil and gas reserves are proven to be there, and the drilling wells are there. However, the wells are not currently operating and producing.

3. **Proven undeveloped**

   The oil and gas reserves are proven to exist. There are no wells on the property.

4. **Exploratory**

   An area is being drilled to find oil and gas. It has not yet been determined if oil and gas reserves exist in the area.

A *producing* well or fund will provide the smallest return of the four types because there is little risk involved. It is already up and running.

The returns are typically higher in a *proved developed* because the oil and gas are there and the wells are drilled. It's simply a matter of getting into production.

The *proven undeveloped* will yield a stronger return on your investment than the developed field or area because of the time and expense of getting the oil and gas out of the ground. Just because an area is proven to have oil and gas does not mean it will be cost effective to get it out of the ground.

You'll find the highest risk in the *exploratory* wells. The experts have done their research, and they *think* there is oil and gas to be found, but they won't know until they drill. They raise investment capital to drill the wells with the expectation that they will strike it, but there are no guarantees.

Oil and gas have never been a highly exciting investment for me. Robert enjoys it more than I do. He's been investing in oil and gas since before we met. Yet, if any of our money is invested there, then it's up to me to get educated about it. I did just that on a trip to Los Angeles. We had just invested in a producing oil and gas field just off the coast of Long Beach, California. The investment company invited Robert and me to view the operation. Hardhat in hand, we boarded a small boat and ten minutes later stepped onto this man-made island. We spent about three hours viewing the site and learning about oil and gas production. For me, actually being on the site and learning about it firsthand did the most to increase my knowledge in the shortest period of time. Oil and gas is still not my favorite of all our investments, but I do have a much greater awareness and appreciation for the oil and gas investments we have.

My Latest Commodity

Jim Rogers, well-known investor and co-founder of the Quantum Fund with George Soros, is one of my favorite investors to follow. He just tells it like it is. He has now founded a commodities fund. Robert and I were interviewing him recently for a radio show, and I asked him what commodities he was investing in. He mentioned gold and silver.

He then talked about food. Jim Rogers predicts there will be a severe shortage of food throughout the world in the near future. He stated that one of the problems is a shortage of farmers. He said that there is not enough profit in farming for young people to get excited about it as a profession. He suggested one solution would be to raise the price of food which would create stronger profits and thereby attract more young people into agriculture. He believes that, with the upcoming shortage, food prices will soar as a result anyway.

So what investment am I now exploring? Food. What kinds of food should I invest in? How specifically should I invest in them?

Financial education never ends.

The Pros of Commodities Investing

- **Easy entry**
  For example, buying gold and silver coins is very easy to do. If you can buy a loaf of bread, then you can buy gold and silver. Buying other commodities has the same level of ease as paper assets.

- **Increase in demand for raw material as economies grow**
  For example, with the growth of China and India, there is a greater demand for oil, gas, food, copper, and aluminum.

- **A hedge against inflation and a falling currency**
  Gold is a good example. When currencies fall in value, commodities usually rise. And when investors lose confidence in currencies, they may run to commodities, especially gold.

- **Tax advantages**
  Different commodities have varying degrees of tax advantages. Almost all are taxed at a lower rate than ordinary earned income, or income from salaries and wages. Oil and gas, for example, can offer terrific tax benefits to the investor.

- **Home-based business**
  A child can easily buy a couple of silver coins and follow daily charts and graphs to check the current price. Involve your children as much as possible as you invest. What a great way for them to get started!

The Cons of Commodities Investing

- **No cash flow**
  Most, not all, commodities do not cash flow. They are a capital-gains investment.

- **No leverage**
  The average investor cannot borrow money to invest in commodities.

- **Dependent on the economy**
  As an economy slows, there is a decreased demand for raw materials.

- **Volatile**
  Commodities can be volatile with extreme ups and downs.

CHAPTER 37

THE SILVER LINING

Trina White-Maduro's Story

Trina grew up in a tough neighborhood in the projects of Chicago. She joked with me once, "Living below my means? That would have been a step up!" A beautiful woman who started with very little, Trina is dedicated to serving others through her faith and by being an example of what it takes to make it. Yes, just like the rest of us, she has had her winning days and her learning days. If you look up the word "persistent" in the dictionary, you'll see Trina's picture. I am grateful to call her my friend.

— Kim Kiyosaki

I was 36 years old when I first heard about precious metals, such as gold and silver—other than in Bible stories. I was uneducated and oblivious to the notion that one could actually invest in them. My story about how I became an investor in silver is rather unusual. My background is in social work, juvenile detention, and youth ministry. I grew up in the ghettos of Chicago, and the only thing we traded was food stamps. I later found myself in the inner core of south Phoenix managing a Boys & Girls Club youth facility and volunteering as a community speaker. One thing that stood out in my office in the midst of youth-development curriculum and piles of kids in trouble was my *Rich Dad Poor Dad* book.

One month prior to meeting Robert and Kim in the fall of 2006, I was a chapel guest speaker for a Phoenix youth-detention center. I had given a spiritual sermon and immediately after the prayer, I made a bold proclamation that I was looking to create 20 millionaires in 20 years in the urban community. Who would want to be one? All of the nearly 40 male inmates enthusiastically raised their hands very high and said, "Pick me!" That youth prison was a most unlikely place to cast a vision for the first time. However, it was confirmation to a vision God put in my heart and on my mind. I told them I don't know how it's going to happen—I just know it will.

One month later, I met Robert Kiyosaki when he came to visit the young people at my south Phoenix Boys & Girls Club and shared his *CASHFLOW* game. After a 45-minute tour, I was able to cast the same vision for Robert as I had with the youth inmates. Twenty-four hours later, a member of the Rich Dad team called to say that Robert wanted to provide the financial education and resources to empower my dream. So I began intense coaching sessions and learning about assets for six months.

Later, Robert told me that I would have to become a millionaire first in order to inspire others and that I needed financial education and good mentors. In all honesty, this was all very overwhelming to me. I was wondering what I had gotten myself into. I thought investing was for rich people who lived in wealthy communities. So I asked myself, "How could I possibly teach wealth principles to a dying community with kids in dire situations?"

As Branch Manager of the Boys & Girls Club, I was fighting the depressing conditions of a community with high drug trafficking and prostitution. Ninety percent of the kids were on free lunch. More than 70 percent were from single-parent households. I began to question how I could compete with the narcotics business on the streets. Working for quick cash for drug dealers was very lucrative. So with fear and trepidation, I gathered the 30 or so teenagers (some against their will) to play the *CASHFLOW* game. Among these teenagers were pimps, prostitutes, and drug dealers. I thought they would start cursing at me and throwing things after the first five minutes, but three hours later, we were still playing. They were mad when we had to quit.

The game showed me many things. I saw that some of the teenagers could barely read the cards and do the simple math on the financial statements. But they didn't let that stop them. They had so much fun making deals, buying houses and businesses, and holding million-dollar bills in their hands! This got their attention and fueled their imaginations—and they began to dream about investing. One kid, Ricky, was a known drug trafficker who wanted to trade that life to learn real estate. Another youth, David, asked his mother to take him out of all his remedial classes and be put in regular classes. That family later purchased a *CASHFLOW* game. These kids were on fire, and it wasn't long before they asked "What's next?" I told them that I didn't know—and that I was learning too.

While going through coaching and mentoring, I learned about commodities like silver. My interest was piqued and then I shouted, "We can do this! Silver! We can invest in silver and learn to watch the market with something simple, tangible, and real." At the time, silver was $11.50 an ounce, so I decided to buy an ounce to get a feel for the process. All of us—the kids, staff, and parents—learned how to watch the market together. All the computers in the learning lab had the website for the precious metals market bookmarked for easy access. The Boys & Girls Club was buzzing with emotion due to the ebb and flow of the market.

The excitement was so intense at times that on payday, my staff, with their slightly above-minimum-wage paycheck, would go buy a one-ounce silver bullion from a local dealer. I said, "We can't all leave at once!" so we took turns buying silver each week until we had nearly 100 ounces. We then started an LLC called the Silver Million to help create micro-businesses from the silver we had accumulated. That experience felt liberating and was empowering. We believed that it was possible to acquire assets and wealth by taking the one small step of buying silver.

In retrospect, I wanted to send Ricky to real estate school so he could have an alternative to selling drugs. I should have had a better plan in place to transition kids to entrepreneurship. However, that vision is still alive, and my dream is to make it happen.

One thing that's certain: I believe all things are possible in any situation and environment. If the kids in the "hood" can get it, anyone can. There are no excuses for not rising to the occasion when opportunity comes. For us, it was silver.

Since playing the *CASHFLOW* game and going through coaching, I have started a business in addition to investing in silver. I realize that passive and residual income is true financial freedom and that my money should work for me.

Applying the Rich Woman principles has had a direct and profound effect on my life, and my passive income is steadily increasing. I own an Internet-marketing company that I operate from home which is virtually paperless. Learning that the new trend is moving from brick-and-mortar to click-and-order further validates the end of the Industrial Age. I own virtual real estate in this Information Age of electronic social-media commerce. In order for me to lead a generation of urban millionaires, I have to first become one myself. I have to be a lifelong student of financial education in order to learn and stay abreast of things as trends change. I cannot have a "typewriter mentality" in this computer age, or I will be left behind.

My goal is a rich life of spiritual fulfillment and healthy living, as well as financial well-being. I thank God that I am well on my way to a rich life of blessings and freedom. It's time for me to rise to the occasion and take action on the opportunity I have to break the negative cycle of scarcity forever.

Trina White-Maduro • Chicago, Illinois • USA

Business woman, investor, social entrepreneur, Trina White-Maduro is an UnFranchise business owner, an investor in precious metals, and an active supporter of community and faith-based organizations. Trina grew up in the midst of violence, drugs, and gangs on the south side of Chicago. She was raised in a single-parent home with 14 other siblings and family members. Her family was very poor and lived on minimal resources. Trina excelled in sports and initially viewed professional basketball as her destiny and vehicle to success. She later chose to pursue a career in social work and ministry through non-profit organizations and churches for 21 years. Today she is a social entrepreneur who understands how to use resources to create opportunities and better the lives of those she serves.

CHAPTER 38

ASSETS ARE
A GIRL'S BEST FRIEND

To rise to your true greatness takes...

Find your asset class of choice. Maybe you already have and are actively pursuing investments. If not, then do some research to discover which asset class speaks to you the most. Which asset class most aligns with who you are and the investments that interest and challenge you?

Practice and get good at investing so that your assets generate cash flow and a healthy return. The smarter you get with your money, the more comfortable you will be in venturing into other asset classes.

We have redefined the traditional meaning of diversification. It is not spreading your investments across just one asset class like paper assets, but across all four asset classes.

Remember that each asset class responds differently to the ever-changing ups and downs of the economy on both the national and global stages. An asset that may be booming today may be crashing tomorrow, and vice versa. The asset column of your balance sheet is your business. As in any business, you have to watch it constantly.

Each asset class has it pros and cons. Paper assets are fast-moving and liquid. Real estate is slower and cannot easily be sold for cash. What is a plus to one investor may be a negative to another. Again, you've got to be true to yourself.

The risk in any investment lies with the investor, not the investment. Putting your money into *anything* that you do not understand is risky. Gaining knowledge by starting small and building experience will reduce your risk.

Finally, we talk about the four *primary* asset classes. The fact is that you can invest in *anything* in which you see the potential of a strong return on your money. People have invested in everything from vintage wines to artwork, from classic cars to Barbie dolls. The world of investing is limited only by your imagination.

So have fun, stay curious, be bold, and embrace your adventure as you explore the asset classes. Here's to rising up to the gifted investor within you!

PART FOUR
ACHIEVE

REALIZING YOUR FINANCIAL DREAMS

ALIGNING ALL THE PIECES

To rise up to the reward of financial freedom takes...

Aspire

Choose your dream. Create a clear vision of what your financial dream and financial freedom look like to you. Hold onto your vision throughout your journey.

Acquire

Acquire the knowledge, the education, the facts, the figures, and the data you need in order to take action. The acquire stage is ongoing because the markets and the economy are always changing.

Apply

Apply the knowledge you've acquired in the real world. Take action. Put into practice what you have learned. With a small amount of acquired knowledge, you can quickly move into the apply stage. Many small *apply* steps lead to more tremendous learning which will produce results.

Achieve

One key to this process is to do one thing every day that gets you closer to your financial dream—which is the fourth "A," *Achieve*. You will achieve throughout your entire journey. You will be achieving with each and every win or success. Be sure to celebrate every win you have along the way. It's those rising moments of success and accomplishment where real joy is found.

Doing, Not Seeing, Is Believing

Robert and I gave ourselves the gift of one week at Canyon Ranch in Tucson, Arizona. Canyon Ranch is a well-know holistic health-and-fitness resort. We went there to recharge our bodies and spirits.

In working with a fitness expert one day, he asked me about my eating habits. I told him I typically eat two meals a day: breakfast or lunch, and dinner. I explained that sometimes I'll look at my watch and it's 6:00 at night, and I'll realize I haven't eaten anything all day. Eating just is not a high priority for me. He looked at me a little disapprovingly and said, "You need to eat three meals a day." Of course, I've heard this before.

"I didn't believe it then, and I don't believe it now," I told him. "My belief is, if I eat three meals every day, I'll gain a lot of weight."

He laughed, "You need to eat more in the day when you're active, like in the morning and early afternoon, and less at dinner when you're less active." Since I'm a pretty active person, he went on to explain that if I don't eat enough, then instead of my body burning fat, it will burn muscle, and I'll never have the level of fitness that I could.

I was still fighting my belief that three meals a day will only put on the pounds, but since I was at Canyon Ranch for my health, I figured I might as well give it a shot.

For seven days I faithfully showed up at the dining room three times I day. I didn't scrimp, by any means. I ate three *full* meals each day. One thing I noticed right away was that my energy was better. My morning grumpiness was less grumpy, and I had more vitality throughout the day. I stuck with the program and, at the end of seven days, not only did I not gain weight, I actually lost a couple of pounds. I'm very fortunate that I do not have a weight problem, so I met with my friend again. To my surprise, he increased the amount of food I need to eat daily. I was amazed.

The point of this story is that I had a set belief. Although I have heard since I was a young girl that I should eat three meals a day, I never believed that the benefits were real. I had the information, but it wasn't until I actually applied it—and ate the three meals a day consistently—

that I had the experience and the true knowledge of what worked best for me.

The quicker and more often you apply what you're learning, the faster the results and your understanding of what works best for you when it comes to money and your investing style.

So Easy an 8-Year-Old Can Do It

The Rich Dad Company was presenting a one-day event in London in 2010. Our driver, Bulent, met us at the airport and drove us to our hotel. We had a lengthy conversation.

We learned that he decided one day to take the leap and, with money he had saved, he started his own limo company. He said he was working hard, but that business was good. Bulent was very familiar with the teaching and philosophy of The Rich Dad Company and was teaching his son, Anil, about money and investing. He told us this story.

I had an appointment with a real estate broker to look at a 10-unit apartment building. A client called for transport to the airport so, instead of canceling the real estate appointment, I told the broker, "I'll send my son in my place."

When Anil showed up for the appointment, the broker was taken aback. He called me, "Sir, you said your son would come look at the property. The boy who is here is only eight!"

"That's right," I replied. "Please show him the property, and he'll report his findings back to me." So the broker and Anil went off to inspect the property.

When I met Anil at our event, I asked him what he saw when he went to the property. He told me about the deferred maintenance, the vacancy was higher than was advertised, and the net operating income did not include several important expenses. His final conclusion was that this property was not a good deal for his dad because he would have to invest more money to repair and increase the occupancy than his father had budgeted.

"Unbelievable," I thought to myself. "And he's only eight!"

Two months later I received an email from Bulent updating me on his business and investments. He told me Anil came home from school the other day and said, "Dad, I have a problem at school." "What's the problem?" Bulent asked.

Anil hesitated and replied, "I know more than my teacher." Bulent just smiled because, when it comes to business, money, and investing, Anil really does know more than his teacher.

Bulent is an outstanding role model for his son. It's time (in fact, it's *rising* time!) we have more and more women role models when it comes to money for our daughters, nieces, and young women throughout the world.

One Young Mother

Six women, myself included, were on a panel discussing investing with a large room full of women. One young woman approached the microphone to ask a question. She started out very timidly, "I feel like I'm a lousy investor and a lousy mother. I so love all that I am learning about the world of stocks and commodities. I've been attending courses and reading, and I've started investing online. I love it!" The more she spoke, the more energized she became. "The problem is, I feel like a bad mother because I think I should be spending every free moment with my three-year-old daughter."

A woman in the audience leaped to her feet and shouted to the young mother, "Oh my goodness, don't you see what an amazing example you are setting for your daughter? I know it's a lot to juggle, but soon you'll be able to teach your daughter. What an incredible advantage you will give her." She turned to the audience excitedly. "How many of you wish you had a mother who could have taught you this when you were young?" she asked. All hands went up.

She turned back to the young mother, "I believe that by passing on your financial knowledge and experience to your daughter, you are doing so much more for your daughter's future than you'll every know. I congratulate you." The room applauded loudly.

The young mother, smiling from ear to ear, simply said, "Thank you. I never looked at it that way. I'll keep going."

Impacting Lives

Earlier in *It's Rising Time!* we talked about the importance of understanding the numbers of an investment. There is power in numbers. As the number of financially savvy women grows throughout the world, the greater power we will have to impact the lives of other women, young and old. Granted, we each face our own unique challenges. Yet when I listen to the stories, I realize many women are going through exactly the same things as I am.

Whenever we can coordinate schedules, I love to get together with my four girlfriends from my bike trip in France. We come together and discuss life. It's uplifting because we are like-minded. We're optimistic about our lives. We all have goals and dreams that we are shooting for. And one of the most important traits that I see in my girlfriends, which I see in many women, is the desire to support and encourage one another to realize their dreams. That feeling of affinity and connection is hard to put into words. *Priceless* comes to mind.

The Rich Woman team and I support and cheer on every woman who is pursuing her financial dream in life. We applaud every woman who is willing to stand up and be a role model for women young and older. And we truly appreciate every woman who is willing to do what it takes today for her freedom and happiness tomorrow.

The Rich Woman community is designed precisely to bring together like-minded, going-for-your-dreams women for the purpose of building each woman's confidence to take that next step on her journey to financial security and independence.

Aspire towards your dream, *acquire* the knowledge, and *apply* that knowledge to *achieve* all that you want in your life.

One final story…

Can't Stop the Waves

Living many years in Hawaii, I always appreciated the men and women who could surf. I never was a surfer. I borrowed my friends' boards a few times, but I just didn't get it. I remember one time, many years ago, when I was practicing on tiny waves and became excited because I was so close to standing up. Not paying attention to a slightly larger wave behind me, I was quickly knocked off my board and right onto a reef of sharp coral. Ouch! That was the end of my surfing career.

Robert was a surfer growing up in Hilo, Hawaii. Living part-time now in Hawaii, he bought a surfboard. He wanted to take his new board out in the waves so we went to Waikiki and, for $10 per hour, I rented one of those long, floatable beginner surfboards. We both paddled out to the waves. For about one hour I struggled, not coming close to catching any waves.

I looked to my left, and I noticed an older local surf instructor working with three young kids about ten years old. I paddled closer to listen. He instructed them through the steps, from lying down on the board, to getting up on their knees, to then standing up. I took in all he was teaching them.

He glanced over at me and said, "You wanna surf today?" I shook my head yes. "Okay," he said, "just do what I say. Turn your board around to face the shore. When I say paddle, paddle as hard as you can. Don't stop. And when I yell, 'Stand up,' you stand up." I shook my head yes.

"I can do this," I thought to myself.

"Get ready," he said. "A wave is coming." I turned and looked, and there was a small wave building. "Paddle!" he yelled. "Paddle! Paddle harder, harder!"

I was paddling as hard as I could, but the wave passed me by. He just looked at me. "When I say paddle, I mean paddle. You quit on the wave. You sure you want to do this?" he asked gruffly.

"Yes!" I shouted.

"Then do what I say, and don't quit," he ordered. "Get in position." "Paddle!" he shouted. "Paddle!"

I started paddling my heart out, and then my board was on the wave, and the wave was pushing my board. I was so excited I almost forgot the next step until I heard the old guy yelling, "Stand up! Stand up now!"

Fearing that he'd hurt me if I didn't do what he said, I got to my knees and then stood up. "Wow!" I thought. "I'm standing up!" And as soon as I had that thought, I fell right off. But I experienced the feel of actually riding a wave. I couldn't wait to paddle out for my next wave.

As he was ending his class with the ten-year-olds he waved to me, "You're on your own now. Well done!"

"Thanks for your teaching!" I shouted back.

I stayed out in that water for the next two hours, and by the end, I was actually standing up and riding waves into the shore. I loved it!

The Moral of the Story

I *aspired* to ride a wave. With no instruction, I was frustrated and confused by the surf. The waves just kept coming… and I didn't know what to do. The waves were winning.

All it took was a little bit of learning, *acquiring* some knowledge, to know what to do.

Paddling, missing waves, and paddling harder until I was on a wave, I *applied* the knowledge until I *achieved* my dream of riding a wave.

And here was the magic—not only did I ride the waves, but I actually loved the experience!

Here's to loving those rising-time moments!

AFTERWORD

It's Rising Time!

Time to rise above whatever gets in your way and deal with it.

Time to rise beyond where you thought you could go in smarts, courage, action, and results.

Time to rise to your financial genius—and create magic in your life.

You've heard from many women throughout this book about what it *really* takes to realize your financial dreams. These are all brilliant women, just like you. Not one of them had any financial education or head start, and most had little, if any, money. The advantage they had was that they were willing to do what it took to bring their dream to life. They certainly faced their rising moments. They encountered turbulence, but they relished in their moments of triumph, small and large. Today they are smarter, stronger, self-fulfilled, and happier because of all their experiences.

I believe this book is important for women at this time because, no matter where you are in your personal and financial life, you know what it is you want to change. The question is simply, "When?" When will you have the courage to truly go for what you want in your life? It is the difference between sitting on the bench or playing in the game.

I believe we women want it all—all of who we are, all that we can give, and all the positive difference we can make in the world. As you rise up and go for your financial dreams, you instantly become a role model to those women around you. And heaven knows, we need strong, positive women role models in this world.

Please use this book as a reference whenever you want assurance along your journey that yes, you are right. You may not always get what you want or expect, but just brush yourself off and keep going.

This journey is a fantastic adventure in wisdom, experience, personal growth, humor (yes, we've got to laugh at ourselves sometimes), astonishing results, and those awe-inspiring rising moments. Embrace all of it, because all of it makes you who you are, and all of it earns you the rewards you deserve.

It is my honor that you chose this book. Our lives are simply the result of the choices we make. Choose wisely for yourself.

It's Rising Time!

FINAL THOUGHT

All our dreams can come true,
if we have the courage to pursue them.
—Walt Disney

ACKNOWLEDGMENTS

Here's to women in cities throughout the world who are rising up to their financial greatness!

Here's to the women who generously and openly shared their stories with us in *It's Rising Time!*

Here's to the Rich Woman team and the Rich Dad team—true team players who do what they do so brilliantly and inspire me to do what I do best.

Here's to Mona Gambetta for going above and beyond to get *It's Rising Time!* into the hands of readers.

Here's to Anita Rodriguez, Rhonda Hitchcock, Marian Van Dyke, and Mike Joe—no better book team in the world.

Here's to Lisa Lannon for giving unconditionally of her time and knowledge to encourage women worldwide to be financially savvy *Rich Women*.

Here's to Robert—my best friend, my business partner, my husband… in that order.

I thank you with all my heart.

ABOUT THE AUTHOR

Kim Kiyosaki
Successful entrepreneur
Best-selling author

As an internationally renowned speaker, author, entrepreneur, and real estate investor, Kim Kiyosaki knows what it takes to succeed and be a financially independent woman. Drawing on a lifetime of experience in business, real estate, and investing to support her mission of financial education for women, Kim is a sought-after speaker, television and radio talk-show guest, the host of a PBS *Rich Woman* show, as well as a columnist for WomanEntrepreneur.com.

Through her international brand, Rich Woman, Kim draws on her lifetime of experience in business, real estate, and investing to be an advocate for women in the marketplace, and is passionate about providing financial education through her Rich Woman products.

A self-made millionaire, Kim is a happily married (but fiercely independent) woman, and often travels and speaks with her husband, Robert Kiyosaki, author of *Rich Dad Poor Dad*. Her first book, *Rich Woman*, was a *Business Week* bestseller and is one of the top 50 best-selling personal-finance books of all time.

References
and Resources

RichWoman.com

RichDad.com

CASHFLOW 101 Board Game

CASHFLOW Clubs
> Look for a CASHFLOW Club in your city where people get together on a regular basis to play the *CASHFLOW* game.

Rich Woman Coaching

Rich Dad Education

Books:

Books by Kim Kiyosaki

Books by Robert Kiyosaki

Books by Robert Kiyosaki and Donald Trump

Business Books
> Garrett Sutton, Rich Dad Advisor
>
> Blair Singer, Rich Dad Advisor
>
> Tom Wheelwright, Rich Dad Advisor

Real Estate Books
> Ken McElroy, Rich Dad Advisor

Paper Asset Books
> Andy Tanner, Rich Dad Advisor

Commodities Books
> Mike Maloney—Gold and Silver

Women Featured in **It's Rising Time!**
Kim Babjak • KimCo LLC
kimbabjak.com

Lesley Brice • MC Residential Communities
mccompanies.com
mcresidential.com

Lisa Lannon • Journey Healing Centers
JourneyRecoveringCenters.com

Kim Snider • Snider Advisors
kimsnider.com
How to Be the Family CFO: Four Simple Steps to Put Your Financial House in Order

Eileen Spitalny • Fairytale Brownies
brownies.com

Other Resources
Kolbe Index
kolbe.com/itsrisingtime

Rich Dad Tools
richdad.com/resources/tools.aspx

INCOME STATEMENT

INCOME

Description	Cash Flow
Salary:	
Interest/Dividends:	
Real Estate/Business:	

Auditor _____

Passive Income : $ _____
(Cash Flow from
Interest/Dividends +
Real Estate/Business)

Total
Income: $ _____

EXPENSES

Taxes:	
Home Mortgage Payment:	
School Loan Payment:	
Car Loan Payment:	
Credit Card Payment:	
Retail Payment:	
Other Expenses:	
Child Expenses:	
Loan Payment:	

Number of
Children: _____

Per Child
Expense: $ _____

**Total
Expenses:** $ _____

BALANCE SHEET

Monthly Cash Flow (PAYCHECK): $ _____
(Total Income - Total Expenses)

ASSETS

Savings:		
Stocks/Funds/CDs:	# of Shares:	Cost/Share:
Real Estate/Business:	Down Pay:	Cost:

LIABILITIES

Home Mortgage:	
School Loans:	
Car Loans:	
Credit Cards:	
Retail Debt:	

Real Estate/Business:	Mortgage/Liability:
Loan:	

G101CTI8.v2

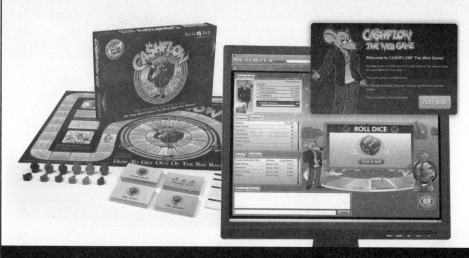

Get Connected to the Rich Dad and Rich Woman Global Community! Join for FREE!

You can expand your world and network in the league of Rich Dad and Rich Woman in one single step. Join the Rich Dad Community FREE at www.richdad.com and continue your journey to financial well-being. Learn, connect, and play games with like-minded people who are committed to increasing their financial IQ, just like you!

Register for free and enjoy

- Inspiring discussion forums
- Access to new releases and events featuring Robert and Kim
- Live web chats with Robert and Kim
- The exchange of ideas and information with others
- Challenging game play with others all around the world

Rich Dad and Rich Woman are committed to communicating with you through social media channels. Follow the inspiration threads on Twitter, connect and participate with a growing fan base in the Rich Dad Facebook community, and enjoy the benefits of the financially literate!

Visit **richdad.com** today and join the
FREE **Rich Dad** Community!

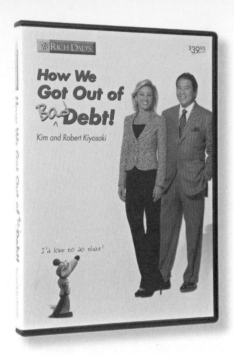